Rules for Compact Urbanism

Rules for Compact Urbanism

Ibn al-Rami's 14th Century Treatise

Edited and Introduced by Besim S. Hakim

Translation by Mohd Dani Muhamad

EmergentCity Press

ISBN: 978-0-9683184-4-7

Library of Congress Control Number: 2017901407

Translation by Mohd Dani Muhamad
Reviewed and edited by Besim S. Hakim
Introduction by Besim S. Hakim

Published by EmergentCity Press, 2017
Available from Amazon.com

Cover: A historic neighborhood in Marrakech, Morocco in the early 1960s. Photo by Papini, M.H.A.T., Rabat, Morocco. First published as Plate 7, in Hakim, B.S. *Arabic-Islamic Cities: Building and Planning Principles*, KPI, London 1986.

Contents

Introduction by Besim S. Hakim vii

Introduction by Ibn al-Rami, the Author 1

Rules for Walls……………………………………....3

Avoiding Damage……………………………........35

Defects in Houses…………………………….....94

Lower and Upper Floors……………………….....114

Water Channels and Sewers………………………125

Property Boundaries………………………………162

Wells…………………………………………….....165

Division of Property……………………………....184

Threshing Floors…………………………….....197

Planting In Other's Property………………………212

Plantation………………………………………….225

Rivers and Irrigation………………………….…...241

Mills……………………………………………….247

Pre-emption……………………………………….257

Damages Caused by Animals,
Birds, and Bees…………………………………...260

List of all 144 Discoursed Cases………………….267

Glossary of selected terms ……………………….281

Bios of the Editor and Translator………………….282

Introduction

This introduction will briefly discuss the author, the treatise and its significance, its structure and composition, the underlying principles that govern the rules, and notes about this English translation of the treatise.

The author

His name is Mohammad bin Ibrahim al-Lakhmi, known as Ibn al-Rami al-Banna (the builder or master-mason), also known as Mohammad al-Banna. He cites his name in numerous locations in his treatise to prevent the loss of his name as its author if the first page of the treatise is lost or altered. He explains his concerns about that in his introduction to the treatise. He grew up and lived in the city of Tunis which he mentions when citing a case that occurred there. He also mentions other locations where he was sent by the judge to investigate a problem.

He states in his introduction that he makes his living as a hired builder. His rank in the local building industry was high as he was often asked by the local judge to investigate on-site issues and especially between proximate neighbors. These problems were presented to a judge to determine an equitable solution. The coverage of the issues and cases in his treatise demonstrates his wide scope of knowledge of the trade. In fact the variety and complexity of the cases that Ibn al-Rami dealt with demonstrates that his rank in the local building trade was considered at the highest level, typically designated as "al-Amin", a term that was known as early as the third century A.H., ninth century C.E. His knowledge in the trade is demonstrated in: (i) the large number of references which he cites, (ii) organizing the vast aspects that the treatise covers in a communicable fashion that is useful as a reference, (iii) abstracting the issues discussed for purposes of clarity, (iv) linking the rules with their underlying principles, and (v) his ability to present his own rational in determining what is the best solution and its underlying rule that convinces the judge to accept it in lieu of other opinions (al-Atram 1995).

No information was discovered about the date of his birth and death. However, based on the citations that he makes to the various judges that he worked for or those that he mentions who were alive during his career, it is assumed that his active professional years were between 701 A.H./1302 C.E. and

733/1333, a period of 31 years (Bin-Slimane 1999). It can be assumed that he died after 1333 C.E.

The treatise and its significance

This is the most comprehensive treatise on building rules within the Mediterranean region. This editor undertook extensive research for sources and manuscripts addressing building rules within the societies located on the southern and northern Mediterranean basin. The languages of those sources can be found in Greek, Latin, Spanish and Arabic. Most of the relevant information on building rules is found in legal treatises written by jurisprudence experts with the exception of one sixth-century treatise written by an architect who lived in Ascalon, Palestine (Hakim 2001, 2014). That treatise documents building rules in a prescriptive fashion, i.e. it tells you what to do based on precedence and customs that are primarily regionally based. It does not articulate the principles that underlie the prescriptions. It also confines itself to the level of the building and does not incorporate streets and the urban fabric. It did however influence urban regulations, 377 years later, in Constantinople as a part of the *Book of the Eparch* and, by extension, other territories under Byzantine rule (Hakim 2001).

What makes Ibn al-Rami's treatise significant is that: a) it was written by a master-mason, b) it draws upon texts that were available to him that date back to the eighth century C.E. from various regions of the Islamic world, specifically from the Arabian peninsula, Iraq, Egypt, Andalus (Islamic Spain), and Tunisia. For a list of primary authors that Ibn al-Rami cites in his treatise see Appendix 2 of (Hakim 1986), c) the author assembled relevant information from a large number of jurisprudence (*Fiqh*) books, thereby presenting the content according to a structure devised by the author that is of value to the building trade and he also addressed the issues that emerge during the on-going process of change and growth, and d) the author interprets various opinions of scholars on specific issues in light of his experience in the building trade within the context of fourteenth century Tunis which was one of the major urban centers in North Africa.

The structure and composition of the treatise
There are fifteen topics that the author addresses as indicated in the table of contents. The study by (Bin-Slimane 1999) indicates five major topic areas that the treatise is structured around; namely, walls, prevention of damage, defects in houses, plantation and mills. Yet Ibn al-Rami does not specifically indicate those five topics as stand-alone separate entities. He does however address those topics in the numerous cases that are discussed in the treatise. Ibn al-Rami clearly states in his introduction to the treatise: ". . . that the reader should understand that I am a builder for hire, and therefore I should be excused for any errors found in words or structure. As for the narration of sources (that I have used), I did my best to carefully check and verify their accuracy."

It should be kept in mind that authoring and writing a treatise in the fourteenth century was limited to pen and paper and if changes were to be made, it would have entailed recopying numerous pages or major portions of the hand written manuscript. Modern word processing tends to spoil the modern reader by criticizing errors or questioning the sequence of presentation of information regarding a specific topic. Ibn al-Rami did not number his cases, and without a numbering system it is difficult to cross check and reference cases that are discussed with those that are presented before or after as they might relate to a specific topic. Therefore in this translation all cases that are clearly indicated by the author as separate items, as when the author provides a title beginning with "Discourse on . . ." were numbered sequentially into 144 cases. The user of this translation will be able to re-group cases, if necessary, according to underlying principles or according to aspects of the built environment. This editor has regrouped Ibn al-Rami's cases into five categories according to the structure and components of the built environment: 1) streets, 2) distribution of land and building uses, 3) micro issues such as overlooking, 4) walls between neighbors, and 5) drainage of rain and wastewater (Hakim 1986). This English translation is designed to keep the presentation of the content of the treatise as close as possible to its original Arabic as presented and narrated by its author Ibn al-Rami. His use of the phrase "Master-mason Mohammad says . . ." when presenting a set of facts or for clarifying an issue is explained in his introduction, namely because 1) fear of loss of his identity as the author if the first pages of his treatise are altered or lost, and 2) to differentiate his opinion from those by other sources that he refers to.

The underlying principles of the rules

This editor has analyzed and published about the principles that were the basis for formulating the rules discussed and presented by Ibn al-Rami (Hakim, 1982, 1983, 1986, 1994, 1997, 2006, 2007, 2008a, 2008b, 2009). The following principles and considerations can be identified by a careful reading of the cases that the author presents, especially the opinions of the numerous jurisprudence experts and the rulings by local judges that Ibn al-Rami relied on in articulating the necessary rules for the cases presented. In general one can identify an underlying goal: to deal with change in the built environment by ensuring that minimum damage occurs to preexisting structures and their owners through stipulating fairness in the distribution of rights and responsibilities among various parties, particularly those who are proximate to each other. This ultimately will ensure the equitable equilibrium of the built environment during the process of change and growth. (Equitable equilibrium is a term that implies that fairness and justice must always be maintained between the rights of proximate neighbors to achieve harmony and good will). This is particularly important given the fact that in principle, property owners have the freedom to do what they please on their own property. Most uses are allowed, particularly those necessary for a livelihood. Nevertheless, the freedom to act within one's property is constrained by preexisting conditions of neighboring properties, neighbors' rights of servitude, and other rights associated with ownership for certain periods of time.

-- Prevention of damage(s) that may occur by the decision/action of one party upon a) adjacent or nearby private properties and structures, and b) upon the public realm such as streets and access paths.

-- That the rights of property owners must be respected and maintained, including the rights of earlier usage that determines the constraints upon what can and cannot be implemented in adjacent or nearby properties. An essential right that was practiced in historic compact built environments was the right of a neighbor to abut a neighboring existing structure, provided its boundaries and the owner's property rights are respected. This triggered detailed study for appropriate rules for these conditions, as it is evident in the treatise of the extensive discourse of rules for walls.

-- Respect of local customary practice (*Urf*) in articulating the necessary rules within the jurisdiction of those customs.

-- The utilization of a space named the *Fina*, which is an invisible space of about 1.00 to 1.50 meters wide alongside all exterior walls of a building, primarily alongside streets and access paths. It extends vertically alongside the walls of the building and allows extensions to be built from upper levels such as balconies, awnings, and even rooms bridging a street called *Sabat*. The extension of the *Fina* vertically plus the space above and within the boundaries of a property is considered air space that belongs to its owner. Ibn al-Rami discusses the rules for the utilization of the air space.

-- The nature of the rules and their impact on the micro environment: the prescriptions in Ibn al-Rami's treatise are primarily proscriptive in nature, meaning that they are an imposed restraint synonymous with prohibition as in "Thou shalt not", e.g. you are free to design and manipulate your property provided you do not create damage on adjacent properties. Prescription, on the other hand, is the laying down of authoritative directions as in "Thou shalt", e.g. you shall setback from your front boundary by (x) meters, and from your side boundaries by (y) meters regardless of site conditions. Only two cases in the treatise, numbers 20 and 76, are prescriptive where specific measurements are indicated. An example of the logic for a proscriptive rule is found in the fourth opinion of case 22 on page 64: (Habib asked Sahnun whether a man whose house is adjacent a public street is allowed to create a door that is facing another man's door or not? He said: He should be prevented from it and the door must be offset from the opposite door. Habib asked again: What is the measurement of the offset, is it one or two cubits? He said: To the extent of what is considered to be enough in removing the harm to the opposite house).

Notes about the English translation of the treatise
Professor Mohd Dani Muhamad undertook the initial translation from the original Arabic to English. Both the translator and the editor of this volume agreed to publish this work so as to make it

available to readers worldwide who cannot access the original Arabic. This editor carefully reviewed and edited the translation by carefully checking it with the original Arabic as published in 1995 by its authenticator Dr. AbdulRahman al-Atram (al-Atram 1995). Al-Atram's work is of very high quality resulting from the process of authentication using five copies of Ibn al-Rami treatise. Those copies all date from after the mid-eighteenth century C.E., and they are all housed in the National Book Archive in Tunis.

The translation is literal, i.e. it translates the actual text and style of writing, including the sequence of sentences, as it is found in the treatise. This will provide the contemporary reader with a reliable source of the original text. The treatise does not number the cases that are indicated for discourse. This editor has numbered the cases sequentially as they are recorded in the treatise for a total of 144 cases. This numbering system will be useful for the reader and researcher and it will make it possible to refer to the content and specific cases by number. It will also be helpful if re-grouping is necessary for research purposes.

References

Al-Atram, AbdulRahman (1995). *Al-Ilan bi Ahkam al-Bunyan* by Ibn al-Rami al-Banna. Authenticated study in two volumes. Dar Ishbilyah, Riyadh, Saudi Arabia. Volume one, pages 1 – 414, volume two, pages 415 – 800 (in Arabic).

Bin-Slimane, Ferid (1999). *Al-Ilan bi Ahkam al-Bunyan* by Ibn al-Rami al-Banna. Authenticated study in one volume. Centre de Publication Universitaire, Tunis, Tunisia (in Arabic).

Hakim, Besim S. (1982). "Arab-Islamic Urban Structure", *The Arabian Journal for Science and Engineering*, Volume 7, No. 2, pp. 69-79.

Hakim, B.S. (1983). "The Representation of Values in Traditional and Contemporary Islamic Cities." Two papers by Besim S. Hakim and Peter G. Rowe combined in one article. *Journal of Architectural Education*, Volume 36, Number 4, pp. 22-28.

Hakim, B.S. (1986). *Arabic-Islamic Cities: Building and Planning Principles*. Kegan Paul International, London. Second revised edition, 1988. Paperback edition, 2008.

Hakim, B.S. (1994). "The 'Urf' and its role in diversifying the architecture of traditional Islamic cities", *Journal of Architectural & Planning Research*, Vol. 11, No. 2, pp. 108-127.

Hakim, B.S. (1997). "Rule systems: Islamic", *Encyclopedia of Vernacular Architecture of the World*, (3 vols.), Edited by Paul Oliver, Cambridge University Press, Vol.1, pp. 566-568.

Hakim, B.S. (2001). "Julian of Ascalon's treatise of construction and design rules from 6th-c. Palestine". *Journal of the Society of Architectural Historians*, Vol. 60, No. 1, pp. 4-25.

Hakim, B.S. (2006). "Rules for the built environment in 19th century Northern Nigeria", with Zubair Ahmed. *Journal of Architectural and Planning Research*, Vol. 23, No. 1, pp. 1-26.

Hakim, B.S. (2007). "Generative processes for revitalizing historic towns or heritage districts", *Urban Design International*, Vol. 12, No. 2/3, pp. 87-99.

Hakim, B.S. (2008a). "Mediterranean urban and building codes: origins, content, impact, and lessons", *Urban Design International*, Vol.13, No.1, pp. 21-40.

Hakim, B.S. (2008b) in volume 1: "Law and the City", pp.71-92, and "The Sub-Saharan City: Rules and Built Form" with Zubair Ahmed, pp. 663-676. Illustrations for both articles in the Plates section of volume 2, in *The City in the Islamic World* (2 volumes), Edited by Jayyusi, Holod, Petruccioli and Raymond, Brill.

Hakim, B.S. (2009). "Built Environment, in Law", *Encyclopedia of Islam Three*, pp. 176-179.

Hakim, B.S. (2014). *Mediterranean Urbanism: Historic Urban/Building Rules and Processes*, Springer.

Besim S. Hakim
Rabi al-Thani 1438 / January 2017

AL-I'LAN
BI AHKAM AL-BUNYAN
(Declaration of Building Rules)

Introduction by Ibn al-Rami, the author of the treatise

In the Name of Allah, the Most Gracious, the Most Merciful.

The poor servant of Allah the Exalted: Muhammad b. Ibrahim al-Lakhmi known as Ibn al-Rami al-Banna', who is also known as Muhammad al-Banna', may Allah forgive him says:

Praise be to Allah, who enlightens the perceptions with His wisdom and uplifts them, and He owns the people with His blessing, mercy and He rules them with kindness and favors, He is their owner. I praise Him highly with a praise that can never be reduced by the oceans or the rain that comes from the clouds or tiny particles of the mountains. I also pray continuously for the Prophet (*al-'ummy*) of 'Arab descent, a Hashimite, may peace be upon him, his family and companions.

In this book I have gathered many matters concerning the constructions of walls, the negation of harm, the planting of trees and the mills from the primary collections (*Ummahat al-Dawawin*), and from late writings and past judgments of judges (*qudat*) and from the questions and answers of *Muftis*. All were recorded in *al-Mudawwanah*, and in *al-Wadihah*[1] and *al-'Utbiyyah*[2]; also from the book of 'Abd Allah b. 'Abd al-Hakam[3] and from the book of Ibn Sahnun[4] and from the book of Ibn 'Abdus[5] and from *al-Nawadir*[6] and *al-Tabsirah*[7]. In it also are some documents that were authenticated by writers of *Wathaiq* such as *Wathaiq* Ibn al-Qasim[8], *Wathaiq* Ibn Mughith,[9]

---

[1] Written by 'Abd al-Malik b. Habib b. Sulayman b. Harun (d. 238 AH/852 CE), **Henceforth dates are indicated in AH (Islamic Hijri calender) and in CE (Common Era year).**
[2] Written by Muhammad b. Ahmad b. 'Abd al-'Aziz al-'Utbi al-Andalusi. (d. 255/869).
[3] He is 'Abd Allah b. 'Abd al-Hakam b. A'yan b. al-Layth (d.191/807)
[4] He is Muhammad b. 'Abd al-Salam b. Said al-Tanukhi (d. 256/870)
[5] Muhammad b. `Ibrahim b. 'Abdus b. Bashir (d. 260/874).
[6] Written by Abi Muhammad 'Abd Allah b. 'Abi Zayd. (d. 386/996)
[7] Written by Abi al-Hasan 'Ali b.Muhammad al-Ruba'I al-Lakhmi (d. 478/1085)
[8] He is Abu al-Hasan 'Ali b. Yahya al-Sonhaji, (d. 585/1189).
[9] Abu Ja'far Ahmad b. Muhammad b. Mughith, (d. 459/1067)

and *al-Mutaytiyyah*[10]. In it also are cases selected by *qudāt* like *al-Ahkām* of Ibn Abi Zimnin[11], *al-Ahkam* of Ibn Hisham[12] and *al-Ahkam* of our teacher *al-Qadi al-Faqih al-Zahid*, the knowledgeable, the righteous, the fearer of Allah Abi Ishāq b 'Abd al-Rafī[13], may Allah bless and guide him. I have chosen what I have mentioned to you of *dawāwin* and the books for the sake of Allah, May He be exalted, because of what I considered to be obligatory to be known to everyone who is seeking knowledge among the scholars, and others who want to deeply understand those matters, and because of what is connected with the protection of those who are looking for them to educate Muslims, for the smallest thing that is in someone's possession therein exists duties (*hukm*) and obligations (*lawāzim*), therefore it is compulsory for someone who is seeking knowledge of such (things) to know what we have gathered (in this book) so that he frees himself from the rights of other Muslims. Hence, it is our hope that by Allah's kindness and honor, this sincerity is what we are looking for.

The reason we say at each heading "the Master mason Muhammad says", is to inform the reader of this book that I am just a Master mason. Thus, the reader would excuse me if he finds any mistake in the words or order. As for the narration, we do not claim that it all comes from me originally: This is because I have made every effort to indicate the source carefully while repeatedly checking the content. The second reason is for the fear of the envious people, who might change the first page of a book, which contains the name of the author, so that the book becomes anonymous; its author not known. May Allah by His grace protect us from the burden of the envious people.

---

[10] Written by al-Qadi Abi al-Hasan 'Ali b. 'Abd Allah al-Ansari, known as al-Mutiti (d. 570/1175)

[11] He is Abu 'Abd Allah Muhammad b. 'Abd Allah b. 'Isa b. `Abi Zimnin (d. 399/1009).

[12] Hisham b. Ahmad b. Hisham al-Hilali (d. 530/1136). His book is known as *Mufid al-Hukkam*.

[13] He is Ibrahim b. Hasan b. 'Abd al-Rafi' (d. 733/1332). His book is *Mu 'in al-Hukkam 'ala al-Qadaya wa al-Ahkam*. The book has been edited by Muhammad bin Qasim bin 'Iyad and published by Dar al-Gharb al-Islami, Beirut. 1989.

1- Discourse On The Wall Between Two Neighbors.

Master mason Muhammad bin Ibrahim al-Lakhmi known as Ibn al-Rami al-Banna' said - may Allah guide him -: The wall that lies between two neighboring houses can be divided into three conditions:

First: A wall that is between the two neighbors while each one claiming it for himself.

Second: A wall that is owned by one neighbor that has collapsed or its owner wants to tear it down. Is he obliged to rebuild it?

Third: A wall shared by two neighbors; does one of them have the right to utilize it without the permission of his partner? Can the wall be divided between both of them?

1a- Discourse On The First Wall:

A wall that exists between two neighbors with each one claiming it: The judgment in such a case is according to the known practice (*'adat al-malek*) i.e. the owner's rights in his property. Because the custom and the practice (*al-'urf wa al-'adat*) of the people is the principle that is referred to in streamlining the dispute when there is no other basis to be referred. On this in the Quran: "*Hold to forgiveness commands what is right."*[14]

Master-mason Muhammad says: The custom (*'urf*)[15] we follow (in deciding the ownership) of a wall is (by looking at) six things:

---

[14] Qur'an, *al-'Araf*: 199. Translations of all Quranic verses in this book are based on 'Abd Allah Yusuf 'Ali, *The Holy Qur'an: text, translation and commentary*, (Maryland: Amana Corporation, 1989). However the proponent of *'urf* translated the above verses as 'bid to what is customary (or accepted by local tradition)'. See for example Othman Ishak, '*URF* and custom as being practiced among the Malay community, *Arabica*, vol: 33 (1986): 352-368.

[15] For the role of *Urf* in the traditional Islamic city see the authoritative article by B.S. Hakim, The role of *'Urf* in shaping the traditional Islamic city, in Chibli Mallat, ed. *Islam and public law*, (London, 1993), 141-155. Also "The *'Urf* and its role in diversifying the architecture of traditional Islamic cities", *Journal of Architectural and Planning Research*, 11/2, 1994, 108-127. For in depth discussion on the role of *'Urf* in Islamic law see Ibn 'Abidin, *Nas al-'urf fi bina' ba'd al-ahkam 'alal 'urf*, in *Majmu'at rasa'il Ibn 'Abidin*. 2 vols. (Beirut: Dar al-Kutub al-'Ilmiyyah, n.d) A good general discussion on the topic can be found in any book of Islamic Jurisprudence written by several contemporary scholars, such as Hashim Kamali, *Principles of Islamic jurisprudence*, (Kuala Lumpur: Ilmiah Publisher, 2nd ed.., 2004), 283-296.

The wall bond (*qimt*)[16], the door in the wall, wooden beams inserted into the wall, the small window, the building on top of the wall and the face of the construction.

Al-Shafi'i said that: All those elements have no influence in our judgments.[17] Abū Hanifah[18] said: The ownership of the wall is determined by the bond (*'aqd*), the direction of closing the door and the inserted beam if there are many. If the beam is only one or two, it is not considered. The opinions of Hanafis were conflicting regarding the small window on the wall. The building on top of the wall did not indicate ownership, nor did the face of the construction.

In our school, some scholars are of the same view as Abū Hanīfah's and we shall mention the detailed differences on the matter and we shall explain the problematic points - God willing - hence we say: the wall can be of four types:

A. The wall with bonds, but no elements.
B. The wall with elements, but no bonds.
C. The wall with elements and bonds.
D. The wall with neither elements nor bonds.

Wall Type A (of the First Wall): with bonds but no elements.
The bonds are either from one side of the two properties or from both sides:

If it is bonded from one side and the other house has no bond or element, then it belongs to the house with which it is bonded.

---

[16] *Qimt / Aqd*: the bond or joint that connects the wall to the house. The connection is permanent and becomes part of the building or house structure. Ibn al-Rami did not differentiate between *'aqd* and *qimt*, however Muhammad b. Ahmad al-Qarnati differentiated these two elements. See *Qawanin al-ahkam al-shar'iyyah*, 369. The dictionary defines *'aqd* as to join, to tie whereas *Qmt* is to swaddle or to bandage. Hans Wehr, *Arabic-English dictionary*, (New York: Ithaca, 1976), 790. Ibn Khaldun rightly described how these two elements were employed to build a strong wall. See quotation above page 35.

[17] He is Abu 'Abd Allah Muhammad b. Idris b. al- 'Abbas b. 'Uthman b. Shafi'i b. al-Saib al-Quraishi al-Hashimy al-Mutlabi, the founder of Shafi'ites School. Born in the year 150/767 and died in Egypt in the year 204/819 Ibn Khallikan, Ahmad b. Muhammad b. Ibrahim. *Wafayat al-a'yan wa anba' abna al-zaman*. trans. M. de Slane. ed. S. Moinul Haq. (New Delhi: Kitab Bhavan., 1996), 4:163.

[18] He is Abu Hanifah Nu'man b. Thabit the founder of Hanafis School (d. 150/767). Ibn Khallikan, 5:405.

This judgment was given by Ibn al-Qāsim [19] in the book of 'Abd Allah b. 'Abd al-Hakam and 'Ashhab [20] in *al-Majmū 'ah*, and in the book of Ibn Sahnun. Mutarrif [21] and Ibn al-Majashun [22] in *al-Wadihah* also had the same opinion. Sahnun [23] also stated thus in *al-'Utbiah* and so too 'Isa bin Dinar [24] and Muhammad Ibn 'Abd al-Hakam [25] and Ibn Habib and Ibn Sha'ban [26].

Al-Fakih al-Qadi Abu Ishaq said in his book *Mu'in al-Qudat wa al-Hukkam*: No consideration is given to the face of the wall and neither is given to the beam of the other owner if any. Master-mason Muhammad says: I do not know of anyone from our contemporary Tunisian scholars having a different opinion from the judgment given above. We also do not know of any judge who has given a judgment that differs from what we have established. The basis for that judgment is as narrated from the Prophet that: Some people quarrelled about the wall and brought the matter to him and he sent to them Huzaifah b. al-Yaman, and he judged in the favor of the one with the bond. They told the Prophet he said: You made the right decision [27].

---

[19] He is Abu 'Abd Allah 'Abd al-Rahman b. al-Qasim b. Janadah al- 'Utaqi (d.191/807). He was Malik's most prominent pupil and he died in Cairo in 191/806. 'Iyad b. Musa ibn 'Iyad, *Tartib al-madarik wa taqrib al-masalik li ma'rifah a'lam mazhab Malik*, ed. Ahmad Bakir Mahmud, (Beirut: Dar Maktabah al-Hayat, 1967), 1:116.

[20] He is 'Ashhab b. 'Abd al-'Aziz al-Qaysi al-'Amiri (d. 204/819) an Egyptian, has his own collection of Mudawwanah, but none survived. 'Iyad, *Tartib al-madarik*, 1:447.

[21] He is Abu Mus'ab Mutarrif b. 'Abd Allah, a Maliki jurist from Madinah (d. 220/835). 'Iyad, *Tartib al-madarik*, 1:358.

[22] He is Abu Marwan 'Abdul al-Malik b. 'Abd al-'Aziz b. 'Abd Allah b. Abi Salmah al-Majashun (d. 213/828) a student of Malik and a leading juristconsult of Medina in his day and studied under Malik and his own father. 'Iyad, *Tartib al-mMadarik,* 1:360.

[23] He is Abu Sa'id 'Abd al-Salam b. Sa'id b. Habib al-Tanukhi (d. 240/854).

[24] Abu Muhammad 'Isa b. Dinar al-Ghafiqi (d.212/ 827) an Andalusian Maliki jurist, an author of *Kitab al-jidar*. 'Iyad, *Tartib al-madarik*, 2:19.

[25] Abu 'Abd Allah Muhammad b. 'Abd Allah b. 'Abd al-Hakam, a Maliki scholar from Egypt, contemporary of al-Shafi'i, died in 268/882. 'Iyad, *Tartib al-madarik*, 2:62.

[26] Abu Ishaq Muhammad b. al-Qasim b. Sha'ban (d. 355/966) a Maliki jurist from Egypt. Muhammad b. M. Makhluf, *Shajarat al-nur al-zakiyyah fi tabaqat al-Malikiyyah*, (Beirut, Dar al-Kutub al-Arabi, 1349/1930), 1:80.

[27] Ibn Majah, Muhammad b. Yazid, *Sunan Ibn Majah*, ed. Muhammad Fuad 'Abd al-Baqi (Beirut: Dar Ihya al-Turath al-Arabiyy, 1975), 2:85.

It is also narrated from 'Ali bin Abi Talib, that he used to judge the ownership of a wall based on the bond or a small recessed window, and if there was a door he judged in the favor of the one who controlled it. The companions of Abu Hanifah judged similarly. Al-Shafi'i said: The bond is not considered in the judgment. It was said that Huzaifah had a good knowledge of building and had experience in it.

As for the meaning of *al-qimt*: It is the bond and both of them are taken from *taqmit al-sabiy* (to bind a baby) and to tighten it from loosing, and *al-'uqūd* is the place where a wall is bonded together and the places of its connections in the corners.

The depiction of the bond: (The expert who is reconciling between the owners of the property) has to look at the layers of the disputed wall and the layers of the neighboring walls, which are connected to form a square corner. If the layers are connected continuously, this shows that they are built together at the same time, provided that the layers of the disputed wall in the corners touches each other like the fingers of a hand. The above is the description of the bond, no matter whether the walls are made of unbaked bricks, stones, burnt bricks or something else. If the walls are made of unbaked bricks, we have to look into the impressions of the forms that were used.

Master-mason Muhammad says: I saw in one of the commentators (*risalah*) of Shaykh Abi Muhammad b. Abi Zayd, that the shape of *al-'aqd* was like this □ (a rectangular shape). When (the expert) examines the way the wall's bonds are connected to the disputed wall, and it appears to him in the same way as we have said, he will look at the connections of the walls (to know) in whose ownership it is, and therefore he judges the wall to be of that person's since the interconnected walls are (considered to be) like one wall built at the same time for one person.

Thereof: Master mason Muhammad says: If one of the two claimants asks the Qadi to send an expert or a specialist to see the wall, is he obliged to do so or not? (Scholars have) two opinions: The first opinion is that he is not obliged to do so unless he chooses to. The second opinion is that he is obliged to do so for the fear of illegally denying the right of the one who asked him, since the Prophet sent Huzaifah b. al-Yaman to look at the binding of the walls, and he judged accordingly.

Thereof: If we say that the wall is for the one with the bonds in his favour does he have to swear under oath in addition to the available evidence or not? Two opinions: Abu al-Walid al-Baji [28] in his Ahkam said: He must swear in addition to the evidence of *al-'aqd*. Even Mutarrif and Ibn al-Majashun in the book of Ibn Habib have the same opinion, because the *'aqd* only stands as a witness; therefore, he has to swear in confirmation of his witness. Others say that he is not obliged to swear under oath because the other person lacks evidence, since the Prophet judged that the wall was for the one who possessed the *'aqd* without asking him to swear under oath.

Master-mason Muhammad says: The above judgment appears to be the correct one because the custom and practice are that if the walls of a house are connected to each other, it means that they have been built before the ones adjacent to it. How can someone who becomes a neighbor to that house claim the ownership of the wall, which has been built before his house? Therefore, the one who is favored by *'aqd* is not obliged to take an oath, and it cannot arise for the second owner that he can build his walls and connect them to the first house. Except when he builds a wall that is touching the first house, which makes each house to have its own wall. Therefore, there will be no claim, for the owner of the separate house, on the wall of the connected house except if he says to the first owner that they have built the wall together. Even then, the words of the one favored by *al-'aqd* accompanied by an oath will be in favor.

Thereof: If the wall is on top of the other, then the bond of the lower floor favors the owner of the lower level and vice-versa. Sahnun said that: The wall at ground level is given to whoever is favored by its bond, as it is also the case for the one on top. That was his answer to Habib[29] in the book of his son (Ibn Sahnun).

Master-mason Muhammad says: It is in *al-Nawadir*, and in the book entitled *Muin al-Qudat wal-Hukkam* written by al-Qadi Abi Ishaq b 'Abd al-Rafi', that this occurred in our place in Tunis and the same judgment was given.

---

[28] He is Sulayman b. Khalaf b. Sa'ad b. Ayyub al-Baji (d. 484/1091), one of the judges of al-Andalus. Al-Shaykh Abi al-Hasan al-Nubahi, *Tarikh qudat al-Andalus*, (Beirut: Manshurat al-Maktab, n.d.), 95.

[29] Habib b. Nasr (d. 287/900), a companion of Sahnun, and was in charge of Mazalim. 'Iyad, *Tartib al-madarik*, 4:369.

Thereof: In the case of the wall between two houses that has no ties with the lower floor while it is being tied to the upper floor; Muhammad bin 'Abd al-Hakam said: The whole wall is for the one who owns the bond.

Master-mason Muhammad says: This happened in our place in Tunis and the Faqih Abu Zayd Ibn al-Qattan [30] was the *Qadi al-Jama'ah* and he asked me to look at the case. I saw a wall that extended from the direction of the *Qiblah* to the northern side and it was separated between the two houses and it was carrying a wooden beam from the house on the western side, while there were about ten beams with one *'aqd* from the top of the wall, from the side of the eastern house. When I told him all those details his judgment was that the wall from the bond and the roofing downwards was for the one that owned the bonds, and the other one has the right to insert beams in it. He (Abu Zayd) mentioned that he narrated this matter from Muhammad Ibn 'Abd al-Hakam.

Thereof: If the wall has bonds on both sides, the judgement gives the ownership of the wall to both claimants, each one owning half of it after he (the judge) asks both of them to take an oath. This was said by Ibn al-Qasim in the book of 'Abd Allah b. 'Abd al-Hakam, it is also narrated by Ibn Habib from Mutarrif and Ibn al-Majashun. They said: If one of them takes the oath and another one does not, the wall is given to the one who takes an oath. If both of them take an oath (or both of them do not), it is owned by both of them equally. Abu Hanifah also said the same as what they said.

Thereof: If their claims differ on the matter where one claims owning all of the walls and the other one claims that it is owned by them equally, (the jurists have) three opinions:

Mutarrif said: The one who claims to own all of it takes 2/3 of it and another 1/3 is for the one who claims owning half of it unless one of them admits that the other one has something which acts as a boundary for the part that he owns. The rest is to be divided equally among them as mentioned.

---

[30] He is Abu Zayd 'Abd al-Rahman b. 'Uthman b. al-Qattan al-Balwi al-Susi. Muhammad b. Ibrahim Al-Zarkashi, *Tarikh al-daulatain*, ed. Muhammad Madur, (Tunis: Maktabah al-Atiqah, n.d.), 80.

Ibn al-Majashun said: No matter whether the boundaries of one side of it are accepted or not, the one who claims to own its half has no share in the other half. (In this case the half that is not claimed by the other is for the one who claims for the whole ownership (and) the other half is divided into four parts) (so that) the one who claims ownership of the half (of the wall) is given ¼ and the one that is claiming the whole ownership is given 3/4 of the wall. That judgment is the same for all other things other than a wall. It does not matter whether the thing is in the hands of the two rivals or not.

The opinion of Mutarrif in this matter agreed with Malik's, and the opinion of Ibn al-Majashun agreed with that of his father 'Abd al-'Aziz b. Abi Salmah[31]. Ibn al-Qasim likewise said the same. Shaykh Abu Muhammad b. Abi Zayd said: Our opinion agrees with the opinion of Mutarrif, which is the opinion of Malik, al-Layth[32], Ibn Kinanah[33], Ashhab, Ibn Wahab[34] and Asbagh[35].

Malik's arguments: Their claims are spread to cover the whole objects, not to the particular half of them (a house or other objects) and not to the other half without touching the other half. This would be like the opinion of Ibn Abi Salamah, but when one of them claims joint ownership of the half of the whole thing, it is necessary to divide it between them to the lowest fraction possible to get a half from it, which would result (into dividing it into) two. The one who claims ownership of the whole wall is given two shares and the one claiming ownership of half of it is given one share out of it. This (division) between the two comes to 2/3 and 1/3, such is also the case if their claims

---

[31] He is 'Abd al-'Aziz b. 'Abd Allah b. Abi Salamah al-Majashun, a faqih from Madinah, died in Baghdad in 164/781. Muhammad Ibn Sa'ad, *Tabaqat al-Kubra*, (Beirut: Dar Sadir, n.d.), 5:323.

[32] He is Abu al-Harith al-Layth b. Sa'ad b. 'Abd al-Rahman al-Fahmi, died in Egypt 175/791. Ibn Sa'ad, 7:517.

[33] Abu 'Amru 'Uthman b. 'Isa b. Kinanah (186/802), from Madinah Kinanah was the protégé of 'Uthman b. 'Affan. 'Iyad, *Tartib al-madarik*, 1:292-293.

[34] He is Abu Muhammad 'Abd Allah b. Ibn Wahb b. Muslim. A jurist from Egypt and a student of Malik, died in Egypt in the year 197/813. Ibrahim bin Farhun, *al-Dibaj al-muzahhab fi a'yan 'ulama al-mazhab*, ed. Muhammad al-Ahmadi Abu Nur, (Tunis: Dar al-Turath, n.d.), 132.

[35] He is Abu 'Abd Allah Asbagh b. Faraj b. Sa'id b. Nafi'. A student of Ibn al-Qasim, Ibn al-Wahb and Ashhab, (d. 225/840). Ibn Khallikan, 1:329.

are less or more than that. (If) one of them says that he owns one third of it and the other one says that he owns all of it, we take the lowest fraction that is possible to get 1/3 out of it which is three multiplied by three for the one who claims to own it wholly and 1/3 multiplied by one for the one who claims to own 1/3 of it. The result that is divided between them squarely. Malik took this in the same way as when the creditors are sharing the wealth of a bankrupt debtor, if he spreads it off for them. Ibn Habib said, "I was informed that the scholars of 'Iraq disagreed in the same way as Malik and Ibn Abi Salamah stated.

The third view: 'Isa b. Dinar said: If one of them says that they own it equally and the other one says that it is entirely his, he said: It is for both of them equally if they take an oath. He was asked, why did you say so here when in another place you said that if two men claimed ownership of a cloth, where one of them claimed it wholly and the other one said that it was for both of them, the one who claimed total ownership received two third (3/4) of it and the other one who claimed owning half of it received one fourth (¼) of it. He said: That was the case where the cloth was not in their possession. However, if they had claimed so and came with it to the Sultan, (in this case) it would have been owned by them equally, because it was the only way that the one who had claimed owning its half would have been able to have it. Again, if someone claims something that is in the hands of somebody else and (at the same time) the one who has it in his possession claims the same thing, and both of them do not have clear evidence, it is for the one who possesses it after swearing under oath. In this case, it is not divided between them, but if it is not in the possession of either of them, it must be divided. Similarly, my view on the wall is that the one who claims owning its half is given half of it while the other half, which he claims to be for him and the other, he is just a claimant who does not own it.

Thereof: If a wall exists between two neighbors, who both claim its ownership, and it is found that the wall is bonded to one house at three places and to the other house at one place, Sahnun in the book of his son said: That should be divided between them according to the number of bonds.

Thereof: In *al-Thamaniyah* of Abu Zayd [36], Ibn al-Majashun said: If there is a wall between the two and each one claims it to be his, we look at whose side is surrounded by the wall and to who's corner on his side is enclosed by the wall. Whoever is found to be in possession of the corner, it is for him. And if it is not in possession of any one of them, its foundation has to be unveiled in order to look at its bond and to see which side is nearer to it so that (the owner) becomes the rightful owner of the wall after he takes an oath, even if there are wooden beams of the neighboring house on it.

Thereof: Habib asked Sahnun about a screened wall between two neighboring houses. Both challenged each other and claimed ownership of the wall and the ownership of the screen. Consequently, two trustworthy experts went and looked at it carefully and then reported that the bond of the lower wall on two sides favored one of them and the bond of the screen on one side were connected to the bond of the lower wall, and on the other side to his rival. Then the owner of the lower wall brought evidence that he had lent it to his neighbor so that he could build the screen on it. Sahnun said: The case should be judged according to the evidence, which indicated that he (the neighbor) borrowed it from the owner of the lower wall. He (Sahnun) would look at the bond only when there was no evidence, even though the bond of the screen from the two sides was directly connected to the house of the owner of the lower wall. This was recorded in *al-Umm* (of al-Shafi'i) and I think should have been (directed) to the house of the other one who did not have any bond that favored him in the lower wall because he (Sahnun) refused to consider (the bond) as an available evidence. He said in answering that query: The judgment is as per evidence and the bond has no value. As a result, the owner of the lower wall has the right to order the owner of the screen to remove it because it is something that is borrowed.

---

[36] 'Abd al-Rahman b. Ibrahim b. 'Isa b. Yahya b. Zayd (d. 258/872) a Maliki jurist from Cordova. Studied under Malik's student such as Ibn Kinanah, Ibn Majashun, Mutarrif and Asbagh. Ibn Farhun, *al-Dibaj al-muhazzab*, 147-148.

Wall Type B (of the First Wall): with elements but no bonds.
Master-mason Muhammad says: The second form of the first wall is a wall between two neighbors, each one of them claiming it, and there is no bond between them. Master-mason Muhammad says: If two neighbors claim ownership of a wall between them and there is no bond, the ownership is determined by (considering) the elements of the wall. There are five elements other than the bond. They include: A small window, a door in the wall, wooden beams, the building on the top of the wall, and (on) the sides of it, according to one opinion. When both of them claim ownership, either all of the above elements or some of them are owned by one of them, or are jointly owned. In case all of them or some of them are owned by one of the two claimants and the other one has nothing, the wall is owned by the one who possesses its elements. This was said by 'Abd Allah b. 'Abd al-Hakam from Ibn al-Qasim. Sahnun also said it in his son's book, so too Ibn Sha'ban. Al-Shafi'i said: Both of them own it equally.
Abu Hanifah said: If the elements are wooden beams or a door, then the ownership is for the one who owns either one of them. If the elements are not of the above then it is not the case. His (Abu Hanifah) consideration for the small windows was not specific, as previously indicated.
Mutarrif and Ibn Majashun said: The wooden beam that is resting on it does not determine the ownership of the wall.
Thereof: If there exists a wall between two neighbors, whereby one of them has inserted in it wooden beams, whereas the other one has nothing in it, and there is no bond for any of them, Ibn al-Qasim, in the book of 'Abd al-Hakam, said that the wall (in this case) should be owned by the owner of the wooden beams, whereas Mutarrif and Ibn al-Majashun said in the book of Ibn Habib that they own the wall equally.
The difference between the two is the known custom that the inserted wood beams are for the owner to show possession of the property. This was the reason for Ibn al-Qasim to judge that the ownership of the wall was for the one who owned the wooden beams.
However, Mutarrif and Ibn al-Majashun did not see any evidence in such argument, because the wood can be inserted by a way of gift or by stealing or by permission, for the Prophet said: Any one of you should not forbid his neighbors from

inserting wooden beams in his wall.[37] The interpretation of the Prophetic saying to mean a recommendation (*nadb*) was the reason for Mutarrif and Ibn Majashun to determine the case as joint ownership.

Master-mason Muhammad says: The wooden beams in our locality are of different types: Some are built by putting them on the wall without holes in it for support. If the beams in the wall are of this type, the owner of the wooden beams owns it. And if they are not connected to the wall, but have been put on it after the wall was built and the process of putting the beam on the wall requires digging into it; for it should be put in those holes, in this case, they do not necessarily compel ownership and the determination of ownership is as was decided by Ibn Habib from Mutarrif.

Thereof: If the wall is between the two neighbors and therein, neither bond nor beams for any of them, but each one has a *Kuwa* in the part that is next to him, Ibn al-Qasim as narrated by Ibn 'Abd al-Hakam said it is jointly owned by both of them. Even al-Shafi'i had the same opinion.

Master-mason Muhammad says: *al-Kuwa*[38] in this situation is a recess (*taqah*) that is built-in to uphold the owner's belongings. It is always built in a stone or a wall built with *jeer*, or *al-baghli*. The small window is usually built simultaneously with the wall. If it is built after the wall is built, then it is not considered (for in that case) it is like creating two small cracks in the wall that is built by unbaked bricks (*tabiah*). Sahnun in *Kitab al-Ikrar* said: The *kuwa*, which is drilled into the wall, is not considered.

Thereof: If the wall exists between two neighbor's houses and each one claims it for himself, and one of them has in it an open door while they both do not have in it a bond or a built-in recess (*kuwa*) or wooden beams, it is for the one that the door opens to his side. It was said by Ibn al-Qasim referenced in Ibn al-Hakam's book, and also by Sahnun, Ashhab and Ibn Nafi'[39]. The

---

[37] Narrated by Muslim from Abi Hurayrah. Muslim Ibn Hajjaj, *Sahih Muslim*, (Beirut: Dar Ihya al-Turath al-Arabi, 1955): 3:1230.

[38] *Taqah*: A recess in the wall that does not penetrate to the other side of the wall. Usually used to place various items on it.

[39] Abu Muhammad 'Abd Allah b. Nafi' b. Thabit b. 'Abd Allah b. al-Zubayr (d. 216/831), a student of Malik and a successor to him in Madinah. 'Iyad, *Tartib al-madarik*, 2:357.

Hanafis also gave the same fatwa. It was also narrated that 'Ali b. Abi Talib followed the same ruling, as was mentioned earlier.

If the door is positioned in a place that is possible for each one of them to claim its ownership, the wall is for the one who possesses the side of its closure, as Sahnun said in *Kitab al-Iqrar* to his son. In case both of them possess a door and the direction of its closure, they then own the wall jointly. Abu Hanifah and Shafi‘i had the same opinion.

Master-mason Muhammad says: A similar case happened in Tunis and *al-Faqih* Abu Zayd b. al-Qattan who was the *Qadi al-Jama‘ah* asked me to look into this matter and I saw a wall which passed from the east to the west and in the middle of the wall there was a door which was used as an entrance and an opening to two places. Abu Zayd had divided it to them equally though one originally owned it. Subsequently, each one separately sold his part to a different person. As a result of that, the wall, which had a door, remained open between the two places, so each one of the neighbors claimed ownership of the wall. Then Abu Zayd judged that the door should be blocked, which forced each one of them to make their own door in another location.

Thereof: If the wall exists between the two neighbors, where one of them has a door in it, whereas another one owns wooden beams, Sahnun in the book of his son Muhammad said: It is for the owner of the door and the other one owns the beam. Abu Hanifah had a similar opinion to Sahnun's, so too with Mutarrif and Ibn al-Majashun. Al-Shafi‘i said that they jointly owned the wall. If such a wall collapses: To rebuild it is the responsibility of the owner of the door, according to the first opinion (of Malikis) and the beam if it was inserted after the fundamental construction then it is not required, but if it was connected to the building (built at the same time), then he is obliged to rebuild it. This was said by Shaykh Muhammad bin Abi Zayd.

Thereof: If the beams on it are for both of them and neither of them has a bond nor a *kuwa* nor a door in the wall; these beams fall (into one) of these two (categories):

Either both of them have an equal number of beams, or one of them has more beams than the other.

If they own an equal number of beams or near equal number of them, say one of them owns ten and the other one owns eight or more, then they are considered to be joint owners. It was said so by Ibn al-Qasim in the book of Ibn 'Abd al-Hakam. Ashhab also shared this opinion in *al-Majmu'ah* and Sahnun in the book of his son.

If one of the men owns ten and the other one owns only one, the opinions of scholars on this differed. Mutarrif, Ibn al-Majashun and Sahnun said: They are considered owning it jointly. Ibn Habib also narrated it and the same was said by Ibn Sha'ban.

Shaykh Abu Muhammad b. Abi Zayd said in *al-Nawadir*: It is for the one owning the ten beams except for the place of the one beam. Ibn Shaʿban also narrated this in his book.

Sahnun said in the book of his son that if the beam has been built simultaneously with the wall it obligates possession, but if it has not then there is no ownership. Abu Hanifah agreed with Ibn al-Qasim, Ashhab and Sahnun. Some of Abu Hanifah's companions differed with Abu Hanifah on the matter. Al-Shafi'i agreed with the opinion of Mutarrif and Ibn al-Majashun.

Thereof: If the wall exists between two neighbors who each claims it to be his own and none of them has in it a bond or elements, and if the wall is joined to a building that belongs to one of them, it is determined that the owner of the building also owns the wall, and after taking an oath, his word is honored. It was said by al-Qadi Abu al-Walid al-Baji in his *Ahkam*. Abu al-Hasan al-Lakhmi[40] also had a similar opinion in *al-Tabsirah*.

Thereof: If there is a wall between two neighbors and one of them has on top of it a screen (*sutrah*) and the other one has beams in it, three opinions were expressed here: Ibn Shaʿban said: It is owned jointly. Al-Qadi Abu al-Walid said: It is for the owner of the building as previously said. It is said: The owner of the beam owns it.

Master-mason Muhammad says: The beams may be prescribed as we have mentioned before (i.e. The beams and the wall was built simultaneously), the owner of the screen (*sutrah*) needs to affirm it.

Master-mason Muhammad says: If the beams have been built contiguously over the width of the wall; so that the wall becomes

---

[40] He is Abu al-Hasan 'Ali b. Muhammad, better known as al-Lakhmi, who died in Qayrawan in 478/1085. He was an early Maliki jurist held in high esteem. He is the author of *al-Tabsirah*, a celebrated commentary on the *Mudawwanah*. 'Iyad, *Tartib al-madarik*, 4:797.

thick because of it, thus the case is like the one where the lower part belongs to a man and the upper part belongs to another; what is below the beams is possessed by one owner while the other possesses what's above that. And if the beams are not built simultaneously with the wall, but have been placed there after the wall has already been completed and the screen utilized the wall thickness, then the lower wall is for the one who builds the screen; this was said by Muhammad bin 'Abd al-Hakam, and the owner of the beams needs to affirm it. If the beams are built into the wall whilst the screen has utilized half of the wall, so the other half of the wall is left unutilized for the owner of the beams, such a case happened to us in Tunis while Abu Zayd al-Qattan was there. He asked me to look at it with an expert. Thereupon we saw a wall inserted with beams owned by one of them, whilst the other one (upper floor's owner) had his structure on the wall, utilizing only half of the wall, and left the other half unutilized, this caused us to disagree with our opinion, and the expert said: He and his neighbor is co-partner in the part that are left unutilized (*isqat*) on his neighbor's side. So the judge said to me: Express your opinion to me. I said: If the owner of the beams owns half of the wall, he will prevent any construction on the wall between them.

The second consideration is that: Inserting the beams does not necessarily mean possession, according to the opinion of Mutarrif and Ibn al-Majashun. In the case of the wall which is between two neighbors where one of them has beams in it and the other one has nothing, (they said that) the wall is jointly owned. They did not consider the insertion of the wood/beams (to be enough reason) for possessing the wall because the insertion can be made by a way of gift or by purchase or by *sadaqah* or by stealing, but the wall cannot be stolen or donated since it is heavy. The wall is for the one who owns a building on top of it. He judged that way and did not go with what was said by other Malikis that: The *isqat* on the wall obligates the ownership.

Wall Type C (of the First Wall): with elements and bonds.
The author says: Discourse on the third form of the first wall: Which is between the two neighbors where one of them has its bonds and the other one owns its elements, or both the bonds and

the elements are owned by one of them and the other one owns nothing, or each one of them owns bonds and elements.

If one of them owns the bonds and the elements of the wall and the other one owns nothing, all the Maliki jurists agreed that its ownership is for the one who owns both of them (i.e. bonds and elements). And if each one has bonds and elements, it is jointly owned.

When its bonds are owned by one of them and the other one owns the elements. (It should be noted that) the elements are of many types. They can be a built-in recess, or a door, or wooden beam or a building on top of the wall.

If one of them possesses its bonds and the other one a recess or a door, which he controls its closure; in this case they jointly own the wall because the built-in recess and the door are similar to the bonds.

If one owns its bonds, and the other owns its wooden beams, the ownership of the wall is for the one who owns the bonds. The other one only possesses the locations of the beams. In case one of the beams is broken, he has the right to replace it with a similar beam. This was said by Ibn al-Qasim, Ashhab, Sahnun and Muhammad b. 'Abd al-Hakam.

Thereof: If the owner of the beams wants to remove them from one place to another, he is governed by two kinds of ownership, either temporary or permanent. If it is temporary or the origin of ownership is not known, he then has no right to change the beams' positions. But if the ownership is permanent, he has the right, even if the removal of the beams can cause harm to the wall. If the origin of ownership is not known, he doesn't have the right.

Thereof: When a wall exists between two neighbors and one of them owns its bonds (at ground level) and on top of the upper level there is a screen (*sutrah*) for a room or something else and both of them claim ownership of the screen. If the screen is connected to the house of either one of them, then, that person becomes the owner of the screen. This was said by Sahnun in *Kitab al-Iqrar*, however, if it has no connection to the upper floor, the owner of the lower floor owns it.

Thereof: If the owner of the bonds wants to build on his wall a screen for rooms, (is it allowed or not?). Sahnun said that in this case we must look at the roof. If it is connected to the building and it can cause harm to the beam of the other person, he is not allowed. If it causes no harm, he has the right to do it. That was how (Sahnun) answered Habib.

Master-mason Muhammad says: What Sahnun meant is that the beam was not built with the wall simultaneously. The beam was connected contiguously with the wall. That was why he gave a condition that if the neighbors building caused harm to the wall, he was not allowed that is, if the beam was not connected to the wall (or built separately), the possession was invalidated.

To examine the harm on the wall is from two view points: Either by saying that: Do not build on the top of my beam because your building will break it or he gives such an excuse. An excuse like that is not considered due to its weakness, because according to our custom, any beam used for roofing can uphold another building on it without causing it any harm. Or if possible to make a reason that the wall is weak, hence, the owner of the beam says: Don't add on my beam another construction because I fear that it may cause the wall to collapse. In such a case, the owner of the wall is not allowed to ignore the concern of his neighbor and say that the wall is his and it does not matter whether he makes it heavy or light. (The experts) have to look into the matter. If the wall is found to be strong, then (the one who wants to build on top of it) is not forbidden from doing so and if it is found to be weak, the one who owns it is ordered to strengthen it first and then he can build on top of it whatever he may wish.

Thereof: If such a wall collapses, it is said that the one who owns its bonds is the one to rebuild it. But does the owner of the beams have the right to rebuild similar ones to what has existed before or not? We have this to say: If the beam that is on the wall is not connected to it, he is not allowed to replace it with other than what has existed before. Mutarrif and Ibn al-Majashun in the book of Ibn Habib said this. However, if the beam(s) that existed before has been built simultaneously with the wall, or its origin is not known, in this case, he has the right to replace it. This was said by Muhammad b. 'Abd al-Hakam.

Thereof: According to Sahnun in the book of his son: If a wall between two houses or between two shops of different owners and both of them have on such a wall beams that support both sides of shops or houses, if both of them claim ownership of the beams and on top of the beams exists a wall, which is owned by one of them, in such a case the ownership of the lower wall is for the one that owns the bonds (provided that he takes an oath). If there are no bonds, both of them will have to take oath and it is declared jointly owned. However, the upper wall of the room is like the bond that is owned by the person who owns the room if he takes oath - while the beams of the other remains on it.

In the book of *al-Jidar* authored by 'Isa b. Musa[41], he said: Isma'il b Muwassil[42] was asked about the fate of the beams that were on a wall of another person, their origin of usage was not known, does the owner of the wall have the right, if he wishes, to extract them from his wall or not? He answered: If the origin is not known, the owner of the wall is not allowed to remove the beams. In case he wants to demolish the wall or rebuilds it, he must replace them in their original places. (On the other hand), the owner of the beams is also not allowed to change their positions. In case the origins are known, he has to follow them strictly.

Wall Type D (of the First Wall): with neither elements nor bonds.

The author says: The fourth type of the first wall is the wall that exists between two neighbors and both claim it, and none of them has a bond or elements in it. In this case it is deemed to be jointly owned. This was said by Ibn al-Qasim in the book of 'Abd Allah b. 'Abd al-Hakam, Ibn Habib from Mutarrif and Ibn al-Majashun, Ashhab, Muhammad b. 'Abd al-Hakam, Sahnun in the book of his son, 'Isa bin Dinar and Ibn Sha'ban.

Another opinion of Ibn al-Qasim, but not from the book of Ibn Habib, and of Ibn Habib from Mutarrif and Ibn al-Majashun say: Each one of them must take an oath. If one of them swears under oath and another abstains from it, it is then owned by the one who takes an oath. And if both of them take the oath or both of them abstain from it, it is then considered jointly owned. Al-Shafi'i also agreed with this judgment.

Thereof: If the wall that exists between two neighbors and it is without bonds or elements, but its finished side faces one of them

---

[41] He is Abu al-Asbagh 'Isa b. Musa b. Ahmad b. Yusuf b. Musa, known as Ibn al-Imam (d. 386/996).

[42] He is Abu Marwan Isma'il b.Muwassil from Toledo (d. 300/913). Abdullah b. Muhammad b. Yusuf, Ibn al-Faradi, *Tarikh 'Ulama' al-Andalus*, (Cairo: Dar al-Misriyyah, 1966), 65.

and its rear side faces the other, there are two approaches of deciding the ownership.

It is said that the wall is for the one who owns the finished side. Ibn Sha's[43], al-Lakhmi[44] and others in the original sources, recorded this.

Sahnun said in *al-Nawadir*: The finished side of the wall is not considered. If the wall is between the two neighbors and there is no bond, one of them owns the finished side and another one owns the rear side, then ownership is divided equally.

Master-mason Muhammad says: This is obvious, for the obverse and rear sides are not, but one structure, especially in a thin wall, either stone or brick wall. If the wall isn't built according to the said feature, the ownership should be considered according to two aspects: -

First aspect: It is not bonded to the corners and there are no divisions. Second aspect: If it is the façade of the wall that has decorations and bonded to the corners, if its front side faces the internal of the house and its rear side faces the external of the house, then this occurrence is rare while rareness is not applied in judgment.

1b- Discourse On The Second Wall:

The author says: It is a wall owned by a man, but it provides privacy to his neighbor. If this wall collapses or the owner wants to bring it down, is he (the owner) obliged to rebuild it or not? We say: For such a wall, there are three conditions: It is either still strong, which is not in danger of collapsing but the owner wants to demolish it. Or it is weak and the owner wants to demolish it out of fear that it may collapse. Or it has collapsed by the will of God.

The first condition: The wall is still strong and not in danger of collapsing, but the owner wants to demolish it.

Master-mason Muhammad says: The intention of the owner to demolish it can either be harmful to his neighbor or beneficial to him. If by demolishing it, he wants to harm the neighbor, then he is not allowed to do so. Ibn al-Qasim in *al-'Utbiah* and *al-*

---

[43] He is Abu Muhammad 'Abd Allah b. Najm b. Sha's b. Nazar b. Asha'ir (d. 610/1213), a jurist from Egypt. Ibn Farhun, *al-Dibaj al-muhadhdhab*, 141.

[44] Abu al-Hasan al-Lakhmi.

Majmu'ah says: He is not allowed to bring it down except when we know that he is not intending to harm (his neighbor). Ashhab, Ibn Nafi, Ibn Kinanah, and Ibn al-Majashun also said the same. It was also the same view of Ibn Habib based on the Prophetic saying: "Do not harm others or yourself, and others should not harm you or themselves"[45].

Thereof: If he demolished it, is he obliged to rebuild it or not. Two opinions: It is said that he is not obliged to rebuild it, and the famous view is that he is obliged to rebuild it.

In the case where he has demolished it for his own benefit, can he be forced to rebuild it? Four opinions:

Isa b. Dinar said in *al-'Utbiah*, narrated from Ibn al-Qasim: If he has torn it down for his own benefit with the intention of rebuilding it and then he finds himself unable to do so due to hardship or feels that he does not need to do so; he is not forced to rebuild it. The neighbor in this case can shield himself within his compound if he is so willing. Ibn al-Qasim in *al-Majmu'ah* also narrated the same view from Malik. Ashhab and Ibn Nafi' had the same opinion.

The second view: In *al-Wadihah*, Ibn al-Majashun, Sahnun and Ibn Kinanah were recorded to have said: The owner is forced to rebuild the wall, whether he likes it or not; for it is harmful to his neighbor's house if it is not built and that is not excusable; because the neighbor has a right upon him since he has built his house with the neighbor's wall as a partition.

Third view: Ibn Habib in *al-Wadihah* said, Mutarrif said: He is obliged to rebuild it but at his own pace. Then his neighbor is required to cover himself by using another partition, but in case he is unable to do so due to poverty, then the owner of the wall is obliged to rebuild the wall, whether he likes it or not. Abu Zayd b. Ibrahim[46] also narrated from Muhammad from 'Abd al- Malik b. Habib from Mutarrif similar to what was said by Ibn al-Majashun.

---

[45] Narrated by Ibn Majah, 2:784; narrated also by al-Daraqutni, 'Ali b. 'Umar, *Sunan al-Daraqutni*, (Beirut: Alam al-Kutub, 1986) 2: 227-228.; Malik also narrated this *hadith* in his *Muwatta'* in *Kitab al-Aqdiah*, 2:745. Imam Ahmad ibn Hanbal narrated this *hadith* in his *Musnad,* 1:313, and 5:327.

[46] He is Abu Zayd 'Abd al-Rahman b. Ibrahim b. 'Isa b. Yahya b. Barid (d. 258/872), the author of *Al-Thamaniyah*.

The fourth view: Yahya[47] narrated that Ibn al-Qasim said: The owner is obliged to rebuild it if he can afford it, but if he cannot, then he is not obliged to do so. The famous view is that he is not obliged to do so and this is what is being practiced.

The second condition: The wall is weak and is in danger of collapse, and the owner wants to demolish it. All scholars agree that he has to demolish it. But if he refuses to demolish it while it is harmful to his neighbors or the people passing near it, in this case, whether he is rich or poor, he is obliged to demolish it. In case he is absent, this matter will be discussed under the topic of the Collapse of the Slanting wall.

Thereof: If after demolishing the wall, is he obliged to rebuild it or not? Two opinions: (according to what has been mentioned). Yahya b. 'Umar[48], 'Abd Allah b. 'Abd al-Hakam, and 'Isa b. Dinar in his book, from Ibn al-Qasim said: If the wall threatens to fall, and the owner is ordered to tear it down, then he should not be forced to rebuild it.

Second opinion: Ibn al-Majashun in the book of Ibn Habib said: He (the owner) is compelled to rebuild it. (Sahnun gave the same opinion in his answer to Habib). The famous of the two opinions is that he is not obliged to rebuild it. Among the preceding four views the first one is generally favoured.

The third condition: The author says: The wall, which is strong or weak, but has fallen due to the will of God; Is the owner obliged to rebuild it? Three different opinions: 'Isa b. Dinar in *al-'Utbiah* narrated from Ibn al-Qasim said: If the collapsed wall is owned by one of them, the owner is not obliged to rebuild it and each one takes care of shielding their properties. Ibn Kinanah, Sahnun and Ibn Majashun said: It is compulsory for the owner to rebuild it.

Mutarrif said: The owner is not obliged to rebuild it and the other is required to shield himself. If he is poor and cannot rebuild the said wall, he is excused. The accepted opinion is that the owner is not obliged to rebuild it and the neighbor makes cover for himself in his property. The difference in the second and third

---

[47] He is Yahya b. Yahya b. Kathir al-Laythi al-Andalusi. He studied under Ibn al-Qasim and died in the year 234/849. Ibn al-Faradi, 2:176-178.

[48] Abu Zakariyya Yahya b. 'Umar b. Yusuf b. Amir al-Kanani, from Qayrawan but resided in Susa and died there in the year 289/902. 'Iyad, *Tartib al-madarik*, 3:234-241.

conditions is covered in the first condition, but the repetition has occurred to make the matter clearer and there is no harm in that.

Thereof: If the wall that is owned by a man collapses due to the will of God, or by the owner's action and then his neighbor tells him: Let me have your site and soil, whereas the bricks and expenses are on me, when I have completed the wall both of us can utilize it as we wish. Sahnun said: It should not be like that, such an act is illegal because both of them are making a contract where its time is not mentioned and none of them has mentioned the items that they will be utilizing the wall for. In such a case, the owner of the site and materials must pay back the expenses incurred for the bricks and labor to his partner and then claim ownership of the wall.

Thereof: If one of the neighbors asks his neighbor to allow him to tear down a leaning wall that is about to fall and rebuild it on his behalf, on condition that he is allowed to put on it his beams, and the owner allows that to happen, Isa b. Dinar said: The owner of the wall will not forever be allowed to request his neighbor to remove his beams even if he is in need of the wall, because of the way that they agreed is taken to be in the category of buy and sell.

1c- Discourse On The Third Wall

The author says: It is a wall that is jointly owned by two neighbors, but one of them decides to use it the way he deems necessary without the permission of the other.

Master-mason Muhammad says: When there is a wall between two neighbors and one of them wants to utilize it without his neighbor's permission, it falls into a few possibilities: He either wants to utilize the full width of the wall or he wants to build on his half and leaves the other half to his neighbor. If he wants to completely build on it, his action is not allowed according to the consensus of all scholars of the *madhhab* and whatever he has built must be pulled down, no matter whether the structure is small or big.

If he requests to build on the side adjacent to his house, there are two opinions: Ibn al-Qasim as narrated by 'Abd Allah b. 'Abd al-Hakam said: That neither of the two partners is allowed to build on it or insert beams or any other use without the permission of the other. This is the accepted opinion, which has been followed in the *fatawa* and in practice.

The other possibility by Ibn Habib in *al-Wadihah* said: I asked Mutarrif and Ibn al-Majashun: A wall owned jointly by two neighbors, one of them wants to build on it, or to erect any building element on it which does not prevent the other partner from utilizing the wall; but finds that the wall is weak for what he wants and thus he wants to demolish it and build a stronger one (is he allowed to do so?) He (Ibn Mutarrif) said: That person is allowed to do it and his neighbor has no right to prohibit him. Then I asked: What is the status of the ownership of the wall (between them) after rebuilding it? They said: The partnership then continues as before. This opinion was also held by Asbagh b. al-Faraj.

Thereof: If two neighbors own a wall and both of them do not differ on the partnership, and both of them have on it their beams, where one of them has beams at a higher level than the other and the person that owns the lower beams wants to raise his wooden beams to the same level as the other's, but is prevented from doing so by his neighbor, Sahnun said in the book of *al-Iqrar* to his son: The owner of the higher level does not have the right to prevent his neighbor from doing so. He (Sahnun) was asked: What if the neighbor who owns a higher (ceiling level) denies that the other one who owns the lower level owns anything above his beams; his word is accepted if he takes the oath because he possesses that part, which is beyond the level of the owner of the lower (ceiling level). What he meant was: The owner of the lower beams does not have the right to increase the level of his beams.

Thereof: If the jointly owned wall collapses; can the two neighbors be compelled to rebuild it (or not)? In such a matter we say: The nature of this wall is either it has a building on top of it for one of the neighbors such as a room or partition of an upper room, or something of the building that makes one of them own the space which is above the wall, or it does not have anything on its top that we have mentioned. The author says that: In that case the one who is refusing to cooperate with his partner is forced to cooperate according to the agreed position of the Maliki School (*ahl al-madhhab*). It is the same as if the lower part of the wall is owned by one man and the upper part by another.

In case it has nothing on its top, there are three approaches: Ibn al-Qasim reported from Malik in *al-Majmu'ah* that: Each one of them must be compelled to cooperate in building the wall with his partner. This was also said by Ibn Habib from Mutarrif and Ibn al-Majashun and Ibn Wahb. The second approach from Ibn al-Qasim, Ibn Kinanah and Ibn 'Abdus in *al-Nawadir* said that: It is not compelled. And Ibn Habib said that: The Sultan (i.e. local authority) can force him to build it. I asked him: What if he is incapable of doing it? He answered: In that case some of his properties or part of his house has to be sold in order for him to be able to do so. Sahnun's stand on that is not certain.

The third approach is by Yahya b. 'Umar reported from Ibn al-Qasim in *al-'Utbiah* that (the one who is refusing to cooperate) is forced to do so if he is capable of doing it and in case he is incapable, he cannot be forced to do it. The author says that al-Qadi Abu al-Hasan b. Yahya al-Qasim, in his *Wathiqah* agreed with the third approach.

Al-Shafi'i said: None of them is compelled to build it. Abu Hanifa's stand is not clear, as that of Sahnun. He once said that it is compelled to do so and on another occasion said that it is not.

Master-mason Muhammad says: The popular practice in the *Madhhab* is that he is not compelled, and our practice and *fatawa* follow this opinion.

The author says: It once happened in Tunis and it was judged not to force the owner to rebuild it. Hence, the two houses remained open to one another until it became unbearable to the owner of the house that had no wall before and he, therefore, built a wall in his compound to protect his privacy. The owner of the first wall was not compelled to rebuild it.

The author says: The logic of not forcing comes from regarding the wall as a possession, which, if no one is sharing it with him; he is not compelled to make any expenditure on it. Therefore the principle is the same when it is jointly owned. Similarly, if they own a piece of land and one of the partners asks another to cultivate it or to build on it together with him, the other partner is not obliged to follow.

On the other hand the logic of compelling is based on the prophetic saying that "Do not harm others or yourself and others should not harm you or themselves", and it is because the partner cannot benefit from his share and cannot be prevented from being harmed unless his partner cooperates with him, and because both of them have interests in it. Hence forcing him becomes compulsory (*wajib*).

Thereof: There was a case where a wall that was jointly owned had collapsed and one of the partners rebuilt it and forbade his neighbor from benefiting from it until he agreed to pay him half of the expenses. Malik said inform the neighbor who did not contribute in the rebuilding thus: either demolish the wall and rebuild it together or pay him half of the expenses he has incurred, and you (the one who refuses) cannot benefit from the wall until you have done one of these two options.

2- Discourse On The Method Of Dividing A Wall And The Method Of Balloting And Whether A Man Has The Right Of Pre-Emption (*Shuf'ah*) In The Wall.

The author says: The wall between two neighbors, one of them wants to divide it and the other wants to build it, we say: this wall falls under one of the following categories:

The wall is either holding (a beam) or a building (on it), or not holding either of them, or holding a beam but not a building. In case it has a beam and a building on top of it, the consensus is that the wall is not allowed to be divided, as previously mentioned.

In case the wall is not holding any beam or building, the opinions of jurists differed into three:

First opinion: Ibn al-Qasim said in *al-Mudawwanah*: It can be divided as long as it does not cause any harm (to either party). Ibn Sha'ban also had the same opinion in his book and it was the popular opinion among Maliki jurists.

Second opinion: Ashhab in *Mudawwanah* said: The wall cannot be divided because its division is harmful to the other partner who refuses to divide it, on which he puts his beam, fastens his peg and to which he ties up his animals. Ibn Habib in *al-Wadihah* said: Mutarrif, Ibn al-Majashun and Asbagh said that: The jointly owned wall cannot be divided except when both partners agree to do so, whether the wall is holding something or not. Fadl[49] and Al-Makhzumi, Ibn Nafi'and others had similar opinions. Sahnun in the book of Muhammad said: (The wall) cannot be divided.

---

[49] He is Abu Salmah Fadl b. Salmah b. Jarir b. Mankhal al-Jahni (d. 319/931). Ibn al-Faradi, 1:352.

Third opinion: 'Isa b. Dinar said in *al-Nawadir*: If the wall is jointly owned and one of them wants to build it while the other wants to divide it, the one who wants to divide it must be ordered by the authority to build it together with the other owner. If he still refuses (to build) he is (then) ordered to accept its division.

The third form: A jointly owned wall, holding beams of both owners. Ibn al-Qasim in *al-Mudawwanah* said: If the stems of their beams are intermixed, so that it is impossible to divide it, and both of the owners have to estimate (their share on them), it is considered to be like goods and animal stock which cannot be divided. Abu al-Hasan al-Lakhmi said: This is not clear; because the wall holding the beams should not be a barrier of division (between them). It is just like the division of upper and lower floor whereas the ground floor holds the upper floor. Ibn al-Qasim allowed the assessment on the condition that whomever the wall goes to becomes the owner of it and the other person owns the right to fix his beam on the said wall. If the assessment is permitted based on the above condition, then the division is advisable.

Thereof: If the division is allowed, how should it be done? Two opinions: Ibn al-Qasim said: A rope extends lengthwise (not height wise) from the beginning of the wall to its end, and its middle is measured and indicated. Then the lot is cast between them and each takes the half of the wall that comes up on their ballot.

The second approach: From 'Isa b. Dinar: It is divided based on the broadness of the wall and each one takes the half that is next to him. Abu al-Hasan al-Lakhmi said: This is not applicable in dividing the whole wall, because the harm and the weight are not specific on the part that is next to either partner. (The above method of division is applicable) when a person wants to divide the upper part, such as if its width is two hand-spans, so each one builds on the top of the existing wall within the part that is next to him of one *shibr* (one hand-span), which will be measured for the upper part only while the whole wall remains to be possessed jointly as it was before.

Master-mason Muhammad says: Or when both owners want to divide the wall after it has collapsed, they should divide the site of the wall equally and each person owns the part which is next to him.

Thereof Master-mason Muhammad says: The method of balloting as described by Ibn al-Qasim is thus: The name of each person is written on a piece of paper (*ruq'at*) and put inside a container made of clay or glass and then each is thrown in a direction so that a person whose name appears on that side will possess it.

Others said: Their names and direction are written, then the first bullet that contains a name on it is taken and thrown in one direction; and whosoever name appears on that side takes it.

Thereof: A wall between two houses and one of them sells his house. Does the right of pre-emption exist on the other half of the jointly owned wall? In this we say:

The wall falls either under the categories of walls that can be divided or walls that cannot be divided. If it falls under the category of walls that cannot be divided then the preemption is not allowed. If it falls under the category of walls that can be divided then pre-emption (*shuf'ah*) is applicable. This issue will be discussed at the end of the book.

3- Discourse On A Man Who Allows His Neighbor To Insert Wooden Beams In A Wall, Or Who Opens A Door Or Passageway And Who Sells The Support for the Beams. Is He Allowed Repossessing It Or Not?

The author says: The principle in inserting the beams is based on the narration by Malik in *Muwatta'* on the authority of Abu Hurayrah[50], which was also narrated by Ibn Nafi' from Malik in *al-Majmu'ah*, and it is also among what Ashhab heard from Malik and recorded it in *al-'Utbiah* and said that it is what the Prophet ordered. The Prophet said that: "None of you should forbid his neighbor from inserting wooden beams in his wall".[51]

Master-mason Muhammad says: Scholars interpreted this *hadith* differently as to whether it should be understood to carry the meaning of *nadb* (recommended) not *wajib* (compulsory). Al-Shafi'i, Ahmad b. Hanbal, Ishaq[52] and Abu Thawr[53] understood

---

[50] He is 'Abd al-Rahman b. Sakhr al-Dusi, one of the companions who died in the year 57/677.

[51] See also Malik b. Anas, *al-Muwatta*, ed. Aisha Bewley, *Kitab al-'aqdiah*, 529.

[52] He is Ishaq b. Ibrahim b. Makhlad, one of the *ahl al-hadith* (d. 238/852). Al-Suyuti, *Tabaqat al-huffaz*, 188-189.

it to mean compulsory (*wajib*) while Malik (and his followers) understood it as recommended (*nadb*).

They also differed on the number of beams, is it one or many? Ibn Battal[54] in his *al-Mufi'* as twenty understood to be many. Abu Ja'far al-Tahawi[55] said: Ruh b. al-Faraj[56] told me: I asked Abu Zayd[57] and al-Harith b. Miskin[58] and Yunus b. 'Abd al-A'la[59]; what about the other narration regarding inserting one's wooden beams? All of them understood that to be read with *tanwin* and *nasb* on *khasbatan wahidatan*. This was taken by Malik and his followers to mean, according to what is known, urging not in a compelling way towards it, and to urge the neighbor who threatens his neighbors to make him aware of the rights of the neighbor without passing judgment against those who refrains from doing it, since it is not good for a Muslim to refuse his neighbors from inserting the wooden beams after knowing the *hadith*. Whoever insists and refuses to follow the *hadith* is considered to be mistaken and to be committing something appalling, but (he) is not compelled, for the *hadith* is taken to carry the meaning of recommendation. The evidence is that the companions did not follow the command since Abu Hurayrah after narrating the *hadith* said that: "Why do I see you not following it?" By the name of Allah, I will throw it upon your shoulders. They were the rightful people who could not turn from the order of the messenger of Allah; and only an ignorant person who could think otherwise.

---

[53] He is Ibrahim b. Khalid b. Abi al-Yaman al-Kalbi (d. 240/854), a Shafi'i scholar from Baghdad. Tajuddin b. Abd al-Wahab al-Subki, *Tabaqat al-Shafi'iyyah al-kubra,* (Beirut: Dar al-Maarifah, n.d.), 1:227-231.

[54] He is Abu al-Hasan Ali b. Khalaf b. 'Abdul-Malik b. Battal, *ahl al-hadith* from Qurtubah (d. 449/1057) 'Iyad, *Tartib al-madarik,* 2:827

[55] Ahmad b. Muhammad b. Salama b. 'Abd al-Malik al-'Azdi al-Tahawi, a well-known leading Hanafi jurist from Egypt (d. 321/933) Ibn Khallikan, 1:107-110.

[56] Abu al-Zanba' Ruh b. al-Faraj al-Qattan al-Misri (d.282/895) a jurist from Egypt, 'Iyad, *Tartib al-madarik,* 2:191.

[57] 'Abdul al-Rahman b. 'Umar b. Abi al-Ghamr (d. 234/849) 'Iyad, *Tartib al-Madarik* 1:525; Ahmad Ibn Hajar al-'Asqalani, *Tahzib al-tahzib* , (Beirut: Dar al-Maarifah, 1325 H), 6:249-250.

[58] He is Abu 'Amru al-Harith b. Miskin b. Muhammad b. Yusuf (d. 250/864). 'Iyad, *Tartib al-madarik,* 1: 569; Ibn Khallikan, 2:56.

[59] Abu Musa Yunus b. 'Abd al-A'la b Musa b. Maisarah b. Hafs b. Hayyan, a Shafi'is jurist from Egypt (d. 264/878) Ibn Hajar, *Tahzib al-tahzib* , 11:440; al-Subki, 1:279.

Further evidence is the Prophetic saying that, "a Muslim's property is not allowed to be used without his consent"[60] and that "Nothing is to be taken from the property of someone except Zakat".[61]

Ibn al-Qasim said in *al-Majmu'ah*: It is not good for him to prevent his neighbor from doing so, but (if he refuses) there is no judgment against him.

Ibn Wahb reported from Malik that: It is something that the Prophet preferred. He said: Ibn al-Mutallib was using (the *hadith*) in his judgments.

Thereof: The author says; if a house is adjacent to a mosque and he wants to insert his beam onto the wall of that mosque, the view of Andalusian jurists in Cordova differed on that.

Ibn Sahl[62] in his book said: I wrote in the month of Sha'ban in the 456th year to the scholars of Cordova asking whether a man who is neighboring a mosque is allowed to insert his wooden beam into the wall of the mosque in the same way as he is allowed to do so into his neighbor's wall.

Ibn 'Itab[63] wrote back and said: The Scholars (al-Shuyukh) allow it if it does not harm the mosque. (On the contrary) Ibn al-Qattan wrote back prohibiting it.

Master-mason Muhammad says: In case a man has inserted a wooden beam into his neighbor's wall, is it possible (for the neighbor) to remove it? On that we say: His insertion has been done either without the permission of the owner of the wall, or with his permission, or with the owner's knowledge but without his permission.

If he has inserted the beam without the owner of the wall's permission or knowledge, the owner is allowed to remove it whether this removal will cause harm to the owner of the beam or not, after a long or a short period of time, because the one who has inserted the beam has used someone else's property illegally, as the Prophet said; 'a Muslim's property is not allowed to be used without his consent'.

---

[60] Narrated by al-Daraqutni, 3:25-26.
[61] Narrated by Ibn Majah, 1: 570.
[62] Abu al-Asbagh 'Isa b. Sahl b. 'Abd Allah al-Asadi, a judge from Granada (d. 486/1093) al-Nubahi, 96-97.
[63] A Maliki jurist from Cordova (d. 462/1070). 'Iyad, *Tartib al-madarik*, 4:810-813.

If it has been done with the owner's permission, the following aspects are possible: Either the period of lending is mentioned or not, or the agreement is quiet about it. If the period of lending is mentioned it must be fulfilled and the owner of the wall is not allowed to remove the beam on his wall until the period agreed upon is covered.

The jurists disagreed in the case where the period is not mentioned and the owner wants to remove the inserted beam. There were four opinions: Malik, Ibn al-Qasim, Ashhab, Ibn Nafi^c, Asbagh and 'Isa b. Dinar said: He is allowed to remove it so long as it is established that he needs his wall to use it for something else and does not intend to harm his neighbor. This is because he has the rights on the building and can remove whatever he wants from his wall, even if this will cause damage to his neighbor.

The second opinion: He is not allowed to remove it until the period of time that is customarily known for such a contract elapses. Ibn Mazin said this in his book *al-Wathaiq*. It was also the opinion of Ibn al-'Attar.

The third opinion: Mutarrif and Ibn al-Majashun in the book of Ibn Habib said: If a man lends his wall to a neighbor to attach his beams, he is not allowed to remove it, whether a long or short period of time has elapsed, whether he is in need of his wall or not, dies or is alive, sold the right, or inherited it, until the wall collapses and the owner rebuilds it. In this case, the borrower is not allowed to reattach his beams unless with a new contract. They (Mutarrif and Ibn al-Majashun) narrated this opinion from Malik and others.

The fourth opinion: Muhammad b. 'Abd al-Hakam said in *al-Tabsirah* that the owner is allowed to revoke his offer and remove it.

Master-mason says: I saw a judgment by al-Qadi Abu al-Hasan b. al-Qasim in his *Wathaiq*: If the wall has collapsed and the owner then rebuilds it, he is required to return all the easement elements as they were before. In case he refuses to do it, it is upon the possessor of the easements to rebuild the wall so that he can benefit from that. If the latter is done and the owner wants to utilize the wall, he cannot do so until he compensates the owner of the beams who has rebuilt the wall. (The rule here is) similar to the rule for sharing a well.

Master-mason Muhammad says: That is not correct, unless the easement, or servitude, was permanent or it is not known how the earlier arrangements were negotiated, so the above solution is correct.

Ibn Mazin said: If he lends his wall to the neighbor and he takes witness on that, the borrower is not allowed to claim more than what he has been allowed to use. If he does not have evidence on the borrowing and the lender denies doing so, he should swear and the evidence should be left as it is.

Thereof: If a man lends his wall to his neighbor to insert wooden beams, and the owner of the beams claims that the place where the beams are inserted belongs to him; his word is taken to be true with an oath. After taking the oath, he becomes a rightful owner.

Thereof: Master mason says it is allowed for a man to buy a location on the wall to place his primary beam (*jawaiz*)[64] from his neighbors. If the location is for permanent use, then it is considered a sale, and if it is for temporary use then it is considered a lease.

4- Discourse On A Man Who Lends His Courtyard (To Another) Who In Turn Develops It and Then the Owner Decides To Remove Him (Or To Sell A Main Beam)

Al-Shaykh *al-Faqih al-Qadi* Abu Ishaq b. 'Abd al-Rafi' said in his *al-Ahkam* that: If a man allows another person to build in his courtyard on *'ariyah*[65] contract and after he (the lessee) has constructed his building, the owner wants to remove him, the owner cannot do so before the expiry of the agreed period, unless the lessee himself wants to go away and to demolish his property. In this situation, the landlord is free to to pay him the value of his demolished building's materials. If the time limit is not mentioned and the tenant has not yet constructed anything, the landlord is allowed to revoke his permission. However, Ibn

---

[64] Cross beam (main beam) between two rows of stone on a wall. From here all the other smaller wood are rested to complete the construction of a roof. Muhammad Amin, 28.

[65] Use of property gratuitously, without a price. *The Majallah*, art. 765.

al-'Attar[66] said: (the landlord's revocation is valid) with a notice and acceptance (by the tenant). If it is done after the tenant has constructed his building, the landlord is not allowed to force him out with such a short notice unless the landlord gives him whatever amount that has been spent on it. He said in another place, *al-Mudawwanah*, that the landlord gives him his expenditures. Ibn Abi Zimnin said: This phrase is not available in some other sources.

Asbagh said: The landlord is not allowed to force him out even if he is willing to give him the construction's standing value until the period known for such a lease elapses. Fadl said (on Asbagh's opinion): His opinion resembles (our opinion) because our scholars agree that he is not allowed to force him out if (they) have agreed on a certain period until it is completed.

And if the lessee stays for a period of time that he is entitled to such a lease, and the landlord wants to vacate him, according to Ibn al-Qasim and those who agree with him among Egyptian scholars, he is entitled to the value of his demolished building only, otherwise, the landlord can give up the demolished parts to him. But according to many *Madaniyyuns* the landlord is not allowed to force him out unless he pays him the building's standing value.

Thereof Ibn Habib said: I asked Mutarrif and Ibn al-Majashun about a man who has requested his neighbor (to allow him to) open a door, or to erect building utilities adjacent to his property or to alter a road or to build an access road in a place which is not proper, and other things that are similar to those mentioned above, as part of a good treatment a Muslim should grant his neighbor, but the neighbor refuses to grant his permission, should he be legally forced to do that? Both of them replied that such a case or cases similar to that should be considered like the case of the consent to insert wooden beams on the neighbor's wall. (The refusal) is not a good signal- as a way of promoting the spirit of kindness for the sake of reward and being kind to a fellow Muslim- whereas there is no harm on him if he agrees and there is no benefit in his refusal. Nevertheless a judge cannot prosecute

---

[66] He is Abu 'Abd Allah Muhammad b. 'Abd al-Aziz b. Yahya (d. 392/1002), an expert in *wathaiq* from Cardova. 'Umar Rida Kuhalah, *Mu'jam al-muallifin*, (Beirut: Dar al-Turath al-Arabi, n.d.), 10:177.

anybody against it because the rights are given to their owner on request and there is none before they make a request. Therefore, it is not compulsory to grant any request. He said: I asked both of them: When a man allows his neighbor to do (the above things), is he forbidden from revoking the permit; just like the case of a man who allows his neighbor to insert wooden beams into his wall is forbidden (from revoking his permission)? They replied that: Both are different. If what is being allowed (to be built) involves labor, expenditures, time and effort, such as inserting wooden beams or building the foundation of a wall on the side of the lender, or sharing water from a spring or well, or growing a tree, or starting seedling or something similar, once the permission is withdrawn it will cause great damage to the neighbor. In this case, he (the lender) is not allowed to withdraw his permission, whether the cost of maintenance is big or small, he cannot revoke it during his lifetime or after his death or if he is inherited, (and whether) he needs it or not; it is like a gift. It does not matter even if during the offer, he makes a provision that he will have the right to revoke his permission; because such stipulation is not valid. Furthermore the stipulation is against the spirit of Muslims because it will harm the other party. By revoking his permission, the other party will suffer both in labor and financial term. The Prophet said: "Do not harm yourself and others and others should not harm themselves and you." No harm is worse than damaging someone after he has completed his work. Therefore the stipulation is not valid. Giving consent after the work has been in progress is permissible and correct, but (giving permission) before the work with the above additional stipulation is not correct.

Both said: However, he (the lender) is allowed to revoke the permission in a case that does not burden the lessee, such as on those things that do not involve major work or expenditures. Among things that do not involve too much expenditures or labors are the construction of a door or of a small window (*kuwa*), or of a passageway through the lender property or of other similar easement rights, or the irrigation of a tree. If the lender has set a definite period in the earlier agreement, he is obliged to honor that. He is also obliged to honor an agreement on an access road to the earlier lender if he sells his house to another buyer with his full knowledge with the condition that he should not build anything, he is entitled to (his) expenditures and a (compensation) if his right is taken over. Ibn Habib said: Ibn Nafi' and Ashhab had the same opinion. However, Asbagh said: In my opinion, it is the same whether it requires a lot of expenditures or not, once the period that is (known) for such a thing is covered, (the owner) has the right to revoke his permission except for cultivation, since he cannot do so after a tree has been planted.

Ibn al-Qasim in *al-Wathaiq* said: If the easement rights are permanent, the owner (*murfiq*) is not allowed to remove (any built element) even though he is in need of it, so too if the letting period is already fixed. But if the contract is ambiguous, he is allowed to remove it if he is in real need of it. Ibn al-'Attar[67] added: Once the period, which is considered to be adequate for the possessor of the easement to take the benefit of his right elapses, the owner (*murfiq*) has the right to revoke his permission 1even though he is not in a hurry to develop his space. If the wall has collapsed and the owner then rebuilds it, he must also reinstate the easement. In case he is unable to rebuild it, the neighbor has the right of doing so to claim his benefits. If he reinstalls it and later on the owner of the wall wants to utilize his wall, he cannot do so unless he pays the neighbor the cost of rebuilding the wall. The above case is like the case of cleaning a jointly owned well, if one of them refuses to clean it when the water dries up; the one who cleans it alone possesses its water until the other party pays half of the expenditure.

A man is allowed to sell the location of the main beam to his neighbor, and if the sale is permanent, then it is a valid transaction and if it is temporary, it is taken as a lease. A man cannot be judged against him if he refuses to allow easement to his neighbor's elements. However, it is recommended that he does not refuse because the hadith is understood to recommend (*nadb*).

5- The Book On the Negation Of Harm, And The Discourse On The Harm And Other (Bad) Things That A Man Can Inflict Upon His Neighbor.

---

[67] Muhammad b. Ahmad b. 'Abd Allah (d.399/1009) a jurist from Cordova wrote a *wathaiq* entitled *Kitab al-wathaiq wa al-sijillat*.

Malik reported in his *Muwatta'* on the authority of 'Amru b. Yahya al-Mazini that the Prophet said: "Do not harm others or yourself, and others should not harm you or themselves."

Master-mason Muhammad b. Ibrahim al-Rami al-Banna said: This *hadith* is *sahih*. It is established from the Prophet in *Muwatta'* and other *ahadith* books. Scholars have interpreted it differently. Some say the (meaning of) "Do not harm others or yourself, and others should not harm you or themselves" is: do not harm yourself and you should also not harm others.

Ibn Habib said: *Al-darar* and *al-dirar* are two words bearing the same meaning which is repeated for emphasis on the prevention of a harmful act. However, they can be morphologically understood differently where *al-darar* can be (understood as) a noun and *al-dirar* as a verb. Therefore, the meaning of *la darar* would be: Harm cannot be inflicted on anybody; whether intended or not; and the meaning of *la dirar* would be: No one should harm another. Al-Khashani[68] said: *Al-darar* is what is beneficial to you but is harmful to your neighbor, (and *al-dirar* is what is not beneficial to you and (at the same time) is harmful to your neighbor. (Meaning) - that *al-darar* is what a man intends for his own benefit and in the process, it causes harm to the others, and *al-dirar* is what he intends to cause harm to the others. Allah said: "And there are those who put up a mosque by way of harm and infidelity."[69]

Others said: It is possible that the meaning of *al-darar* is: A neighbor having the intention to harm his neighbor, and the meaning of *al-dirar* is each one of them harms the other. Hence, the Prophet prohibited both possibilities.

Ibn al-Mawwaz said that: It means that a person claims something, which he has a right in it and it is not beneficial to him but at the same time causes harm to the defendant. This is the essence of *'la darar wa la dirar.'* He added: If the harm caused by his act only benefits him, he has no right to do it and it must be stopped.

Shaykh *al-Faqih* Qadi al-Jama'ah Abu Ishaq b. 'Abd al-Rafi' in his book *Mu'in al-Qudat wa al-Hukkam* said: The meaning of *al-*

---

[68] He is Muhammad b. 'Abd al-Salam al-Qurtubi, a jurist from Andalus (d.286/899). Imam Abi 'Abdullah Shamsuddin al-Dhahabi, *Tazkirah al-huffaz*, (Beirut: Dar Ihya al-Turath al-Arabi, n.d.), 2:200.

[69] Al-Qur'an, *al-Taubah*: 107.

dirar is: To harm yourself so that you cause harm to somebody else."

Ashhab said: If two damages are concurrent, then the lesser should lapse for the greater. (Therefore) it is said, the biggest harm in this case is to forbid a man from doing something beneficial in his property. And the small harm: Is his neighbor's objection to him for doing something that causes harm to himself.

Master-mason Muhammad says: Harms are of many kinds and can be categorized into two: Old and new.

The old is of two types: One is that which has already existed before it causes damage, and the other one is that which will cause damage in the future. For the harm which comes from the structure that already exists before the damage is done, its position cannot be changed even if the neighbors are being harmed by it. This is the agreed opinion among scholars. An action which can potentially damage others in the near future and it is long lasting is either worthy to be continued or not worthy to be continued even if it has been there since a long time before.

Among the ones that are not worthy to be continued even if they have been in existence for a long time before, are the smoke of public baths (*hammam*) and bakeries, and the dust from floor threshing, and the offensive smell of the tan of the tanners. This opinion was narrated by al-Qadi Abu al-Walid Ibn Rushd; Ibn Hisham also narrated this in *Kitab Mufid al-Hukkam*, and also narrated by al-Shaykh *al-Faqih al-Qadi* Abu Ishaq b. 'Abd al-Rafi' in his *Mu'in al-Qudat wa al-Hukkam*. Ibn Hisham added that: If the damaging elements harm the neighbors, the one causing it is told to control it or to stop it, no matter whether it is old or new because being old does not make the harm worthy unless if it has been in existence before the damage is caused. The one creating the harm cannot use the right of possessing (*hiyazah*) a damaging act as a strong argument, but rather his damaging precedents do not add on him other than proof of aggression and hostility.

Master-mason Muhammad says: Aspects of harm are countless. It will become clear when judging them (individually), and we shall now give details on what have been briefly presented, putting each one under an appropriate chapter.

6- Discourse On The Harm Of Smoke And The Judgment On It.

Master-mason Muhammad says: Smoke is of two types; the one which is forbidden and the one that is not forbidden. The one that is forbidden is: The smoke of public baths and bakeries and whatever similar to that.

The non-forbidden smoke includes the smoke from the ovens (*tanur*) and kitchens (*matabikh*) and whatever is similar to that, which fall under necessities that cannot be avoided like cooking of food and other things that must go on.

Master-mason Muhammad says: The principle of preventing the smoke is from Allah's saying:

"Then watch thou for the day that the sky will bring forth a kind of smoke (or mist) plainly visible enveloping the people: This will be a penalty grievous."[70]

Sahnun said in *al-Mudawwanah*: I asked Ibn al-Qasim: If I own a vacant lot adjacent to some houses and I want to make a *hammam* or a bakery (*furun*) on that lot and the neighbors prevent me, do they have the right of doing so? according to Malik (He said): If your action causes harm to the neighbors like producing smoke and something similar to that, they have the right to prevent you from doing it because Malik said: (a neighbor) is prevented from doing something which is harmful to his neighbor. I asked him: Even if he is a blacksmith (*haddad*) and he operates a bellow or ovens to melt the silver and gold, is he prevented from doing so? He said: Yes, Malik said so on many occasions on matters of smoke and others.

Ibn 'Abdus narrated from Ibn al-Qasim: And in *al-'Utbiah* a saying of Sahnun: On someone who operates an oven or an ironsmith inside his premise and as a result of that, causes harm to his neighbors, he must be prevented from it and action has to be taken against him.

It was reported in *al-Wadihah* that: Ibn Habib reported from Mutarrif and Ibn al-Majashun and Asbagh about the newly created oven and public bath (*hammam*) inside a man's property which emitted harmful smoke to his neighbors. The one that created them was prevented from doing so without the permission of the neighbors who were being harmed by the

---

[70] Al-Qur'an, *al-Dukkhan*: 10-11.

smoke. Because it was a newly created harm, which did not fall under the things that someone should not be prevented from doing; there was no dispute on the matter.

Master-mason Muhammad says: Our saying that: No dispute on the matter as narrated by Ibn Rushd.

In the book of Ibn Sahnun, Muhammad said: Sulayman has written to Sahnun inquiring about ovens, which are being used to burn clay, some are old and others are newly made. Can the neighbors complain about the smoke or should they keep quiet? Sahnun wrote to him saying: The old ovens cannot be prevented.

Master-mason Muhammad says: From *al-Ahkam* of al-Baji- narrated by Ibn Hisham- it is said: The scholars disagree in the case of an oven (*furun*) and a public bath (*hammam*) that are newly created near a house and the owner of the house is not harmed by such an act but it reduces the value of the said property. Some say that reducing the value is a harm, which should be prevented. (The prospective buyer) will fear the fire (from the *hammam*) and the gathering of people because of their frequent visits near his house. The evidence is Allah's saying: "and reduce not the things that are due to the people."[71]

Others said that: He is not forbidden from doing so. In *al-Mudawwanah* Sahnun is quoted to have said: I asked Ibn al-Qasim, do you, according to Malik, see any harm in a furnace (*tanur*)? He answered, I did not hear anything on that matter from Malik and I consider the the harm from a *tanur* to be minor. Ibn 'Abdus narrated the same opinion from Ibn al-Qasim. Also from *al-Majmu'ah* similar to what was said by Ibn al-Qasim and was quoted by Ibn Hisham in *Mufid al-Hukkam*.

Master-mason Muhammad says: *Al-Sinfaj*[72] is also harmful, and also *al-Tawajin*[73] which is designed to fry flour in markets and homes. It happened in our town Tunis and some people complained to Shaykh *al-Faqih al-Qadi* Abu Ishaq b. 'Abd al-Rafi' and he told us to look into the matter. We wrote (our findings) in a document saying that: Its smoke is harmful to the

---

[71] Al-Qur'an, *Hud*: 85.
[72] *Sinfaj* is a kind of small furnace used to fry food called *sinfajah*, and it creates smoke.
[73] *Tawajin* (pl), the singular is *Tajin* referring to frying pan.

neighbors, and he consequently ordered not to be used. Smoke is harmful and it is prohibited with the consensus of opinions.

Shaykh *al-Faqih al-Qadi* Abu Ishaq b. 'Abd al-Rafi' said: The judgment for the smoke from public baths and furnaces or the smell of tan of the tanners is to order them to stop it (or) otherwise, they are told to control it so that it does not harm the neighbors, no matter whether it is old or new, because the harm in (such things) cannot be justified by being old."

Master-mason Muhammad says: If we say that the recently created smoke is prohibited and the old one is not, as explained before, and the one who owns the old one wants to enlarge it (Is he allowed to do so?). This case occurred in Tunis. One man had a *kusha* (a bakery stove), which had in it one fireplace and he wanted to create another fireplace and to channel its smoke into the chimney of the first fireplace, and the neighbors prevented him and they said to him: You have created on us additional smoke different from the old one. They took the matter to Qadi Abu Zayd 'Abd al-Rahman b. al-Qattan and he then shut down the newly created fireplace.

Master-mason Muhammad says: I asked *al-Faqih* Abu 'Abd Allah ibn al-Ghammaz[74] about this case and he answered that: It must be shut down because of the additional harm it causes to the neighbors.

Master-mason Muhammad says: If the tenant of a house builds an oven (*tanur*), which he is allowed to do so, and it causes fire to the house and the houses of his neighbors, he is not held responsible for it. However, if the owner of the house made a condition to the tenant that he should not build an oven and he neglects the condition and the house catches fire, he is held responsible for whatever is burnt down. This opinion is attributed to Ibn al-Qasim from *al-Mudawwanah*.

7- Discourse On The Harm Of Bad Smell And Judgment On It.

---

[74] He is Abu 'Abd Allah Muhammad b. Abi al-'Abbas Ahmad b. Muhammad b. al-Husain b. al-Ghammaz (d. 785/1383). Appointed as Qadi al-Jama'ah in 718/1318, Ibn Farhun, *al-Dibaj al-muhazzab*, 2:323. al-Zarkashi, *Tarikh al-daulatain*, 66.

Master-mason Muhammad says: The principle in removing the harm of a bad smell is from the Prophetic saying: "Whoever eats from this tree should not come near our mosque, to harm us with the smell of garlic."[75]

Ibn Habib in *al-Wadihah* said: I asked Mutarrif and Ibn al-Majashun, about a person who operates a tannery to dye the hide, and his neighbors complain about the harm of the smell which reaches them, do they have the right to prevent him in order to remove the harm? Both of them answered: Yes, he must be prevented from that and the harm, which comes from such a place, is like the harm of the *hammam* and the furnace.

Thereof in *al-Tarar*: Whoever opens near his neighbor a toilet or an uncovered wastewater channel, or anything that harms his neighbors with bad smell, he is prevented from doing so or he must be forced to cover it so that his neighbors are not harmed by its smell, for the offensive smell hurts their noses and it is offensive to human beings in general. Ibn 'At said: It was said by Ibn 'Abd al-Ghafur (d. 440/1048) in (*Kitab*) *al-Istighna'*, Abu 'Amr said: That is what is being practiced.

8- Discourse On The Harm From The Tailor (*Kammadin*)[76] And The Vibration Of The Mills.

Master-mason Muhammad says: In *al-Mudawwanah* Sahnun said: I asked Ibn al-Qasim: If I have a plot of land that neighbors' other houses, and I want to build on that plot a mill, which will cause harm to the neighbors' walls, am I prohibited from doing that? He answered: Yes, thus Malik told me.

Master-mason Muhammad says: The harms of tailors (*kammadin*) and mills are of different types. Some cause harm to the walls by vibration and others cause harm by frequent thumping. That which causes harm to the walls is prohibited by consensus. This was the view of al-Qadi Abu al-Walid b. Rushd.

---

[75] Narrated by Malik in *al-Muwatta'*, 37 from Sa'id al-Musayyab; see also Ibn Majah, 1: 324-325.

[76] *Kammadin* is translated as "tailors". *Kammad*, according to Ibn Manzur is the hammerer of the fabric. By comparing *Kammad* and *Qassar* it means a tailor who hammers or beat the cloth. Ibn Manzur, *Lisan al-arab al-muhit*, ed. Y. Khayyat and N. Mar'ashli, (Beirut, Dar Lisan al-Arab, 1304/1887), 3:101and 295, for *naddaf* see 3:608.

As to the harm caused by hammering, scholars differed about it. There were two opinions: Ibn Habib in *al-Wadihah* said: I asked Mutarrif and Ibn al-Majashun and Asbagh: The laundryman and the bleacher, who harm their neighbors by the sound of their trade, should they be prevented from doing so? They answered: Our opinion is that none of them should be prevented.

Thereof: Master-mason Muhammad says: It was reported in *al-Tarar* and in *al-Majalis* that: The scholars (*al-shuyukh*) of Toledo gave verdicts preventing the *kammadin* from their trade if the neighbors were harmed by its sound.

Ibn al-Qasim said in *al-Mudawwanah*: A man has the right to do whatever he wants in a rented house, like selling goods, keeping animals, being a blacksmith or a bleacher (*qassarin*) as long as he does not cause any harm to the house.

Ibn 'Abd al-Ghafur said: Based on that, the landlord has the right to operate a trade of his wish in his house as long as he does not cause any harm to his neighbors premises. As to the sound or vibration of the trade, it cannot be prevented.

Al-Mushawir[77] had similar opinions. This was quoted from *al-Tarar* of Ibn 'At. Al-Qadi Ibn Rushd said: Some of our contemporaries are of the view that he is prevented from doing so due to the harmful effects of the sound. They base their argument on what is reported from Sa'id b. Al-Musayyab who said to Bard: "expel this reader from me, he has harmed me."[78] The reader was 'Umar b. 'Abd al- 'Aziz.

Master-mason Muhammad says: From *al-Mufid al-Hukkam* by Ibn Hisham: No one is prevented from establishing a mill in his house. And he also says: From *al-Thamaniyah* of Abu Zayd: A blacksmith is not prevented from doing his trade in his house, even if he does it day and night, for his livelihood.

Master-mason Muhammad says: *Al-Faqih al-Qadi* Abu Zayd bin al-Qattan has given me a question and its answer written in his own handwriting, and it says; What do you say about a man who owns a ruined site, on which there used to be a mill, and his heir wants to rebuild it as a bakery (*furun*) and not as a mill like

---

[77] An officer in judicial office, at that time the holder was Ibn al-Fakhhar. He is Abu 'Abd Allah Muhammad b. 'Umar b. Yusuf b. al-Fakhhar (d.419/1028). Ibn Bashkawal, Khalaf b. Abd al-Malik *al-Silah*, (2:510).

[78] The *athar* was narrated by Ibn Rushd from Malik in *al-Bayan wa al-tahsil*, 1:466-467

before. The abutting neighbor stops him, claiming he did not know about any such previous function and that the right to build a bakery will cause harm to his wall once he builds it. He also wants a wall built inside the ruined site abutting his house to strengthen his wall and counteract the damage that will be caused by the bakery. Does the neighbor have a say in the way of building that wall? Or does he have the right of preventing the inheritor from building a mill? And how about if the owner of an existing house, which has a mill, that was built according to known measurements, wants to replace it with a larger one. Does he have the right of doing it? And does the heir have the right to replace the old mill with a bakery or not?

He answered that: Since the house has not been used as a bakery for a long time, and is eliminated and demolished, and it is left in that situation for a long time, and the neighbor has built a new house adjacent to the bakery, and it is established that the renovation will cause harm to the neighbor's wall, he (the neighbor) has the right to prevent it unless the heir builds (for the neighbor) a wall, as mentioned. If the house was used as a bakery quite recently or if the neighbor's house existed while the bakery was functioning, then the heir would have the right to reinstate the function even if the neighbor did not know about it.

And what has been mentioned that: If the owner of the bakery wants to replace it with a larger one, he cannot be prevented from doing so as long as he is doing it in his own plot and it does not cause harm to his neighbor, if he wants to change the place of the mill to another place (of his possession), he cannot be prevented if it is not harmful to his neighbor. It was written so by 'Abd Allah b. Yahya al-Zawawi.

Thereof, Master-mason Muhammad says: I asked the *Fakih* Abu 'Abd Allah Muhammad b. al-Ghammaz about (the measurements to be considered by) a man who wants to set a mill in his house and has been asked (by his neighbor) to put the mill at a distance, which will make it far from the neighbor's wall, and he said: I do not have any measurement to be followed, you the professional know the measurements of how far the mill should be located from the neighbor's wall, and we do not know of any measurement to be followed in this case.

Master-mason Muhammad says: In my opinion the one who wants to make a mill in his house has to make it a distance of eight hand-spans from the limit of the rotating animals to the wall of the neighbor, and that space should be occupied by a building, a house, a store or a corridor. The building of a barrier between the boundaries of the rotating animals and the wall of the neighbor is a must because it will prevent the causation of harm to the neighbor's wall.

Thereof, Master-mason Muhammad says: I asked al-Shaykh *al-Faqih al-Qadi* Abu Ishaq ibn 'Abd al-Rafi' about a man who builds a mill in his house and then the neighbor complains about the harm to his wall caused by the mill, what formula is used to determine the vibration of that wall? And at what location should be determined? Is it on the ground or on the wall? He answered: Take a rectangular dish of paper *(tabaqan min kaghid)*, connect threads to its four corners, and hang it on the ceiling that rests on the wall between the mill and the house. You should then put dried coriander seeds on the paper dish and then ask the owner of the mill to operate his mill. If the seeds move tell the owner of the mill to remove it; if the seeds remain still, tell the owner of the house: Let the owner of the mill operate, because it causes no harm to the house.

I asked him: If the wall, which works as a barrier between the mill and the house, does not have beams on it, where should we hang the paper? He said to me; dig a hole half a hand's width in the party wall and insert a thick stalk in it and hang the paper on it (put the dried coriander seeds onto the paper dish), ask the owner of the mill to operate his mill, if the coriander seeds move, prevent him from operating his mill, and if the seeds are still, he is not prevented from doing so.

I asked him: If the owner of the mill owns the separating wall between the mill and the house, and the wall shakes whenever he operates the mill, is he prevented from operating his mill or not? He said: If the wall of the neighbor does not shake, but the wall owned by the owner of the mill shakes, he is not prevented from doing so.

9- Discourse On A Man Who Builds A Stable To Secure Animals.

The author says: In *Kitab Mu'in al-Hukkam 'ala al-Qadaya wa al-Ahkam*: *Al-Shaykh al-Faqih al-Qadi* Abu Ishaq b. 'Abd al-Rafi' said: A man is prevented from building a stable adjacent to a neighbor's house because of the harm that comes from the animals' urine and from their movements during the day and night which prevents (the neighbor) from sleeping.[79] Similar opinion is found in Ibn Hisham's book.

Master-mason Muhammad says: This case happened in our area when al-Shaykh *al-Faqih* Abu Ishaq b. 'Abd al-Rafi' was the Qadi al-Jama'ah of Tunis. When a man constructed behind his neighbor's house, a stable (*riwa*) for his small animals, the owner of the house complained because of the harm that came from the *riwa'*. *al-Faqih al-Qadi* asked us to look into the matter. After we saw it and reported to him that it was newly created, he ordered it to be removed and also the animals released from it. The owner of the animals pleaded and waited many days without implementing the orders, and then told me, "I cannot do without the animals because they are my source of income, maybe I should ask for professional advice on how to prevent harm towards my neighbor". Consequently, we ascended from the order of *al-Faqih al-Qadi* and he ordered the man to build a wall parallel to his neighbor's wall. The wall's foundation was to be one *qamah* (a person's height)[80] deep; between the two walls there should be half a hand-span of space (*tarwih*). This space should exten five hand-spans above ground level and the width of this wall should be two hand-spans. We reported the matter to the Qadi about his order to the owner of the animals. When the man did what he was asked to do; the transmission of harm to the neighbor was prevented. *Al-Qadi al-Faqih* Abu Ishaq told me to get witnesses to observe the action of the owner of the animals so that he would not remove the wall in the future to claim later on that his stable had existed a long time ago.

Thereof Master-mason Muhammad says: It also happened on a ruined site, and the owner wanted to make it a stable. However the owner of the adjacent house prevented him from doing so and took the matter to Shaykh *al-Faqih al-Qadi* Abu Ishaq b. 'Abd al-Rafi' and he consequently asked me to look at it. We saw a large area, which was bounded by a street on the west and north sides, and by the houses on its eastern and *qiblah* sides. The stable was adjacent to the *qiblah* side. The owner of the stable admitted his action and his eastern side neighbors protested that.

---

[79] Ibn 'Abd al-Rafi', *Mu'in al-hukkam*, 2: 1503, 786.
[80] One *qamah* is equal to 199.5cm or around 2 meters. Ismail Marcinkowski, *Measures and Weight in the Islamic world*, (Kuala Lumpur: ISTAC, International Islamic University, 2003), 80.

We ordered the owner of the stable to build a room (*bayt*) between the eastern side neighbor's house and where he wanted to make a stable. The width of the room should be 9 hand-spans and the width of the wall should be 2 hand-spans. Consequently, I reported the matter to the Qadi Abu Ishaq, who was by that time the Qadi al-Jama'ah, and he then asked me: Does the precaution taken have prevented the transmission of the harm to (the house) and I answered: Yes, it does. He said: Get witnesses on the matter so that later on the room would not be removed to make the whole area a stable. Those events happened and judgments were given accordingly.

However, a man is prevented from turning his portico into a stable or to turn a house into a ranch to keep animals inside it. All kinds of *riwa'* are prevented because they cause harm and disgrace.

Problem: Master-mason Muhammad says: I asked *al-Faqih* Abu 'Abd Allah b. al-Ghammaz who was by then the *Qadi al-Jama'ah* in Tunis about a person who makes a stable near his neighbor's house, mentioned at the beginning of this case, is he prevented from setting a stable adjacent to the rest of the house? Since the boundaries of the erected *riwa'* may not be the wall of the house itself, but such as a wall adjacent to the center of the house, or adjacent to the entry or adjacent to any particular space or something else that is not the house itself, is the neighbor permitted to build a stable behind it or not? He said: If any of those places harm the neighbor's wall or causes it to be moist, he is prevented from doing so; and if it is not harmed, he is not prevented from doing what he wants. I asked him; what about the movements that prevented the owner of the house from sleeping, which was mentioned by Ibn Hisham: Is he prevented from establishing a stable? He said: I do not believe that he should be prevented (from doing that) because the noise is not, according to the popular opinion, considered as harm. I asked him; what is the limit for the harm to be prevented from being transmitted to the wall? He said: That is your responsibility (to see according to your profession) what you may consider (as enough) to remove the harm, of the vibration and the dampness of the wall. Then I told him about the case that happened and it was the one before this case, in which we asked the owner of the animals to build a wall behind the wall of the neighboring house to make him feel comfortable. He said: If the measure being taken is effective in preventing the harm, then the other has no right to prevent him from that which benefits him (the owner of the animals).

10- Discourse On The Harm Caused By Overlooking From Small Windows And Doors And the Judgment Therein.

Master-mason Muhammad says: Small windows (*kuwa'*)[81] are of two types: Old (*qadim*) and recent (*muhdath*). There are two opinions in the closing of the old *kuwa'*. The most famous among them is to keep it as it was. Two opinions are cited for the closing of the recent ones: The common rule is to shut them permanently.

The author says: The first opinion regarding the closing of the recent *kuwa'* is found in *al-Mudawwanah* where Sahnun said that: I asked Ibn al-Qasim: What do you have to say about a man who builds a palace (*qusuran*) adjacent to my house and heighten his building so that it is taller than mine and opens in them, doors and a window, which he uses to look at my family and house, do I have the right to prevent him from doing so according to the teachings of Malik? He answered: Yes, you must prevent him (the neighbor). Malik said: It was the opinion of 'Umar b. al-Khattab. Malik said: Ibn Luhay'ah told us that he wrote to 'Umar b. al-Khattab inquiring about a man who built a new room adjacent to his neighbor and he opened in it a small window, 'Umar wrote to him ordering him to place a bed beneath the small window, and to ask a man to stand on that bed, if he could see what was inside the neighbor's house, the owner must be prevented from using that small window, but if he could not see through it, the window would be allowed to remain.

Master-mason Muhammad says: The word *sarir* has two meanings: Ibn Abi Zimnin said: *al-Sarir* is the bedroom furniture (bed). Ibn Shas in his book, *al-Jawahir* said: *Al-Sarir* is a ladder. Some people said: *Al-Sarir* means a chair or anything similar to it.

Master-mason Muhammad says: My view is that its height should be that of something that can be used to gaze through:

---

[81] *Kuwa'* plural of *kiwa* refers to small windows or apertures on the wall. 'Abd al-Rahim Ghaleb, *Encyclopedie l'architecture Islamique, Arabe-Francais-Anglais*, (Beirut: Jarrous Press, 1988), 328.

The maximum of it is five hand-spans and the minimum are four hand-spans.

Al-Lakhmi said in *al-Tabsirah*: The man who looks must be of strong vision. The second opinion: Ibn Hisham in his *Ahkam* said: Ashhab, Ibn al-Majashun and al-Makhzumi said: No one should be prevented from opening doors and small windows (*kuwa*) on their rooms, whoever feels offended by that should cover and protect themselves from being looked upon. However, he said: The practice is different from this opinion.

Al-Qadi Abu al-Walid b. Rushd also reported the same opinion, and similar to his report is also found in *Mu'in al-Qudat wa al-Hukkam* by *al-Faqih* Abu Ishaq: That this opinion is not followed, the famous opinion is to close the recent openings.[82] The others (i.e. neighbors) are not to be burdened by having to build a wall to cover their privacy.

Master-mason Muhammad says: When we say: The onlooker should be prevented from overlooking as per popular opinion, what should the height of the wall be, which prevents the viewer from it? Two opinions:

First opinion: It is as what Malik said in *al-Mudawwanah*, about the bed, which has been mentioned at the beginning of this problem.

Second opinion: In *al-'Utbiah*, Abu al-Hasan said: Ashhab said: My opinion is to prevent him if a passing person can glance through and order him to heighten his building to the extent that prevented passer-by from peeking. Ibn Wahb also had a similar opinion but added: He has to be disciplined if he overlooks unnecessarily after a warning, but the door should not be shut. The position of the (*kuwa*) is like on the backside of a house or at its rooftop (*sutuh*) or when someone heightens his house over his neighbor's house; all (of these elements) would later on invite complain. (The petitioner) would say: I am afraid that you will infringe upon our privacy through the above elements. The openings, which the man creates in his house for the purpose of admitting light and fresh air will later on invite complain. However, the neighbor has no right to complain about such thing.

---

[82] Ibn 'Abd al-Rafi', *Mu'in al-hukkam*, 2: 785.

Master-mason Muhammad says: Seven hand-spans are enough to prevent overlooking by passers-by if he is not staring and has no intention to spy.

The Master said: The practice in Tunis and which is applied in the judgment of such cases is: To prevent a neighbor from gazing and overlooking. This was practiced by al-Qadi Abu Ishaq b. 'Abd al-Rafi' in his frequent verdicts during his tenure. He ordered the closure of small windows.

From *Kitab Mu'in al-Qudat* by Abu Ishaq: Some trustworthy scholars said: The harm that is ordered to be removed is: That which exposes the faces of people inside the house to another person who stands next to the door or in front of the windows. If the faces are not exposed, (the small windows) are not considered harmful.[83]

Master-mason Muhammad says: If the view is far and the distance in between is quite far, and the small window is an old one, which has been in the house of the man who overlooks the neighbor's house, there are two opinions in closing it:

From *al-Mudawwanah* Sahnun said: I asked Ibn al-Qasim: What is your opinion about a man who has an old small window above his neighbor's house or an old door that he is not benefiting from it, while at the same time causes harm to his neighbor, is he compelled to close it? Ibn al-Qasim said: I will not force him to do so, because it is something that has already existed; not newly created, therefore, it is not applicable to him. I did not hear this from Malik but it is my opinion.

Master-mason Muhammad says: Similar opinion of what Ibn al-Qasim said can be found in *al-Wadihah*.

However, al-Shaykh Abu Bakr Muhammad bin Yunus[84] in his *Diwan* said: "Some of our scholars recommend that he be prevented from overlooking even if the opening is an old one and even if both parties are satisfied with it because they are satisfied with something that is not legal.

Master-mason Muhammad says: This is different from what is recorded and from practice: Which is not to close it, it is what has been followed by our judges and I have not seen any of the

---

[83] Ibn 'Abd al-Rafi', *Mu'in al-hukkam*, 2: 785.
[84] He is Abu Bakr Muhammad b. 'Abd Allah b. Yunus al-Tamimi from Sicily (d. 451/1059). The *Diwan* is his commentary to *al-Mudawwanah*. Ibn Farhun, *al-Dibaj al-muzahhab*, 2:240.

judge's orders to close it, and I have not heard anyone saying differently from that. However, the other one is ordered to heighten his building so that the other neighbor cannot see him.

11- Discourse On The Vacant Lot without Any Building.

The author says: About a vacant lot that is owned by a man who does not have any building on it, and his neighbor builds a room with a small window through which he overlooks his neighbor's vacant lot.

Master-mason Muhammad says: The opinion Of *al-Madaniyyun* on that issue, as found in *al-Wadihah*, differed in two: Ibn Habib said: Ibn al-Majashun said that a door or a small window, which is in someone's house and through which he looks at his neighbor, is not to be shut if it has existed before the exposed (neighbors) house. It is the responsibility of his neighbor to protect his privacy. But if the door or the small window has been recently built, the owner is prevented from using it and he should be ordered to block it by putting in front of it a screen (so that it cannot be seen through). Ibn al-Majashun said: If the opening of the room has existed earlier, before the neighbor develops his land, but he (the neighbor) wants to prevent him (from opening the *kuwa*) which will harm him in the future, he (the neighbor) does not have any right to do so; neither before he builds nor after he has completed the building (on the empty plot); since at the time of the opening (of the *kuwa*) it did not expose and did not cause harm to anybody. It is a benefit, which he has possessed and acquired before the other person.

Ibn Habib said: Mutarrif told me: The owner of the house should be prevented from utilizing his window once the owner of the vacant lot had built his house. His prior permission cannot, by now, be an excuse to nullify his neighbor's right to privacy. However, if at the time the owner of the room bought (the house), the small window had already existed, he (the owner of the vacant lot) could not prevent him from using it. But if it had not existed at the time he bought the house and now he wants to create it, the owner of the vacant lot has the right to prevent him. If he (the owner of the vacant lot) allows him to create it on the condition he has the right to prevent the owner of the window from using it whenever he feels like doing so, (such agreement) is valid between them. Master-mason Muhammad says: Asbagh and Ibn Habib follow the opinion of Mutarrif.

12- Discourse On Someone Who Creates A Small Window (*kuwa*), Which Enables Him To Look At The Courtyard Of His Neighbor.

Master-mason Muhammad says: Ibn 'At said in *al-Tarar*: Whoever creates a room, which enables him to overlook the the courtyard of his neighbor, must be prevented from doing so.

Master-mason Muhammad says: Among the questions answered by al-Qadi Abu 'Abd Allah b. al-Hajj[85] as reported by Ibn al-Hindi: Whoever opens a small window in his room and the window enables him to look at the courtyard of his neighbor or his private room, must be prevented from doing it on the ground that it can be used to look at what is going on in the neighbor's house. Therefore, that window must be blocked, and the way of blocking it is by removing the window's lintel; because if it is left in its place, after some time, the owner may use it as evidence to reopen it, when he feels like doing so. Al-Qadi Abu 'Abd Allah said: Ibn Rushd told me that: If the builder builds a small opening (*sharjaban*)[86] to the extent of not being able to put his head through it, the scholars' opinions differ, some allow it whereas others do not.

Master-mason Muhammad says: Whoever approves of the small opening (*sharjab*) is misguided because looking through a *sharjab* is more harmful than looking through an ordinary window. Through it, someone can see you while you are unable to see him or to protect yourself from him, whereas you can protect yourself if he protrudes his head through it. Moreover, it is not a practice here. However, if the small opening (*sharjab*) can totally prevent the harm (of overlooking), the above problem is solved. But if someone can stare through the *sharjab* that has a screen on it, then its harm is stronger than the opening itself.

Master-mason Muhammad says: I asked all the scholars of our country and the *muftis* regarding a man who builds a room with a small window (*kuwa*) that enables him to see what is inside his neighbor's portico whenever he opens the door. Does the owner of the exposed house have the right to prevent him while they are separated by a wide street used by many people? And does the

---

[85] He is Abu 'Abd Allah Muhammad b. Ahmad b. Khalaf b. Ibrahim al-Tujibi (d. 529/1135), *Qadi al-Jama'ah* in Cardova. al-Nubahi, 102.

[86] Small opening finely meshed with screen. Muhammad Amin, 69-70.

owner of the window have the right to say: My window opens to the street just like a door opens to the street, which is not prevented. Does he have the right to say to him: I and my next door neighbor have the same view of your door. *Al-Faqih* Abu 'Abd Allah b. al-Ghammaz said that: A neighbor is prevented from creating small openings (*kuwa*), which enables him to see his neighbor's portico. The small opening (*kuwa*) and the door are not the same (in causing harm to the neighbor). The door is a necessity for entrance and exit; whereas the neighbor cannot protect himself from the small window, and the one with a *kuwa* can see you without you seeing him. He is also unseen to the passers-by, all his activities are hidden therefore the harm of a *kuwa* (which enables the owner) to sit (and watch the others) is bigger.

Master-mason Muhammad says: All our scholars answered this problem in the same way and I do not know of any *qadi* who judged differently. He also says: There is no excuse for someone saying that: I see the same as those other owners of small openings (*kuwa*) nearby see. It was quoted by Ibn 'At in *al-Tarar*, he said: Whoever creates a *kuwa* that enables him to view what others are viewing, which must be stopped, must also be prevented. The opportunity of others to stare cannot be used as an excuse. Whether it is a through street used by many or is a dead-end street, he has no excuse to stare.

Ibn 'At also said in *al-Tarar*: Regarding the small windows (*kuwa*) which expose (other people's house): The *kuwa* must be prevented if people are clearly seen but if they are not, the openings are permitted. Ibn al-Talla'[87] also expressed the same view in his *Wathaiq* (as mentioned before by the Qadi (Ibn 'Abd al-Rafiᶜ). The author says: The window is not prohibited if the people who are in the *saqif* (entrance hall) are not seen.

13- Discourse On Two Small Windows *(kuwa)* Facing Each Other.

Master-mason Muhammad says: In the book of Ibn Sahnun, Muhammad said: Sahnun was asked about the two houses that

---

[87] He is Abu 'Abd Allah Muhammad b. Ahmad b Farj al-Qurtubi, better known as Ibn Talla'(d. 497/1104), the author of *Ahkam al-Nabiyy*, Kuhalah, 11:123-124.

were separated by a public lane (*zuqaq masluk*) or through street, and in one of the houses there was a *kuwa* that enabled the owner to see what was in the other house, then the one who did not have a *kuwa* in his house decided to build a room and opened in it a window facing the other one, and he could see through that window what was in the room of the other. The owner of the first house asked his neighbor to close the newly created window, but the neighbor said: Close your old *kuwa*, so far I have kept quiet for five or four years for the sake of maintaining good neighborly relationship although the condition has been unfavorable to me. He (Sahnun) said: The owner of the newly created window has to swear to confirm that he did not oppose the old *kuwa* to exist for all that period of time for the sake of keeping good relationships with his neighbor without giving up his rights. The two openings then have to be closed.

Master-mason Muhammad says: A similar case happened in Tunis during the period of Abu Yahya al-Nuri[88] and he gathered some jurists, and he was notified about this issue and consequently passed the judgment accordingly and blocked the two small windows (*kuwa*).

14- Discourse On Small Windows For Light And Doors Of Roof Terraces.

Master-mason Muhammad says: It is reported in *al-ᶜUtbiah* that Asbagh said (through audition): Ibn Nafi' was asked whether a man is allowed to put an elevated small opening (*kuwa*) in his wall, which is opposite the house of his neighbor, if the neighbor is uncomfortable with it? The *kuwa* is only accessible through a ladder. Is there any harm to the neighbor? Ibn Nafi' answered that: If it does not harm his neighbor I do not see any problem with it because it is beneficial to him and at the same time the other one is not harmed (by it), but in case it is harmful, he is prevented from doing so. It was also the opinion of Ibn Wahb and Asbagh.

Master-mason Muhammad says: (If) someone puts a small window (*kuwa*) in his house that is overlooking the neighbor's house, and he cannot look through it, but he can hear their

---

[88] He is Abu Yahya b. Abi Bakr al-Nuri al-Safaqasi, one of the *Qadi al-Jamaʻah* of Tunis (d.699/1300). al-Zarkashi, 54.

conversations, and the neighbor complains that he is being harmed by it (What is the solution?). Master-mason Muhammad says: This case happened in Tunis and the opinions of our scholars differed about it. Some considered the hearing of the conversations and movements in the residence to be harmful and others did not. Someone said: He should not be prevented and the judges used not to shut it and based their opinion on those who did not consider it as harmful.

Master-mason Muhammad says: The same rule applies to the door on the roof terrace (of the house). If it is created (with the intention) of staring at the neighbor's house, it must be prevented. However, if it is in conformity with the agreed location then it should not be prevented. If the neighbor argues that: "We fear that you may stare at us when you come out (of the door)", the said argument cannot be considered.

Ibn Wahb said: If the opening of the door on the roof terrace is harmful to the neighbor in a way that the owner can look at his neighbor's activities once he utilizes his roof terrace, in such a case the owner must be prevented from doing so and he should not be allowed to open it. If it is not as prescribed above, but the neighbor has a fear that the other one may stare at him, he is not prevented and his door cannot be closed at all and the neighbors' fear is not an excuse to prevent the other from opening his door.

Master-mason Muhammad says: The owner of the roof terrace door is not obliged to screen his roof terrace to protect the owner from overlooking his neighbor.

This case happened in Tunis. A man had access to his roof terrace and there was a screen to protect the owner from overlooking his neighbor. Consequently, the screen fell down and whoever used the roof terrace was able to stare at the neighbor' house. The exposed neighbor asked the owner of the screen to rebuild his screen. Both of them took the matter to the judge who did not order the owner to rebuild it and said: It is not compulsory for him to do so, but he should forewarn his neighbor whenever he wants to go to his roof terrace.

15- Discourse On A Man Who Wants To Close The Window *(kuwa)* That Harms Him While The Owner Does Not Benefit From It.

Master-mason Muhammad says: Sahnun said in *al-Mudawwanah*: I asked Ibn al-Qasim on his opinion regarding a neighbor who has an old *kuwa* or an old door, which is not beneficial to him and is harmful to his neighbor; will you force him to close it? He answered: I will not force him (to close it), because it is something that he did not create recently. I asked him again: What if the man who owns the old (door or window) does not benefit from it and it is harmful to his neighbor? He said; I will not force him. However, I did not hear it from Malik, and it is my own view.

16- Discourse On A Man Who Wants To Renovate (His House) And By Doing So It Blocks His Neighbor's Window (*kuwa)* And Cuts Him From Fresh Air And Light.

Master-mason Muhammad says: Sahnun said in *al-Mudawwanah*: I asked Ibn al-Qasim: What is your opinion of a man who heightens his building and blocks the window(s) (*kuwa*) of his neighbor, and hence darkens his neighbor's room? He said: I had not heard anything from Malik (on that matter), and my view is that he should not be prevented from increasing the height of his building.

'Abd Allah b. 'Abd al-Hakam said in his book: I asked Ibn al-Qasim: What is your opinion if I own a house and I heighten its wall and block the window of my neighbor and prevent them from getting fresh air and light, am I forbidden from doing that? He answered: That is your right to heighten your building as you wish, even if your act will block their *kuwa*, darken their homes and prevent them from getting fresh air and light. The reason is that to obstruct you from exercising your right will cause harm to you, whereas your building will cause harm to them, therefore for them to bear the harm is better than to deprive you of your right to extend your building, provided that your act will not destroy anything of their homes.

Thereof: Master-mason Muhammad says: Al-'Utbi said: It is reported in *Kitab al-Madaniyyin*: Malik was asked about a man who had created in his wall a *kuwa* towards another house or towards the street for light and sunlight. But his neighbor, then heightened his wall to the extent of blocking the *kuwa* from sunlight, and Malik said: The neighbor cannot be prevented from heightening his wall, and if that is not allowed it would mean that the one who first opened the *kuwa* will be ordered to shut it.

Thereof: Master-mason Muhammad says it is reported in *al-Mustakhrajah*, Ashhab said: Malik was asked about a man who built a house which prevented his neighbors from getting fresh air and light and he said: That is his right and he has the right to benefit from his property. He (Ashhab) also said: Malik was also asked about a man who wanted to build his wall taller which would harm his neighbor by doing that. Malik answered that he is free to heighten his wall as he wishes.

Ashhab said: I asked: What is your view regarding someone next to whom I open a window to get some light and he has no way of blocking it except by building inside his area a house taller than mine and thus blocking my window, does he have the right to do so? He said: Yes, it is allowed and you do not have the right to prevent him from doing it. Since he cannot prevent you from heightening your building within your property, similarly, you also do not have the right to prevent him from heightening his building inside his property.

Thereof the author says: Malik generalized this opinion and said that: A man has the right to heighten his building, and Malik did not discriminate between a Muslim and a *Dhimmi* (not a Muslim), and according to my knowledge, there is nothing in the *madhhab* that forbids a *dhimmi* from heightening his building over a Muslim's building. In Shafi'i School, there are three opinions: first opinion: Permissible. Second opinion: Not Permissible, because it allows a *kafir* to be higher than a Muslim. Third Opinion: If it is already built, it is permissible, and if it is to be built, it is not permissible.[89]

Thereof Master-mason Muhammad says: No disagreement on what we have said before, except the opinion of Ibn Kinanah in *al-Nawadir*, he said: If someone wants to heighten his building for the sake of causing damage (to others), he should be prevented. Some scholars disputed whether Ibn Kinanah's statement was a different opinion or not.

Ibn Kinanah said: No one is allowed to prevent another from heightening his building if he is indeed doing it out of need, but if his intention is to harm his neighbor and he is not going to benefit from it, he should be prevented. However, as for the wall, he is allowed to heighten it to the extent that it ensures his security. If he heightens it more than that with the intention of

---

[89] See the opinion of the Shafi'i school in al-Nawawi, *Raudah al-talibin,* 10:324, al-Shirazi, *al-Muhazzab*, 2:255 and al-Ramli, *Nihayah al-muhtaj*, 8:99-100.

causing harm to his neighbor and without him benefiting from such an act, he must be prevented.

Master-mason Muhammad says: I saw the same (ruling) in *al-'Utbiah* from Ibn Nafi', However, Ibn al-Qasim denied it to be from Ibn Nafi' and said: I do not know that.

Master-mason Muhammad says: The practice is this: Everybody is allowed to heighten his building as he wishes. This judgment and *fatwa* are based on this opinion.

Master-mason Muhammad says: In *Kitab al-Mu^{c}in* by al-Shaykh *al-Faqih al-Qadi* Abu Ishaq b. 'Abd al-Rafi' it is reported that Ibn 'Itab said: My opinion, which I follow in the *madhhab* of Malik, is that all the harm must be prevented except from heightening a building that would stop the flow of fresh air and light, unless it is proven that its intention is to cause harm to others.

Master-mason Muhammad says: Such a matter happened to me when a man who had a higher building than mine opened a *kuwa*, which he used to look at the street. As I decided to build on my property, I heightened my building and it blocked my neighbor's *kuwa*. Hence, he took the matter to *Qadi al-Jama'ah* and stated to him that my building which had been heightened over his building had blocked his window, the one through which he used to look at passers-by and other things and that its closure had invalidated the room. The *Qadi* asked me whether what had been said against me was correct. I accepted the charge. Then the *Qadi* told him that he did not have the right to prevent me from what I did because what I did was legal.

Master-mason Muhammad says: Such cases frequently happen at our place and I did not see any of the judges giving a different judgment from that.

Fatwa on a similar case: Master-mason Muhammad says: I asked *al-Faqih al-Mufti Qadi al-Jama'ah* Abu Ishaq b. 'Abd al-Rafi' regarding a man who built a room with a *kuwa*, which enabled him to see the roof terrace (*sutuh*) of his neighbor where some of them hang their laundry. Should he be prevented from using that *kuwa* because of the usage of the neighbor of their roof terrace? He said: He should not be prevented. I asked him: If the owner of the top-floor builds another level on it, and the window exposes those on the second level, does he have the right to block the window that overlooks the first level? He said: No one can block his *kuwa*, since it has been there earlier and he deserves to benefit from it. I also asked *al-Faqih* Abu 'Abd Allah b. al-Ghammaz, and he said the same. They said that, it is the responsibility of the owners of the roof terrace to cover themselves.

Master-mason Muhammad says: Everyone I asked, answered in the same way. Master-mason says: That *fatwa* agrees with what was said by Ibn al-Majashun in *al-Wadihah* as discussed earlier.

Once in Tunis there was a man who built a factory to make *Tiraz*[90]. He opened a *kuwa* that enabled him to overlook his neighbor on the roof terrace, which was surrounded by a screen wall. It was the highest building before the factory was completed. Its owner then complained against the owner of the factory and they took their matter to *al-Shaykh al-Faqih al-Qadi* Abu Ishaq b. 'Abd al-Rafi', *Qadi al-Jama'ah* in Tunis and he ordered the owner of the factory to shut the *kuwa* and told him that: His (owner of the house) roof terrace was invisible, you do not have the right of unveiling it, go and shut your *kuwa*.

17- Discourse On Shutting The Window (*kuwa*) By Judgment.

In the book of Ibn Sahnun, Muhammad said: My father was asked about a man who had been ordered to shut the *kuwa* in his house that enabled him to see through his neighbor's house. He requested to be allowed to shut the *kuwa* from the inside. Sahnun answered that the owner of the house is not allowed to do so. He must remove its covering and block it from the outside. If he leaves the sill, he may reclaim it later by producing a witness to claim that the covering has existed a long time earlier, so he may claim the right of precedent (*hiyazah*). Therefore, he must remove the sill.

Master-mason Muhammad says: In *al-Ahkam* by Ibn Zimnin it is reported that: The owner must remove the sill.

Some scholars said: He must also remove all the things related to the covering and shut it by using similar building materials so that its place cannot be differentiated from that of the wall itself. If the wall is made of bricks, the blocked part cannot be built using stones (for it must be built using bricks) and (similarly) if it is made of stones, the blocked area cannot be built with bricks,

---

[90] A kind of embroidery patched on the cloth of Sultan or high-ranking official.

since it will be depicted differently and as a result will cause suspicion.

A case like this happened to us in Tunis: A *kuwa* was shut by blocking its sill and the decoration on it looked old. The owner then reopened it again. Although it was in a dead-end street, it resulted in exposing other people's entrance halls. Consequently, their owners stood against him and asked him to shut it by judgment. The owner of the *kuwa* pleaded and brought with him witnesses who claimed that it was an old blocked *kuwa* (and its sill still remained and the decoration on its edges were still there without any changes). It is only that the owner of the house had shut it for some time. As a result, the *Qadi al-Jama'ah* ordered it to be opened because of the doubt, which existed, namely in the sill, the remaining carved decorations and the lintel, helped the owner claim the right of precedence and reclaimed his window. Therefore the sill must be removed (as explained in the first paragraph).

18- Discourse On Someone Who Opened A Window *(kuwa)* On A Rented House.

Master-mason Muhammad says: Ibn 'At in his *al-Tarar* said: If the house is rented, and a neighbor builds a room and opens a *kuwa* that exposes the rented house, and the tenant asks the owner: Defend my rights, and the owner says: It is not my responsibility. Ibn 'At in *al-Tarar* said: It is upon the owner of the house to defend the rights of the tenant and to avoid the harm. If he refuses to take responsibility, the tenant is free to terminate the contract if he wishes, just as he is free to do so as in the case when something collapses and causes harm to him and the owner refuses to rebuild.

19- Discourse On The Window Of Towers In The Gardens And Vineyards.

Master-mason Muhammad says: In *Kitab As'ilat al-Faqih al-Qadi* Abu 'Abd Allah b. al-Hajj al-Tujibi al-Qurtubi, he said:
The principles of overlooking from buildings are of three types: On houses: No disagreement in forbidding it. Master-mason Muhammad says: This is according to his knowledge because disagreements did exist as have been elaborated before. He said: However, for farms, all agree on allowing buildings that enable

someone to overlook the others. As for gardens, opinions differed. He also told me thereby from Ibn Talla' regarding vineyards near residential areas, that they are considered as gardens, especially in our place because people frequently visit their vineyards together with their families. (The quotation is correct from the questions of Ibn al-Hajj.)

Fatwa: Master-mason Muhammad says: I asked the opinion of *al-Faqih al-Mufti* Abu 'Abd Allah b. al-Ghammaz regarding owners of vineyards who built towers and opened *kuwa* to enable them to enjoy their gardens, but at the same time they overlooked the others' gardens and vineyards, are they forbidden from opening the *kuwa* or not? He said to me: If the gardens have buildings to live in and are protected, to me they are like houses, therefore any *kuwa* facing them must be shut, so that their owner is prevented from overlooking. But as for the gardens which have no building and which do not have anything in them other than the fruit trees, the owners of the towers are not prevented from opening the *kuwa* in their towers. I asked him: If a man owns a vineyard, and has in it a tower that is surrounded by a fence, and has a neighboring vineyard, whose owner has decided to build a tower with a *kuwa*, which will enable him to overlook the compound of the other, should he be prevented from that? He said: Yes, he should be prevented from that, because the neighbor surrounded himself with a fence, so the other one must be prevented from watching him just as the case with houses. I asked him: If the other one does not have a fence surrounding his tower and the other neighbor wants to build a tower that will enable him to overlook at the courtyard of the neighbor's tower or at those who come and go, should he be forbidden from it? He said: No one can be prevented to do that unless (the other neighbor) has a building that covers him.

Master-mason Muhammad says: I also asked Shaykh *al-Faqih al-Qadi* Abu Ishaq b. 'Abd al-Rafi' regarding a man who wants to open in his tower a *kuwa*, which will enable him to look at his neighbor's vineyard, should he be prevented from doing it or not? He answered: No one is prevented from doing that, except if it faces an occupied area like a courtyard and others, but if he is looking at the vineyard without any building in it, he is not forbidden.

Al-Faqih al-'Adl Abu 'Ali b. 'Abd al-Sayyid,[91] who was *Qadi al-Jama^ah* in Tunis said: All *kuwa* facing gardens and vineyards must be shut, and it is forbidden to create a *kuwa* in such areas. There is no difference between vineyards and gardens, because a vineyard, which has no building enables the owner to walk freely in it either with his family or alone, or to sleep under the trees, or to eat or to ease himself in it, or to do anything he likes inside his property, while being unaware that someone is watching him, and he cannot guard himself from the one who watches from the *kuwa* of the tower. It is too much and also a clear harm to him. He added: This is also the opinion of *al-Faqih al-Qadi* Abu al-Qasim Ibn Zaytun,[92] which he used in his *fatwa* and judgments.

20- Discourse On Someone Who Builds On Higher Ground Overlooking Neighboring Houses.

The author says: A discourse on someone who builds on a higher site exposing those houses or other structures built before.
Master-mason Muhammad says: The jurists disagree on that matter and there are two opinions:
In *al-Wadihah*, Ibn Habib said: Ibn al-Majashun, Mutarrif and Asbagh said: If a man builds on a higher ground, exposing the watering place of the village from a distance of one *ghalwah* (400 cubits that is equal to 184.8 meters), or two *ghalwah* and if the building has a door or a *kuwa* or anything of that kind facing the watering place, it has to be prevented. The reason is that he chooses his site on the second hill, exposing the villagers' watering place. It is not wrong for him to build on the higher ground, even if he has another site to choose from. However, if his house has been built earlier than the others, then he cannot be prevented even though others are exposed through his *kuwa*.
The second opinion: 'Isa b. Dinar said in *al-Nawadir*: If the place does not have any communal facility other than the building, my opinion is not to prevent him, and if the place is

---

[91] He is Abu 'Ali 'Umar b. Muhammad b. Ibrahim b. 'Abd al-Sayyid al-Hashimi (d. 731/1331). He was the Qadi of Marriage (Qadi *al-Ankihah*). al-Zarkashi, 68-69.
[92] He is Abu al-Qasim b. Abi Bakr b. Musafir al-Yemeni al-Tunisi (d. 691/1292), the *Qadi al-Jama'ah* in Tunis in the year 679/1280 to 680/1281, Ibn Farhun, *al-Dibaj al-muzahhab*, 1:310.

planted and he has no other choice, and he cannot do without it, he also cannot be prevented. But if he can do without it and it does not harm him in any way, my opinion is that he should be prevented if it is really harmful to others. Sahnun has the same opinion as in *al-'Utbiah*, so too Ibn 'Asim[93] who based his opinion on Ashhab.

Master-mason Muhammad says: *Al-Sharaf*: A high place from which the neighbors' houses and other properties (other than buildings) can be seen, and the owner of the mound wants to build a house on it, and whoever stays there will be able to stare at the village's watering place or other peoples' houses.

The author says: *Al-Mawridah* is a place where the community fetch their water supply, the distance between the high place and the watering place is one or two *ghalwah*. The disagreement in that matter is as reported earlier, especially regarding the house. However, if he builds on the mound or opens a *kuwa* in addition to what has already existed in the house, there is no disagreement in preventing that.

Master-mason Muhammad says: *Al-ghalwah*[94] is the distance of a released horse and it is equivalent to two hundred (200) cubits (*zira'*). There is no disagreement on this.

Al-Baji in *al-Muntaqa* and Qadi 'Iyad in *al-Tanbihat* said: A mile is composed of ten *ghala'*, and a *ghalwah* is the distance of a released horse -as mentioned above- and it is two hundred (200) cubits (*zira'*), therefore in a mile there are 1000 spans which is two-thousand (2000) cubits (*zira'*). Ibn Habib said to me: I understood it as: The span of an animal, but the span of a person is the length of his two arms and the width of his chest, therefore, it is four cubits long, and it is called *qamah*. Others said: A mile is 3500 cubits.

Ibn 'Abd al-Barr[95] said: This is the best among all opinions. Al-Zanati in *Sharh al-Risalah* of Ibn Abi Zayd said: One *dhira'* is

---

[93] He is Husain b. 'Asim b. Kaab b. al-Thaqafi (d. 208/823), a jurist from Cordova. 'Iyad, *Tartib al-madarik*, 2:28.

[94] One *ghalwah* is equivalent to 184.8 meters. Muhammad Abd Satar Uthman, *I'lan bi ahkam al-aunyan, Dirasah 'athariyyah mi'mariyyah*, (Iskandariyyah: Dar al-Wafa, 2002), 207.

[95] Yusuf b. 'Abd Allah b. Muhammad b. 'Abd al-Barr (d. 368-463/979-1071), a jurist from Cordova, who has written several well-known books such as *al-Istizkar*, *al-Kafi fi al-fiqh* and *al-Tamhid*. 'Iyad, *Tartib al-madarik*, 2:808.

equal to two hand-spans, and one hand-span is equal to 12 fingers, and a finger is equal to five seeds of barley being put on the surface. Someone else said: A finger is equal to 6 seeds of barley being put on the surface, and one *farsakh* is equal to 12000 cubits.

21- Discourse On A Man Who Builds A Minaret That Overlooks Neighboring Houses Or From The Roof Terrace Of A Mosque.

Master-mason Muhammad says: From *al-'Utbiah* it is reported that Ashhab and Ibn Nafi' heard Sahnun being asked about a mosque, which had a minaret and whenever the *muezzin* (caller for prayer) went up the minaret, he overlooked people's houses. The owners of the surrounding houses wanted to prevent him from using the minaret. Some of the houses were at a distant from the mosque and a street between them. Sahnun answered: Access to the minaret must be prevented because it causes harm (to the neighboring houses) and the Prophet forbids all kinds of harm.

Master-mason Muhammad says: If people are not clearly seen and the houses are at a fair distance from the mosque, it is not prevented, as reported by Ibn 'At in *al-Tarar*. But if people can be clearly seen, the *Muezzin* is forbidden from ascending the minaret until further precaution is taken to avoid overlooking. This is the judgment of *al-Faqih al-Qadi* Abu Zayd b. al-Qattan on the matter.

Thereof: Master-mason Muhammad says: From the book of Ibn Sahnun: Habib asked Sahnun about a person who had built a mosque on his roof terrace adjacent to his neighbor's wall, which enabled anyone who went up there to overlook the neighbor's house. Hence, the neighbor protested. Sahnun said: The one who builds the mosque must be compelled to cover his roof terrace, and the people must be prevented from praying in that mosque until his neighbor is well protected (from exposure).

22- Discourse On A Man Who Wants To Create A Door On A Main Road.

Master-mason Muhammad says: If a man wants to open a door onto a main public lane (*zuqaq nafid*), his action falls under one of three conditions:

It is either facing another door of an opposite neighbor, or it is near to the door of an adjacent neighbor and will be troubling to the neighbor, or his new opening is neither opposite nor near an adjacent door, then in this third condition, the Maliki jurists agreed that he should not be prevented from doing so.

However, they differed in the case where his door is adjacent to the door of his neighbor by three opinions:

It was said that: He should be prevented because he contraints his neighbor by the position of his door. The second opinion: He should not be prevented. The third opinion: He should be prevented if he is damaging his neighbor's wall by opening and closing of his door. However, if it is not causing any harm, he should not be prevented. The author says: This is also my opinion.

The scholars also disagreed in the case where someone opens a door opposite another. There were four opinions on that:

Ibn al-Qasim said in *al-Mudawwanah* from Malik: If it is a public street (*sikkah nafid*), he is free to open whatever he likes, and to locate his door to any side without any limitations. Al-Shaykh *al-Faqih al-Qadi* Abu Ishaq b. 'Abd al-Rafi' in his book said on (the) matter with a brief statement: it is allowed to whoever wants to open a door opposite another. Ashhab in *al-'Utbiah* had a similar opinion as to what was reported by Ibn al-Qasim from Malik in *al-Mudawwanah*, the same opinion of Ibn al-Qasim was also reported in *al-Nawadir*.

The second opinion: Ibn Wahb said in *al-Mustakhrajah* from the book of *al-Sultan*: He should not be prevented from opening the door if the street is wide and used by many people, and he is free to do whatever he wants. But if the street is narrow, he is prevented from doing it.

The third opinion: In *al-Nawadir* Ashhab said: Malik was asked about a man who wanted to open a door in his house, which was situated on a street used by many people, and the door would face his opposite neighbor's door or be offset from it. Ashhab said: Malik answered that: If the neighbor is harmed by it in such a way that the one behind the open door can see people entering and exiting the opposite house, he should be prevented from opening the door. Ibn al-Qasim in the book of Ibn 'Abd al-Hakam also had a similar opinion, so too Ibn Kinanah as reported in *al-Majmu'ah*.

The fourth opinion: From the book of Ibn Sahnun, Muhammad said: Habib asked Sahnun whether a man whose house is adjacent a public street is allowed to create a door that is facing another man's door or not? He said: He should be prevented from it and the door must be offset from the opposite door. Habib asked again: What is the measurement of the offset, is it one or two cubits? He said: To the extent of what is considered to be enough in removing the harm to the opposite house.

The author says: *Al-Faqih al-Qadi* Abu Ishaq b. 'Abd al-Rafi' said in his book: He who makes a door facing an opposite door is ordered to offset his door a little bit from the opposite neighbor's door unless the street is too wide to the extent that people at the opposite door cannot be clearly seen from it other than what is seen in the street. He is free to open and locate the door where he wishes if the street is very wide.

Master-mason Muhammad says: People disagreed on which is the most famous among the above-mentioned opinions. However, what is being practiced and used in judgment in our place is this: If the street is used by many and it is wide, he is not forbidden from creating a door, even if it is opposite to another man's door. The author says: *Al-Faqih al-Qadi* Ibn 'Abd al-Rafi' applied this opinion when he judged between two neighbors. One of them created a door opposite to his neighbor's door and as a result of that they took the matter to the above-mentioned judge *(Qadi)*. The one who was facing the new door said: This man has opened a door opposite mine that damages me. The Qadi asked him: Is the street wide and used by many people? He said: Yes. The Qadi replied: You can go; you have no right to stop your neighbor from opening the door. The man said: The door, which has existed before, was small and now he has made it wider. The Qadi replied: Leave him; he can even open his entire wall. (That recent door was created because the owner wanted to operate a bakery and to pound wheat).

Master-mason Muhammad says: The saying of *al-Faqih al-Qadi* "Leave him, he can even open his entire wall" is to stress the right of opening the door. I have also read the famous opinions of some scholars from Qairawan, the text is: *Al-Faqih* Abu al-Qasim Khalaf b. Abi Firas al-Qurawi was asked (on the same case) and he said: *Al-Madaniyyun* (the tradition in the city of Medina) disagreed on the issue of opening a door in a house which faces the door of an opposite house. However, what is being practiced in our place and the opinion of our scholars (as have been discussed above) is that he should be prevented. That is what our followers choose after their masters, and I agree with them, and it is the popular view, and it is the real stand of the Maliki *madhhab*. I also think that our scholars are following the previous scholars' opinion, and I have not heard anyone before them who has chosen other than this opinion. The method used to determine the harm: A man is to stand at the opening of the entrance hall (*uskufah*) of the earlier house. If the viewer from the location of the opposite door can see what is behind the man, then the prevention is certain. If the one standing at the door of the entrance hall is not seen and nothing is exposed until the standing man moves from his position, then the prevention is not necessary. The situation is therefore like the position of a passer-by, which is unnecessary for self protection from being exposed.

This is my opinion apart from what have been mentioned regarding the views of our masters and their followers who were before us, and it is the practice in the past and present.

Master-mason Muhammad says: His saying is that: Until the one standing at the door of the entrance hall is exposed: Means the place where the door is allowed to turn as it is being opened and closed, which is also the thickness of the wall to which the door is attached.

That is a good and genuine question, which I have abbreviated and removed the questioning and have mentioned only the answer.

In *Kitab al-Tarar* by Ibn 'At it is reported that there are three approaches concerning someone who wants to create or relocate a door facing the open-ended street: Generally he is allowed to do so, without any explanation given. He is not allowed, also without any explanation given. The third: To allow him if the road is wide and to prevent him if the road is narrow.

Master-mason Muhammad says: Regarding the opinion of Sahnun, which is at the beginning of the problem, some jurists said: It is a recommendation (*mustahab*) as implied through the saying of al-Qadi Abu Ishaq b. 'Abd al-Rafi' in his book. However, to me it is compulsory (*wajib*).

Master-mason Muhammad says: It is also clear from the saying of al-Qadi Abu al-Walid b. Rushd that the offsetting (of the new door), which was mentioned by Sahnun, is preferred (*mustahab*).

Master-mason Muhammad says: To me it is compulsory (*wajib*) if the opening is recent and the street is used by a small number of people and the door is facing the opposite door. He must offset his door- as said by Sahnun- to the extent that it is enough to remove the harm incurred on the opposite door, because those are the rights obtainable by the rule of *hiyazah*. No one is allowed to harm the earlier user and no one is allowed to deprive him of his right. This rule is applicable to the rights to create doors and windows (*kuwa*), digging wells or something similar.

Master-mason Muhammad says: From *al-Tarar* of Ibn ᶜAt: The street is considered wide if its width is seven cubits.

Master-mason says: If the width of the street (*zuqaq*) is less than seven cubits it is considered to be narrow, and opening a door there is harmful for the opposite neighbor's door, and the one doing it must be prevented from doing so.

23- Discourse On A Man Who Wants To Open A Shop Or Shops Opposite His Neighbor's Door.

Master-mason Muhammad says: The opening of shops is as the opening of doors of houses; however it is more damaging.

Master-mason Muhammad says: From *al-'Utbiah* in the chapter of *al-Sultan* 'Abd al- Malik b. al-Hasan[96] said: I asked 'Abd Allah b. Wahb about a man who opens beside his house shops facing a public street, while another man has a house opposite those shops and its door facing the street (*zuqaq*) and those shops. As a result, the opposite neighbor complains that he is being harmed by the owner of the shops for being able to see his servants and family coming out of the door, Is he prevented? Ibn Wahb answered: If it is not obstructing the road and the road is wide to the extent that he (the claimant) and other passers-by are having the same exposure, the shop owner is allowed to open whatever he wants, be it a shop or other utilities. Ashhab had a similar opinion as reported in the *Kitab al-Sultan* in *al-'Utbiah*.

Fatwa: Master-mason Muhammad says: The contemporary scholars disagree on that matter. Among them: From *Nawazil* of

---

[96] He is 'Abd al-Malik b.al-Hasan b. Muhammad b. Yunus b. 'Ubaidullah (d. 232/847), a Maliki jurist from Andalus. He studied under Ashhab, Ibn al-Qasim and 'Abd Allah b. Wahb and was appointed as judge of Toledo. 'Iyad, *Tartib al-madarik*, 2:20.

Ibn Rushd (the popular opinion from him), it was stated that he was asked about two neighbors facing each other, separated by the public street (*zuqaq nafid*), one of them opens a door and two shops, facing the house of the other, and no one can come in and out of that house unless he is exposed to those who sit in the two mentioned shops doing their work, and that is a clear harm, which the owner of the house can justly establish. Is the owner obliged to close his two shops because of the damage to the other, and shut the newly opened door? Please give us your verdict on this particular matter.

He answered: He should be ordered to offset his door and his two shops so that they do not face the neighbor's door. In case he cannot do it, and he has no way of doing it, he is allowed to continue without having to close the shops.

Another *fatwa* by *al-faqih al-salih* Abu al-Qasim Khalaf b. Abi Firas al-Qurawi, the author said: He was asked concerning a man who owned a house and on the left side was a shop. Opposite him was another house whose owner wanted to open on the right side of his door, three shops by opening a room that was attached to his house. He claimed that it was his right because the two houses facing each other were on the main road and it is one of the major roads in town. However the opposite neighbor protested and said: Doors are allowed on wide public streets, but previously only the door of the house faced the main road, but now shops were added and it is more damaging. People continuously sat around it, therefore the harm and exposure became greater. Also, there was evidence that the first shop, when operated, exposed the entrance of the opposite house and whoever entered it, and as for the second shop: It exposed whoever came out and also exposed part of the entry hall, and as for the third shop, it exposed the door of the house only.

He (Abu al-Qasim) answered: Scholars of the Maliki School (*madhhab*) disagreed on the issue of opening a door that faces another. However the current practice of our people is to prevent it and to protect the owner of the door that existed earlier. This opinion is chosen by our companions after analyzing the views of their teachers, and we have seen those views before, and I agree with them and it is also the popular view of the Malik school, because it is the right of whoever opens the door earlier and no one should be allowed to appropriate and cause damage to the earlier user. This ruling is also applicable to: Digging of wells, developing dead land (*mawat*) for farming, running a river and several others. The principle applied here is that whoever comes earlier is the rightful owner, based on the popular view and which is also the pillar of the *Madhhab*. I believe that our scholars follow the practice of those before them since I have not heard of any alternative opinion. However, in the interest of solving a problem, a deviation is indeed necessary. Since the issue here is about doors of houses; the opinion, which allows the shop to be operated in front of someone else's door, argues that the exposure while exiting from the house is unavoidable just like for passers-by on the street. But there is a clear difference between a passer-by and the one who is coming out from his house. The exposure caused by opening the shops is more severe and the damage is not only from a single source, but many. Once we prevent someone from opening a door that is opposite to another door, the rule should also be applied to opening shops that are facing someone else's door because of several reasons.

The method used to determine the harm: A man is to stand at the opening of the entrance hall (*uskufah*) of the earlier house. If the viewer from outside can see what is behind the man, then the prevention is certain. If the one standing at the door of the entrance hall is not seen and nothing is exposed unless the standing man moves from his position, then the prevention is not necessary. His situation is therefore like the position of a passer-by, which is unnecessary for self-protection from being exposed. In this case if the other person is being prevented from opening a door, it will cause damage to him since he cannot benefit from his own property. This is my opinion apart from what has been mentioned regarding the views of our masters and their followers who were before us, and it is the practice of the past and the present.

Master-mason Muhammad says: From a question to al-Qadi Abu 'Abd Allah bin al-Haj: He was asked about someone who had opened a shop facing another man's door and he could look at the entrance hall. al-Qadi Abu 'Abd Allah answered: I have studied the question and have ordered the owner of the shop to offset his shop from his neighbor's door, for the harm of the shop is more severe, and the Prophet prohibited any harm.

Master-mason Muhammad says: This opinion is different from what Ibn Rushd said at the beginning of this case.

Master-mason Muhammad says: I also agree with what he (Ibn al-Haj) has said in this *fatwa* and disagree with the opinion of Ibn Rushd. However, if the neighbor can see the entrance hall (*saqifah*) of the house from the shop, then this is considered to be harmful, as mentioned before and he must be prevented from opening the shop, but if he cannot see it, he is not to be prevented from doing so. With this, al-Shaykh *al-Faqih al-Qadi* Abu Ishaq b. 'Abd al-Rafi' resolved the issue of a man who had opened a shop facing a street used by passers-by from east to west, and in front of the shop there was a dead-end street (*zuqaq ghayr nafid*), and in the *zuqaq* there was a house that opened to the east on the right hand of the person entering the house. The owner of the house complained about the harm coming from the shop, and they took the matter to the Shaykh *al-Faqih al-Qadi* Abu Ishaq b. 'Abd al-Rafi'. After looking into the matter, he discovered that a person in the shop could not see the people in the entrance hall (*saqifah*) but could only see someone coming out of the house through its door. The Qadi judged that the shop should remain.

Al-Faqih al-Qadi Abu Ishaq b. 'Abed al-Rafi', however, reported in his book that: Ibn ʿItab said: My opinion and what I follow in the Madhhab of Malik is that all harm must be prevented except the one caused by the heightening of a building that prevents fresh air and sunlight to his neighbor, unless it is established that the builder of the building intends to harm his neighbor.

Master-mason Muhammad says: The harm of someone sitting in a shop and staring or looking at those in the entrance hall opposite him, whereby such behavior or act is unavoidable, such as in the market area or near a wide street used by many people, cannot be prevented.

Master-mason Muhammad says: *Al-Faqih al-Qadi* Abu Zayd b. al-Qattan told me that this case happened to him and he gave the judgment that the shops must be shut. He said: I also have a note in the handwriting of Imam Abu al-Qasim al-Qamudi with a question on the matter, and with which he answered that: If the shops expose the entrance hall (*saqifah*) of a house, the one establishing them should be prevented from doing so.

24- Discourse On A Man Who Wants To Open A Door On A Dead-End Street And His Neighbor Protests.

The author said: The one who wants to open a door in a dead-end street (*zuqaq ghair nafid*) will either cause harm to his neighbor or not.

If he causes harm to his neighbor by cutting off his *marfaq* that his neighbor has been utilized, or by staring through his door towards the entrance hall (*saqifah*) of the neighbor, he is prevented from doing so and in the case he has done it he should be ordered to shut it. This is the known legal opinion of the *madhhab*, (*marfaq* is the area adjacent to a doorway on the street that is used for temporary purposes).

In case he is not harming his neighbor by any of the methods mentioned above and wants to open it, he is either creating it with the consent of all the dead-end street users or the consent of some of them or the refusal of all of them. If all of them approve his action, then he is allowed to open it and none has the right to revoke it. But if he does it with the approval of some and the refusal of others, and the ones who allow him are at the end of the dead-end street and they have to pass by the newly created door, there were two opinions on this:

Sahnun in the book of his son said: No one is allowed to open a door in a dead-end street except with the consent of all owners.

This was also the opinion of Abu Muhammad 'Abd Allah b. Abi Zayd in *al-Nawadir* who narrated it from Yusuf b. Yahya.[97]

Second opinion: Abu 'Umar b. 'Abd. al-Bar in *al-Kafi* and Ibn 'At in *al-Tarar* said: If the ones who allow it are at the end of the street and their passage is by the newly created door, their permission is legal and the weight of whoever refuses is negligible. If all the co-owners of the dead-end street refuse him, there are three opinions:

First Opinion: He is allowed to do so as long as his door does not face the door of his neighbor or located near an adjacent neighbor by damaging the use of his *marfaq*. This was the opinion of Ibn al-Qasim in *al-Mudawwanah*. It was also the opinion of Ibn Zarb and quoted by Ibn 'At.

In *al-Mudawwanah* Sahnun said: I asked Ibn al-Qasim: What is your view on a dead-end street or a through street which has

---

[97] He is Abu 'Umar Yusuf b. Yahya b. Yusuf b. Muhammad (d.288/901), a Maliki jurist from Toledo but lived and died in Qayrawan. Ibn al-Faradi, 2:201.

many houses on it and some of the owners want to open a door for their houses facing the street? He answered: One should not create a door opposite to his neighbor's door or near to it if the street is a dead-end street; because his neighbor will say: "This part of the street, which is adjacent to my house is for my use and you want to open a door in a place where I have an opportunity of opening a door. Furthermore, presently my privacy is well protected (from any exposure) and it is the nearest place for me to unload my burden, so I do not harm anybody. Hence, I will never let you open a door near my house since it will attract people to gather near my property or something like that." If it is certain that, once open, the door will cause damage, then he is not allowed to create what is damaging to his neighbor.

Second opinion: He is not allowed. It was reported in *al-Nawadir* that 'Abd Allah Ibn Abi Zayd said: Ashhab said: Malik was asked: What if I want to open in a dead-end street a door other than the one that has already existed or a toilet other than the one that has already existed or to bring my door nearer to my neighbor's door? He answered: You do not have any right to do that.

Ashhab also reported in *al-Majmu'ah* from Malik about two people whose houses were located on a dead-end street; one of the houses was located at the beginning of the street and the other one at the extreme end of it. If the owner of the one at the extreme end wants to bring his door forward, within his *fina*, is he allowed doing so? He answered that: If the action causes damage to others, he is not allowed to do so because people will be coming and going and the damage may be of that kind.

Ibn Zarb also said: He is not allowed to open it unless all the house owners on the dead-end street give him their permission. He raised this issue in *Kitab al-Qismah* in *al-Mudawwanah*: Regarding two houses, one of them is within the interior of the other and the owner of the interior has to access through the outer house. The owner of the interior house, then divides his property into smaller houses, and all of the new owners want to have access for each of their houses from the outer house, but they are not allowed to do so. However, all of them have the right to use the access, which they used before the division of the house.

In *Kitab Mu'in al-Hukkam 'ala al-Qadaya wa al-Ahkam* by Shaykh *al-Faqih al-Qadi* Abu Ishaq b. 'Abd al-Rafi', it is said:

No one is allowed to open a door in a dead-end street except with the consent of all the other house owners on the street, it is like a jointly owned property.

Thereof Master-mason Muhammad says: In *al-Nawadir*, Shaykh Abu Muhammad 'Abd Allah said: Yusuf b. Yahya said: Dead-end lanes and inclined dead-end paths are shared by their occupants. No renovation, either inside or outside facing the street can be done unless all of them agree with it, be it opening of a door or creating an upper extension cover from the wall, or a well to be dug or to be covered.

Master-mason Muhammad says: Judgments are based on the above opinion, and it is the popular opinion, which is being practiced. Many similar cases happened in our place and I did not see any of the judges giving a different verdict.

Third opinion: In *al-'Utbiah* from *Kitab al-Sultan*, Ashhab said: He is allowed to open a new door if he shuts the previous one, and does not cause any harm to his neighbor by opening the door next to the neighbor's place of holding his animals and off-loading his belongings. If the neighbor is harmed by his act, then he should be prevented. Ibn Hisham, Ibn 'At and al-Qadi Abu Ishaq b. 'Abd al-Rafi' also have similar opinions.

Thereof: Master-mason Muhammad says: From the book of Ibn Sahnun it is reported that: Qadi Shajarah[98] wrote to Sahnun asking him about two men who occupied a big mansion, each one lived in a part of it, and between the two residencies there was a path used by one of them while going out. The other neighbor wanted to open a door so that he could also use it to go out, but his co-owner protested and prevented him from doing so, thus both of them shared one exit (what is the solution?). He said: The door is a shared (*musha'*)[99] property between them, and they live together on common understanding (*muhaya'ah*)[100] and nothing can be done on the *musha^c* property except when both of them agree.

---

[98] He is Abu Zayd Shajarah b. 'Isa al- Ma'afiri (d. 262/876) a judge from Tunis. 'Iyad, *Tartib al-madarik*, 2:12.

[99] *Musha'* is a jointly owned undivided property in which no co-owner can declare that his interest is attached to any specific portion of the property.

[100] *Muhaya'ah* refers to subdividing the utilization of a property by agreement, such as a house owned by two persons in which each of them will reside alternately for a specific period without subdividing the property.

Thereof Master-mason says: If a man lives in a dead-end street and wants to create a door that has not existed before, and he asks the permission of the owners of the houses on the street (*zanqah*) and they all grant him except the one at the end of the street who owns a house with the entrance door facing another street and its backside facing the street under question. Does that owner's objection prevent him (what is the view of '*Ulama*'?). Some Andalusian scholars said: The man has the right to prevent him because he has the right (*haq*) on the street by the fact that he shares with them a backside wall. Others said: He does not have that power to prevent the other one from making a door in the street under question. This is because his main door is facing the other street. If his door faces the *zuqaq*, he has the right to prevent him.

Thereof Master-mason Muhammad says: From *Kitab As'ilah* of al- Qadi Abu 'Abd Allah b. al-Haj, it was reported that Abu 'Abd Allah b. Faraj said: The two knowledgeable jurists, Abu 'Abd Allah b. 'Itab and Abu 'Umar Ibn al-Qattan disagreed regarding a person who owned a solid wall without a door on a dead-end street. Does he have the right to prevent a neighbor who wanted to make a door adjacent to his wall or not? Abu 'Umar b al-Qattan thought that he did not have that power if he does not have a door facing that street. Whereas Abu 'Abd Allah b. 'Itab thought that he had the authority to prevent anyone from opening a door adjacent to his wall, as he would be having if he had a door facing the street.

Master-mason Muhammad says: It appears that he does not have the legal standing to prevent the other owner because he has no say on the street based on the assumption that if he wants to create a door on his wall facing the street, the other co-owners have the legal right to prevent him. Hence, how could someone who does not have a say on something that benefits him can prevent the other who has already been granted permission to open a door by the rest of the house owners on the street. This opinion is the more popular.

Master-mason Muhammad says: *Al-Faqih al-Qadi* Abu Zayd b. al-Qattan gave me a *fatwa* written in his own handwriting about a man who had wanted to open a door in a dead-end street or in one of it's open sides and the neighbors protested. He then agreed that he would not open the said door in that particular place. Then he sold the house and the new owner also wanted to open a door in the previous place and again the neighbors protested. The new owner claimed that he did not know about the agreement by the previous owner on the matter. Did he have any say on the matter or not? Ibn Ziyadatullah al-Qabisi answered: If the seller has dropped his right of creating the door it becomes the rights of the neighbors, and then he sells the house to the new purchaser, the new owner is treated like the previous one. If the seller has not explained the agreement to the purchaser, the new owner has the right of asking the previous owner to compensate him.

25- Discourse On A Man Who's Building Encroaches Onto A Public Street.

Master-mason Muhammad says: Regarding a man whose building protrudes onto the public road, he is either causing damage to the public or not. If his action harms the passers-by, then the building needs to be demolished, be it small or big (regardless of its size), this is the undisputed opinion of Maliki scholars.

If it does not harm the people where the road is very wide, there are three different opinions: some scholars said: Demolish it. Others said: Retain it. Another view depends on the width of the road: If the road is less than seven cubits wide, then the building should be demolished, if the road is wider than that, then it should be retained.

Master-mason Muhammad says: The basis of the rule is that it is prohibited; the argument of the group who prefer it to be demolished is from *al-Majmu'ah* and *al-Wadihah*. Ibn Wahb narrated that The Prophet said: Those who take illegally a piece of land from public roads or their space (*fina*) or land which was as small as a hand-span, on the Day of Resurrection, Allah would submerge him to the seventh layer of the earth.[101]

Ibn Wahb said: 'Uthman[102] narrated to me that 'Abd Allah bin al-Hakam narrated it from Abi Hazim[103]: During the time of

---

[101] Wensick, A.J. *Mu'jam al-Mufahras li alfaz al-ahadith al-Nabawiyy*, (Leiden: E.J. Brill, 1936-1988), 5:470.

[102] He is 'Uthman b. al-Hakkam al-Jazami (d.163/780), from Egypt and the one who was responsible for introducing the teachings of Malik to Egypt. 'Iyad, *Tartib al-madarik*, 1:309.

'Umar, a blacksmith built a furnace in the market, then 'Umar told him: You have narrowed the market and afterwards he gave an order to demolish the furnace.[104]

Thereof Master-mason Muhammad says: From *al-Wadihah*, Malik narrated that 'Umar bin al-Khattab passed by Abu Sufyan who was building his house in Madinah. While Abu Sufyan was setting the foundation of the wall and a part of it was infringing the right-of-way of the street, 'Umar said to him: O! Abu Sufyan You have exceeded your right and protruded into the rights of others, so remove your infringement. Abu Sufyan obeyed and began to remove the stones one by one with his bare hands until finished. Abu Sufyan said to 'Umar: 'O! Leader of the believers! Where do you want me to place the wall? 'Umar said, 'I want what is right'. While 'Umar saw Abu Sufyan comply with the order, he raised his hand and said: 'All praise be to God who exalted Islam with truth and I did not expect that Abu Sufyan would obey this order'.

Master-mason Muhammad says: The above text is proof for those saying that it should be demolished.

Ibn Wahb said: It is reported to me from Rabi'ah[105] that someone has asked him concerning a man who has built a mosque in the corner of his house. Does he have the right to extend his building onto the road? Ibn Wahb said: He should not do that. Ibn 'Abdus narrated from Ibn al-Qasim from Malik: It is not appropriate for someone to expand the building (onto the road) even if (the road) is wide and even more so if the road is narrow.

Al-ʿUtbi said: Ashhab said: Yes, the ruler should command it to be demolished once a passer-by or a neighbor protests. Therefore, no one can encroach upon the public road, be it wide or narrow, harmful or not as we have explained before. Thereupon any building that protrudes into the road should be demolished and it is necessary for the ruler to warn the public that they are not allowed to protrude into any public road.

Al-ʿUtbi reported from Ashhab and Asbagh a different view on the subject matter. Thereof Master mason says: In *al-'Utbiah*,

---

[103] He is Abu Hazim Salmah b. Dinar al-A'araj al-Timar al-Madani (d.140/757). Ibn Hajar al-'Asqalani, 4:143.

[104] This citation (*athar*) is mentioned by 'Isa b. Musa in *Kitab al-jidar*, 81.

[105] Rabi'ah 'Abd al-Rahman (d. 136/753) a leading figure of *Muhaddithun* of Madinah. al-Suyuti, *Tabaqat al-huffaz*, 53-54.

Sahnun was asked about someone who had built a tower on the public road attached to his wall. Should he be prevented from doing so and should he be instructed to demolish it if it has already been built? He said: Yes! No one can make any incursion narrowing the road and restricting the movements of passers-by. Ibn Habib had a similar opinion in *al-Wadihah* where he narrated from Mutarrif and Ibn al-Majashun.

Thereof: Master-mason Muhammad says: From the book of Ibn Sahnun, Muhammad bin Sahnun said: Shajarah wrote to Sahnun asking him about the shops which were located in the east of the *fina* of the grand mosque. In front of the shops were a roof passage supported by columns close to the road and people were walking below it as a public road. There were benches between the shops, and there was another road between the benches and the pillars. The owners of the shops wished to block the other road by extending their walls on both sides up to the columns and to make the shop entrance through the columns. Sahnun wrote back saying: They have no right to partition the roofed passage into becoming a building for each store if some of the owners disliked that.

Thereof Master-mason Muhammad says: It was also written to him (Sahnun) a question about the stores as in the previous case. The owners of the stores wanted to block the road from the roofed passage by taking the benches from the front of the columns and planting another column in each of their places. Sahnun answered: Reverse back to the original condition since it is not allowed to narrow the road. As for the stores, they belong to their owners. When they divided this road into parts, they added in front of the columns something harmful to the road. What they did was not in their rights. Their customers entered their shops through the covered *fina'*. If they did as what I described, their *fina'* would extend to the road. But what was in front of those stores was actually a roofed *fina'*, and the *fina'* is indivisible and should remain like that as it was in the past.

Master-mason Muhammad says: When we discuss the above-mentioned topic the practice and verdict is based on that, therefore whoever protrudes his building onto the public street, the building will be demolished, according to the established opinions (*mashhur*).

Master-mason Muhammad says: There were a lot of cases like this that happened to us; the judge commanded me to demolish them. The markets were regularly inspected to check for any protrusion of buildings or others. I brought up a case to the judge where some people whose houses were adjacent to the public road subdivided their properties into several units towards the road. They opened their doors facing the road and set up pillars or columns on the road. The distance between the pillars and their walls was either five (5) hand-spans, more than five (5), or sometimes less than five (5), and they each built a structure within the area between the columns and their walls. After that they covered the structure with a roof until it resembled a store and they built the door to their houses in the said store. He said to me: Demolish whatever protrudes onto the road; either buildings or others until there is nothing in the front part of the houses. After that, I said to him: Some of the structures are harmful because they have narrowed the street and some are not because the street is wide. He replied to me: Demolish whatever protrudes onto the road, be it harmful or not: Whether the road is wide or narrow.

Thereof: Master-mason Muhammad says: From *al-'Utbiah*, Abu al-Hasan said: I asked Ashhab about a man who had enlarged his house until it encroached onto the road one or two cubits. After that he built a wall, spent on it, and raised on it a structure, his opposite neighbor from the other side of the road complained. The neighbor wanted the protrusion to be demolished. Since he refused to do so, the case was brought up before the Sultan and the Sultan ordered it to be demolished. However the man argued that the width of the road was included in his *fina'* and it was a location for his animals. The rest was the public street, which was eight (8) cubits wide. Should he demand his neighbor to demolish the protruding structure or should some passers-by, who frequents the road, demand to demolish it?

He replied: Of course it should be demolished, be the road eight (8) or seven (7) cubits, as I explained to you. No one can build a structure that protrudes onto the public road and it is necessary for the judge to inform and emphasize to the public that no one is allowed to make any extension that encroaches onto the public road be it wide or not.

Thereof Master-mason Muhammad says: From *an-Nawadir*, al-Shaykh Abu Muhammad bin Abu Zayd said: Ibn 'Abdus narrated from Ibn al-Qasim, that Malik said: No one can protrude into the open space (*al-fadha or al-fina*), even though the space is wide.

Al-'Utbi said: Ashhab said: Yes! The ruler should order the demolition when such a case is brought up to him; either from a passerby or a neighbor, and no one is allowed to extend their building that it encroaches onto the street. Whether the road is wide or not, or whether the protrusion is harmful or not, they should be asked to demolish it. It is necessary for the Sultan to inform the public, emphasizing not to encroach onto the public street.

26- Discourse About A Man Who Makes A Protrusion Onto The Road Without Damaging Others.

Master-mason Muhammad says: The opinions of Maliki scholars of someone whose building encroaches onto the public road differed in three: Permissible, prohibited, and detested.

Abu al-Hasan al-Lakhmi said in *al-Tabsirah* and other books: Permitted and disliked were the obvious opinions of Ibn al-Qasim and Asbagh. Meanwhile, the opinions of Ashhab were two: Prohibited and disliked, whereas Ibn Habib and Ibn al-Majashun were on the opinion of prohibition. Prohibition was the famous opinion and the practice is based on that.

Master-mason Muhammad says: Proof of permission: From Ibn Wahb who said, 'I asked Malik about a man who had built a mosque on the corner of his house. Thereupon he wished to expand his building onto the road. Ibn Wahb said: Malik said: If it is not harmful to the street then I do not have any objection on that.

In *al-Nawadir*, Ibn al-Qasim said it was reported from Malik about a man had built a house and he intended to incorporate parts of his wide *fina'* into his house. Malik said: I do not like that.

Thereof: Master-mason Muhammad says: Asbagh said in *al-'Utbiah* about someone who had demolished his house, which had a wide *fina'*. He rebuilt his house and integrated parts of the *fina'* into his building. He (Asbagh) said: There is no objection to him if his *fina'* is wide and spacious and the building does not damage the road. Indeed Malik disliked that and I also dislike it, and I do not recommend it, and I do not ask it to be demolished when the road is wide and spacious, and it is not harmful to others.

Thereof Master-mason Muhammad says: The opinions differed about a tower attached to the wall. Ibn Habib said in *al-Wadihah*: I asked Mutarrif and Ibn al-Majashun about someone who constructs a tower attached to his wall on the street, should he be prevented from doing so and if the building has been built, should it be demolished? He replied: Yes! That man has no right to build anything on the street; which will narrow it even though the rest of the street is still wide enough for passers-by.

In *al-'Utbiah*, (Al-'Utbi) said: Sahnun was asked about a tower, which was attached to a wall. Should that person be prevented from building it, and should he be asked to demolish it, if he has built one? He replied: Yes! That person has no right to build anything on the road that will narrow it or cause restrictions to passers-by.

Second opinion: In *al-Wadihah*, Ibn Habib said that Asbagh said: If the road is wide, then he has the right to do it. That was the way 'Umar bin al-Khatab judged. The *fina* belongs to the house owner. Asbagh said: The *fina'* belongs to the adjacent property, whether it is in the front or rear. The owner can benefit from it as long as it does not narrow the road, block the passers-by, and harm the public. Since they possess it, they can build on it, and they can incorporate the *fina'* for building a tower, or to fence it. I do not think that he should be prevented. The owner should not be prevented if the adjacent street is very spacious, not being harmed and does not become narrow. He (Asbagh) continued: Initially I dislike it if he (the property owner) puts a fence around it or incorporates it into his property for fear of transgression (*al-ithm*), but if he has done so, I will not judge against him and I will not prevent him. I follow what was handed over to me and I realize that Malik disliked someone to build on the *fina'*. In consequence, I initially dislike the matter but if the possibility to cause damage disappears, there is no objection and I do not prevent him

Asbagh said: Such a case happened to us and the Sultan consulted me asking my opinion. When I examined it, I saw that the *fina'* was very spacious and the owner also had in front of his house on the street a bench and a place for the traders to trade. Following that, the owner demolished the bench and incorporated its area into his building. I saw that all were very spacious, and I advised the Sultan to approve the action. And I asked Ashhab about the matter at that time, and his opinion was the same as mine.

Master-mason Muhammad says: Ibn Habib rejected and did not accept that view, on the other hand he accepted the views of Mutarrif, Ibn al-Majashun and Sahnun. He said: The person has no right to protrude onto the street; for the space belongs to all Muslims, where no one can infringe upon it as it is, if it is the property of someone. No one can infringe upon it without the permission and consent of its owner. On that matter The Prophet said: Whosoever took a hand-span of a land without rights, on the Day of Resurrection, Allah would submerge him to the seventh layer of the earth.[106]

Ibn Habib said: Indeed the interpretation of 'Umar's decree on *fina'*, that it belongs to the house owner is for the following purpose: As a place of gathering and assembly and as a place for the traders to run their small businesses, and it does not include any building or fencing. This is the interpretation of the declaration that the *fina'* belongs to the house owner. That was what I heard from other scholars on the interpretation of 'Umar's decree.

Master-mason Muhammad says: Abu al-Hasan al-Lakhmi said in *al-Tabsirah*: The argument of those saying that the building should not be demolished if it is not damaging to others is based on The Prophet's saying: If people disagree about the width of a street, make it seven cubits; this *hadith* was narrated by Abu Hurayrah which was reported by al-Bukhari.

Abu al-Hasan al-Lakhmi said: As for the *hadith* mentioned by Ibn Habib: "Whosoever infringed a hand-span of the Muslim street", it is not reliable and not authentic. He (al-Lakhmi) said that as in the *hadith* of Abu Hurayrah: It is about disagreements that occur during the initial construction of houses, and not when they are already built. The acquisition of the road is for it to be utilized and as a passageway or other purpose. The case here is ambiguous because the owner does not know whether his reserved land benefits the passers-by and others. Consequently that empty space becomes an inalienable property, and cannot be changed once people occupy it. Even though a legal transaction will cause the house to change hands, the condition of the

---

[106] Muslim, 3: 1231

reserved space stays. Therefore whoever makes an extension should be ordered to demolish it or to leave it as it was before, either an area for (tying) animals or to unload belongings or reserved for an unexpected need. However, when the matter carries two possibilities, the first possibility should not be carried out for the fear of the second possibility; i.e. it might be an inalienable property; but if he has done it, it should not be demolished. Indeed, no space should be left without any purpose and what is meant by *al-manafi'* (benefits) refers to something that is particularly for them (the owners).

Thereof Master-mason Muhammad says: If we say that the *fina'* belongs to the house owner; in the front or at the back, based on the narration from 'Umar al-Khattab, how wide should the *fina'* be? Abu al-Hasan al-Lakhmi said in *al-Tabsirah*: For the house that is situated adjacent to a dead land (*mawat*), its *fina'* is according to local custom: The spot where rainwater drops from a waterspout, and space for access.

Master-mason Muhammad says: The spot where water spouts pours to the ground depends on the amount of rainwater and the size (long or short) of the gutters. In my opinion, it should be between four to six hand-spans.

Thereof Master-mason Muhammad says: If the houses are close to each other, the *fina'* are jointly shared according to local custom. Each of the owners can benefit from it without creating any harm to his neighbor.

27- Discourse On Renting And Dividing The *Fina'*

The author says: Regarding someone who wishes to rent a *fina'*, should he be prevented or not?

Master-mason Muhammad says: Different opinions were recorded from Malik. In *Al-'Utbiah*: Ibn al-Qasim said: Malik was asked about a *fina'* that was adjacent to a street and the man who was staying adjacent to the *fina'* leased it. Do you think he has the right to do that, whereas the *fina'* is on the public street? He replied: If something that is placed on the *fina'* narrows the street and harms passers-by, I do not think that someone can take benefit from it, so he should be prevented from doing so.

The owner can benefit from a wide *fina'*, so long as it does not narrow the road for the passers-by to pass through. I do not have any objection to that, for The Prophet said: "Do not harm yourself and others and others should not harm themselves and you". If any obstruction causing narrowness is placed on the public road, it will harm the passers-by. This was the opinion of Ibn 'Abdus as he narrated from Ibn al-Qasim from Malik. Master-mason Muhammad says: There is a different opinion in al-*'Utbiah* from Malik (regarding the same issue).

Ibn Habib said in *al-Wadihah*: I heard Mutarrif and Ibn al-Majashun said: Malik would not allow the division of *fina'* and the resting places (*al-marah*) located in front of the people's houses and adjacent to the road even though the people agree with the division; for such a place is a public utility. Moreover, once the street is crowded with people and animals, those riding or wishing to stop by, for example, would like to approach the *fina'* and *rihab* (empty space) located in front of the gates which are sufficiently wide for them. Therefore the *fina'* should not be narrowed and modified from its original condition.

Ibn Habib said: I asked Asbagh about it and he replied with the same view. He said: If they have already partitioned the *fina'*, leave it to them; for they have the right of priority over others, and indeed sometimes people take benefit from it. They have the right of possession over others if they want to. Ibn Habib said: I do not like that.

28- Discourse On Building A Gate On A Dead End Street.

Master-mason Muhammad says: Ibn Hisham said in al-*Ahkam*: If there are several houses located on a dead end street and some of them (the owners) wish to build a door (gate) at the mouth of the dead end street, then the ones who wish to do so, should not do it without the consent of the others.

Master-mason Muhammad says: A similar case happened to us in Tunis regarding a man who owned several houses on a dead end street except one, which was owned by another man. He then built a gate (*darb*) at the opening of the dead end street. Afterwards, the owner of the other house protested to al-Qadi Abu Ishaq bin 'Abd al-Rafi'. Consequently al-Qadi commanded me to take the protestor with me and to remove the door and to demolish the gate. Having been commanded, I went straight toward the place but could not find the owner of the house who built the gate and with whom to speak. After that, I returned back to al-Qadi informing him that the said man made himself unavailable and he commanded me to demolish what was built, and to sell the wreckage for paying the workers.

Master-mason Muhammad says: And the gate (*darb*) on the dead end street is part of our custom and I do not see anyone rejecting it except when the owners of the walls to which the gate is supposed to be attached, prevent those who are building the gate (*darb*) from doing so. Indeed, if the owners of the walls prevent that, it is their right since the opening and closing of the gate may damage their walls.

Master-mason Muhammad says: This case also happened to us on a group who agreed to work together to build a gate by attaching it to a wall that belonged to a man who lived on the upper floor. Later, the owner of the wall made a complaint over the harm of vibration caused by the opening and closing of the gate. Thus the judge commanded us to look into it and see if it was really harmful. One of us opened and shut the gate while the other observed the wall to see whether it vibrated or not. The wall did shake during the opening and closing of the gate. As a result, we informed the *Qadi* and he ordered us to remove and demolish the gate.

29- Discourse On The Residents Of A Dead End Street Who Want To Repair Their Gate While Some Of Them Refuse (And About Those Who Want To Protect Their Houses With Walls Or Others).

Master-mason Muhammad says: In the book of *Masa'il*, *al-Qadi* Abu al-Hasan Abu 'Abd Allah bin al-Haj was asked about the above problem and he replied: If the neighbors agree on hiring someone to guard their farms and gardens, while others refuse to do so, the ones who refuse can be forced to join the others to hire someone. Similarly, Muhammad bin ʿItab issued a *fatwa* on a gate, which some neighbors agreed to repair, but others refused, and he compelled those who refused to participate with their neighbors.

Master-mason Muhammad says: The above-mentioned cases occurred to us often. Some of the residents of a dead-end street who wished to repair their gate requested me to decide for them their shares of the responsibility and to put pressure on the few who refused to participate. Thereby I informed *al-Qadi* Abu Ishaq bin 'Abd al-Rafiʿ asking him: Can those who refuse be forced or not? He replied to me: No one can be forced to do so, and no repair can be done on their gate until they reach consensus on the matter.

Master-mason Muhammad says: Apparently the aforementioned judgment was based on the application of *qiyas* (interpretation based on previous judgments) on many problems. Originally, a partner should not be forced to do anything with a co-partner on shared property; such as a house, a garden, a piece of land or a wall, and the dead-end street is not owned by any individual, thus no one can be forced.

Thereof Master-mason Muhammad says: When we say that no one can be forced until they have reached consensus over the matter, how will the funding (*gharam*) be allocated? I asked that to Abu 'Abd Allah bin al-Ghammaz, the jurist and *mufti*, and he replied: The funding is the responsibility of those who have money, not depending on the number of the houses; for the benefit of fortification (*al-tahsin*) is of benefit to the rich, not the poor who fear nothing.

Master-mason Muhammad says: Fortification is an essential part of a house. Since a fortified house will increase in value, the poor should contribute according to the appreciation in value of their house, so too with the rich, and at the same time, it protects life and assets and lessens the burden on the poor.

Master-mason Muhammad says: The case happened to us with a group of residents who desired to fortify their homes and they disagreed on how to arrange the funding among them. So the case was brought to *al-Qadi* and he was asked by them to make a decision. Thereby I was asked by *al-Qadi* to go to their residential area asking them about the type of fortification that they want. They said: We want to encircle our area with a trench or a wall. Then I said to them: To achieve such an intention, it is the obligation of the rich. So they wrote down the name of the richest among them followed by the second and the third. The rich would pay a much higher percentage of the cost compared to the poor. Afterwards, I informed *al-Qadi* on what I had obliged upon them and *al-Qadi* said to me: That is not the way, the obligation should be based on what they have agreed and consented upon, whether it is based on wealth or the number of the houses. And they should not be burdened except on what they have agreed upon without being forced.

The author says: I also asked Abu 'Abd Allah bin Rashid[107]: A group of residents wish to fortify themselves either by building a gate, a fence or a trench, or whatever else that can protect themselves or their wealth from adversaries. It happens that some of them agree while others refuse. As for those who refuse, can they be forced to participate or not? He replied to me: Yes, they can be forced to participate; for people are obliged to participate for their own benefit and interest; thus whoever refuses must be forced. I asked him: How should the cost be divided among them. He replied: According to the number of houses; every house has its own value; a new house with its own assessment and so with an old one. Subsequently the value of every house is added up for a total sum; the estimated cost of the gate or the trench or the fence should be taken; each of their costs should be counted in a total sum; the cost is divided by the total sum of the value of the houses; everyone has to carry out the work according to their amount of share either big or small.

Here is an example of that: The total value of the houses is 100 *dinars* and total cost is 10 *dinars*. The percentage comes to be: One *dirham* of the cost is for one *dinar* of the value, so whoever possesses the equivalent to 10 *dinar*, should spend 10 *dirham* and whoever possesses the equivalent to 10 *dirham*, should spend one *dirham* in accordance to its calculation.

The author says: I asked al-Qadi Abu ʿAli bin Qadah[108], and he gave the same opinion: People should be forced to protect their wealth. I said to him: How should the funding for it be? He replied: Equally distributed among them according to their houses. I said to him: Some have very expensive houses while others have less valuable ones. Should their expenses be the same? He replied: Yes, this contract necessitates it.

The author says: I asked al-Qadi bin 'Abd al-Salam[109] about the fortification. He replied: The ones who refuse to participate cannot be forced. I said to him: How to implement that? He said: Indeed, we like the protection, but dislike to force those who refuse. I said to him: People differ on that; some of them agree to

---

[107] He is Abu 'Abd Allah Muhammad b 'Abd Allah b Rashid al-Qafsi, died in Tunis (d.736/ 1336).
[108] He is 'Umar b. 'Ali b. Qadah al-Hawari al-Tunisi (d. 736/ 1336).
[109] He is Abu 'Abd Allah Muhammad b. 'Abd al-Salam b. Yusuf b. Kathir al-Tunisi (d.749/1348).

participate while others refuse. Then he said: Talk gently to those who refuse to participate, and advise them gently and pleasantly until they soften their stand and are willing to participate without any difficulties. Once a man came to the Prophet and the Prophet asked him: What is your name? He replied: Al-Hakam. The Prophet disliked the name al-Hakam; for the name is one of God's names. Then the Prophet said to him: Why do they call you by that name? The man replied: O! Messenger of God, indeed I belong to a tribe and I am their judge (*hakam*). The Prophet said to him: How do you judge? The man replied: Two men who quarrelled came to me and I consulted both of them gently until they left fully pleased, this is my approach. That amazed the Prophet and he did not ask the man to change his name. The Prophet said to him: Do you have any children? The man replied: Yes. He said: What is the name of the eldest? The man replied: His name is ʿAli. The Prophet said to him: May you be called Abu ʿAli. The man said: Yes.[110] The Prophet did not change his name for it was his function to judge gently among his tribe. Likewise those who refuse should be consulted gently until they are willing to join their fellows.

Master-mason Muhammad says: My opinion is that after they agree, then to divide the cost of the fortification by two-halves; the first half to be fairly distributed based on the value of the houses, as previously mentioned, and the other half to be allocated to the rich, according to their wealth status; first, second and third.

For example, if there are three people; half of the expense is 6 *dirhams*, thus the first of them -the richest among them- should spend 3 *dirhams*; the second richest should spend 2 *dirhams*; and one *dirham* for the third richest and so forth; the proportion is to be according to that principle.

30- Discourse On The Defamation (*tajrih*) Of Someone Whose Building Protrudes Onto A Public Street (And Is It Possible To Reclaim A Part Of The *Fina'* To Expand The Street).

---

[110] Abi Daud, Sulayman b. al-'Ash'at, *Sunan Abi Daud*, (Dar Ihya al-Sunnah al-Nabawiyyah, n.d.), 4:289.

Master-mason Muhammad says: Two different opinions were recorded regarding a person whose building protrudes onto the public street; whether such a matter invalidates (*jurhah*) his testimony or not.

The author says: In *al-Mustakhrajah* and *al-Nawadir,* Ibn Habib said: Asbagh said, concerning a man whose house encroaches onto the street, should his testimony be invalidated or not?

He said: If his encroachment causes harm to the street and he realizes the effect of his encroachment, then he should not be discredited for his testimony and the protruding element should be demolished, if it harms the public.

Ibn ᶜAt reported in *al-Tarar*: Ibn Sahl said: It will damage his reputation if he knowingly encroaches onto the public street and the encroachment harms the public. But if it is not harmful, then his reputation is not damaged. In the second chapter of Ibn Sahl's book, Sahnun has the same opinion as in the earlier problem.

Second opinion: Al-Baji[111] said in his *Wathaiq*: It will damage his reputation if the infringement is done intentionally and with deliberation; even though it does not harm or narrows the street. Ibn Rushd has the same opinion.

Thereof: Master-mason says: For those whose building should not be demolished, should the man who encroaches onto the road pay the rent in the same way as the rent is in the main street? Two opinions:

Ibn al-Jazar[112] as reported by the author of *al-Tarar* said: If rent is taken from the main street, then the doer of the infringement should pay the rent.

Ibn ᶜAt said: No rent should be imposed upon him. Ibn Rushd has the same opinion. His argument was that: For the unalienable (*hubs*) property that is subjected to the yield (*al-ghillat*), if a member of the group exploits it alone; then he who is accountable for that should be judged based on the time going forward of the encroachment, not the time that past. The question is, how about a public street, which is not subjected to yield?

---

[111] He is Abu 'Abd Allah Muhammad b. Ahmad b. 'Abd Allah b. al-Baji (d.431/1040).

[112] He was a Maliki jurist from Andalus (d. 297/910). Ibn Farhun, *al-Dibaj al-mudhahhab*, 358.

Thereof Master-mason Muhammad says: In *Nawazil* of *al-Qadi* Abu al-Walid ibn Rushd, he answered that: If a local mosque becomes too small (because of the growing population), making it necessary to expand it, the owners of the surrounding land have to be compensated, and that is the judgment. Likewise, as narrated from Sahnun regarding the expansion of the road, if the adjacent owner wants to bequeath it as a religious endowment (*waqf*), then the property would be acquired without payment, unless the said property is donated for a certain period of time only.

31- Discourse On Someone Who Possesses The Right of Precedence (*Hiyazah*) Over his Neighbor On Building Or Damaging Act, Which Is Limited For Several Years, Does He Have The Right To Claim Ownership On That Or Not?

Master-mason Muhammad says: I had originally taken this from *al-Wadihah*: 'Abd al-Malik Ibn Habib said: Ibn 'Abd al-Hakam and Asbagh bin al-Faraj narrated to me through Ibn Wahb through 'Abd al-Jabbar bin 'Umar through Rabi'ah bin Abu 'Abd al-Rahman through Sa'id bin al-Musayyab that The Prophet said: He who has possessed a thing over his opponent for ten years, is rightful to it. Ibn Habib also said: Mutarrif narrated to me through Muslim bin Khalid through Zayd bin Aslam from the Prophet, the same *hadith*.

Ibn Habib also said that: Ibn al-Hakam and Asbagh narrated to me through Ibn Wahb through Muslim bin Khalid, a similar *hadith*. Ibn Wahb and Ibn al-Qasim and Ibn 'Abd al-Hakam narrated the same *hadith*.

Ibn Habib said: I saw Mutarrif applying that in fixing the time; that it should be ten years or what is approximately ten years, these opinions strengthen each other. Ibn al-Qasim said: My opinion is that nine or eight or what is near to ten years is equivalent to ten years.

Ibn al-Qasim said: Malik did not fix any time limit on possession (*hiyazah*)[113]; neither ten years nor any length of time, and resolved each case independently based on his own opinion. He used to say that the *al-hiyazah* could occur in a short time or less than 10 years.

---

[113] Possession as a means of acquiring ownership.

Master-mason Muhammad says: Possession (*al-hiyazah*) is divided into three types: The first type, in which the owner is in full possession, on this subject we only deal with it briefly for fear of being too detailed, and we only select what we need of it.

The second type, in which the owner only has partial control, such as the wall, the roof, the use of beam and the building attached to a neighbor's property. The third type, is about the right of possessing damage.

The concept of the owner having only partial control, and the right of possessing damages will be clear after we explain and elaborate.

Master-mason Muhammad says: The harm is divided the same way as what we have mentioned before. Many features of the harm will be explained during the judgment of each case; some of them are the smoke from public baths (*hammam*) and ovens, the dust from threshing floors and the smell of tanners.

Al-Qadi Abu Ishaq bin 'Abd al-Rafi' said in his *al-Ahkam*: The judgment on that is to tell the owner of the *hammam* or the others: Reduce the smoke, the dust and the smell of the tanners until those things no longer harm your neighbors; if not, eliminate it! Whether it is old or recent; for the owner of the source of harm in such a case does not have the right to claim that it is a pre-existing damage (or an old damage), so he has no right to continue it.

Ibn Hisham added in his *Ahkam*: The damaging source has no claim to the right of precedence except when it is earlier than the suffering, and the possession (*al-hiyazah*) of something that causes damage (possession of damage) should not be used as a proof to strengthen the argument of the claimant; rather in the course of time the harm does not increase anything except cruelty and enmity.

Al-Qadi Abu Ishaq bin 'Abd al-Rafi' said in his *Ahkam*: Indeed *al-hiyazah* together with the lapse of time (*taqadum*) is based on what came from the *hadith*: He who has possessed a thing over his opponent for ten years, is more rightful to it.

From *al-Tarar* of Ibn 'At: As regard to the right of possession over another's property, the original owner's right is not dissolved except after the property has been possessed by another person and that person then holds on to it for ten years, whereas the original owner knows about it, but does not ask for a change or protest it or does not find an excuse which prevents him from protesting. As a consequence, his right to protest has expired. But, if he does not know about it, his right to protest is still valid. This view is taken from *al-Istighna'* [114]. Others said: The original owner still has the right to protest if they swear that their silence does not mean that they have forfeited their right.

Thereof Master-mason Muhammad says: As for the smoke, the dust from threshing floors and the smell of the tanners, the scholars have unanimously agreed that these three harms cannot be claimed as a right of precedence except when they have existed earlier (a long time before) than the suffering as previously mentioned. Ibn Rushd and others narrated that such things cannot be possessed by consensus.

Master-mason Muhammad says: There are disputes about other harms apart from what have been mentioned above; meanwhile, Ibn Hisham mentioned five views in his *Ahkam*:

The harm cannot be possessed, according to Ibn Habib. The harm can be possessed as all other rights are possessed, according to Ashhab and Ibn Nafi'. It can be possessed after twenty years, according to Asbagh.

Ibn Mazin said: If the degree of the harm does not increase such as from opening a door or a small window (*kuwa*), it deserves to be possessed just as much as properties deserve to be possessed, especially when one knows who created it. This is in contrast to a toilet, an underground storage site or a ditch in which water is collected. Those things do not deserve to be possessed because the harm intensifies with the increase of time.

Husin bin 'Asim said: If someone sees his neighbor doing something would harm him and does not protest until the time when the construction or the building has been completed, then he can no longer protest about it; for his continuous silence during the neighbor's initiating the action and accomplishing it, is considered as a consent.

Thereof Master-mason Muhammad says: Al-Qadi Abu Ishaq bin 'Abd al-Rafi', as quoted from his *al-Ahkam*, has a similar view with Ibn 'Asim: Whoever protests against someone who has built something that (damages) him or any other things that can harm him after it has been completed, then he (the protester) must take

---

[114] *Kitab al-Istighna'* authored by Khalaf b. Maslamah ibn 'Abd al-Ghafur (d. 440/1048). 'Iyad, *Tartib al-madarik*, 2:760.

an oath that his silence is not meant to forfeit his right and to prevent damage to him.

Thereof Master-mason Muhammad says: In *al-ʿUtbiah*, al-ʿUtbi said: Asbagh bin al-Faraj was asked: If a man builds a room in his house and opens a small window (*kuwa*) overlooking his neighbor and opens a door towards the other's *fina'*, while the owner of the *fina'* witnesses it; or creates a mill causing harm to someone in the house or in the garden; or channels water (*mizab al-ma'*) on someone else's property; or builds something on the other's wall as we have stated; and then later on someone complains and as a result, he is asked to shut the door and discontinue from doing everything that he has done illegally; and he has no other arguments to counteract it except by saying that all along people have known what he has been doing: Do you think such an argument will benefit him (the builder)? Can he counter the arguments of the protester with it, or is such an argument not beneficial to him? What is the time limit for the ones who are being harmed to protest after which their silence is considered consent? Do you consider him to be like the case of a man who builds on someone else's property while the owner witnesses it, but only protests about it after several years? Indeed Ibn al-Qasim thought that the owner of the vacant property could make a protest after six or seven years and he could accuse him (the builder) as a usurper (*ghasib*). Do you think this opinion that I mentioned to you from Ibn al-Qasim is reasonable? That the owner still has the right to protest even after many years; such as six or seven years?

Asbagh replied: He has no authority (to continually harm others) and there is no benefit for him to continue, and there is harm to the others because of it. They have the right to prevent him (the builder) and to stop him if that space belongs to them. It is not necessary for them to protest at the beginning (to protest early). Both are the same (to protest early or late), since the action (by the builder) is not by consent or by the right of possession (*hiyazah*). The above condition cannot remain permanent unless he acquires the permissions, approvals or acknowledgements (from the owners); or he has clear evidence of his action. In such a matter, there is no time limit for their protest to be void unless it takes too long that their silence appears as a consent and the right of possession (*hiyazah*) is applicable, but neither five years nor more than that can be considered (as long) in this matter, for it is still too short; not even ten years, and after they swear to him, such a long time does not signify their consent and permission.

Thereof Master-mason Muhammad says: Ibn Hisham reported in his *Ahkam*: Ibn Lubabah[115] said: Ten years as the period for the harm on the street is too short. The same opinion is also narrated from Asbagh, and what is known from Asbagh's own opinion, and by which all jurists in Cordova have used in applying their *fatwa*, that the right of precedence is still not applicable even after twenty years unless it is more than that.

Thereof Master-mason Muhammad says: Ibn Habib asked Sahnun about a man whose house protruded onto the main street and no one protested except after twenty years. He (Sahnun) said: If the evidence is acceptable, then return back to what has been taken from the street, since the public street cannot be possessed. Abu Muhammad [116] said: I know from another passage: If the evidence is clear that there is damage caused to the street and there is no clear excuse for not protesting, then that is a crime (*jurhat*).

Thereof Master-mason Muhammad says: The opinion differs regarding a man who finds defects in the house which he has purchased. Does he have the right to complain to get rid of the defect or not? Ibn Habib said in *al-Wadihah*: I heard Mutarrif and Ibn al-Majashun saying: Anyone who buys a house while the neighbor has already opened a small window (*kuwa*) (overlooking him) or there is a water channel or any other kinds of damaging aspects which has existed before the purchase, and which he (the buyer) should have spoken about it, but did not discuss it or ask the seller about it, and did not protest or ask for those harms to be removed, but instead does all that only after the sale is completed, then he has no right on the matter. However, if the seller has discussed it or has argued over it before the transaction, then the purchaser does not have a case to rectify the defect.

Master-mason Muhammad says: Al-Qadi Abu Ishaq bin 'Abd al-Rafi' said in his *Ahkam*: He has no right to ask again, adding

---

[115] Abu 'Abd Allah Muhammad b. 'Umar b. Lubabah al-Qurtubi (d. 341/952), a jurist from Cordova. Ibn a-Faradi, *Tarikh 'ulama' al-Andalus*, 34.

[116] He is Abu Muhammad 'Abd Allah b Abi Zayd al-Qayrawani the author of *an-Nawadir wa al-ziyadat*.

that: This evidence is from *al-Mudawwanah* about a slave owner who sold his slave without knowing that the slave was already married; the buyer had no right to nullify the marriage of the said slave. Thereby Ibn ꜥItab issued a *fatwa* on the problem of damage: If he sells after acknowledging the (defect), then the buyer has consented with the condition and there is no further discussion on that matter, the same goes with the buyer. He (Abu Ishaq) said in *'Utbiah*: The buyer has no evidence to dispute against the recent harm.

Master-mason Muhammad says: Yahya bin Mazin said: One has no right to reclaim and protest against others who open a small window (*kuwa*) or doors that overlook him, or (a protruding) shelf (*raff*); or to protest about the neighbor's water channel that is running through his property; or about the road that is running through his land, if the original owner claims that he has allowed such things on the basis of neighborly relationship and he swears on that. In the first place, all of these things do not deserve to be done. If someone opens a window or a door facing his neighbor's property or creates a passage through his land and the owner wants to develop his land and to stop the harm, he (the owner) has the right to do so. Similarly, if someone builds a protruding shelf or a gutter or something similar towards another's property, and the owner wants to develop his property and to end the damage on him; he is entitled to do so. As mentioned, in the first place, all of these things should not have happened except when a long time has passed, making it difficult to identify the limit of toleration and kindness (toward neighbors) and therefore the longer period of time has abrogated such claim. Furthermore, transactions, inheritance rights and change of ownership (will) take place, so the condition should be left unperturbed.

32- Book Of Defects In Houses.

Master-mason Muhammad bin Ibrahim al-Rami said: The principle of defect is stated in the Quran and the saying of His Prophet. God says: "O believers! Do not eat up your property among yourselves in vanities."[117] And the Messenger said in his well known sermon during the conquest of Makkah and at *Hujjat al-wida*ᶜ in Arafah and in the day of *'id* at Mina: "Be reminded

---

[117] Al-Qur'an, *al-Nisa'*: 29.

that your blood, your wealth, and your dignity are sacred upon you as today's sacredness, in this month of yours, in this country of yours; did I have informed, did I have informed, did I have informed."[118] The Messenger said: "The property of a Muslim is unlawful without his consent."

Concealing any defect is regarded as taking people's wealth illegally, which Allah has prohibited as stated in His sacred book and through the saying of His Messenger. The Prophet said: "Do not hate, do not envy, and do not oppose each other but be amicable servants of Allah."[119]

It is not allowed for a Muslim to sell a slave or goods or a house or a land property or gold or silver or any other things, while he knows there are defects therein, regardless whether they are minor or major until he describes the defects to the buyer. After doing that, the buyer should know about the goods as much as the seller. However, if he does not tell the truth and he hides the defects and tries to defraud, he will endure God's wrath together with the angels' curse.

Master-mason Muhammad says: It is narrated that Wathilah bin al-Asqaᶜ said: I heard The Prophet said: He who sells defective (goods) without declaring its defects, will endure God's wrath together with the curse from angels.[120]

Al-Faqih al-Qadi Ibn Rushd said: Perhaps the apparent meaning of the Prophet's saying that: He who cheats us is not one of us[121], stands for the defrauding Muslims who conceal defects; for he who sanctions the concealing of defects (*tadlis*) while cheating in a transaction (and others), is an unbeliever (*kafir*) and his blood is *halal*; after he agrees to repent he is freed, but if he refuses then he can be killed.

Master-mason Muhammad says: The above introduction is also applicable to houses and others; however we only focus on what we have mentioned previously, and we will discuss the defects of houses according to the structure of this book, its sections and its order will be stated afterwards.

Master mason says: In al-*Muqaddimat* of al-Qadi Ibn Rushd said: There are three kinds of defects: -

---

[118] Narrated by al-Bukhari, 3:573.
[119] Narrated by al-Bukhari, 10:481.
[120] Narrated by Ibn Majah, 2:755.
[121] Narrated by Muslim, 1: 99.

Firstly, a defect that does not lower the value; since it can be easily removed or because it is indissoluble from the goods. Secondly, a defect that causes a small decrease in value. Thirdly, a defect that causes a great decrease in value. As for the defect that does not lower the value since it can be easily removed or it's inseparable from the goods, there is no ruling on that.

Master-mason Muhammad says: I regard the first type of defect as like a crack on a plastered wall, or a crack on the waterproofing layer (*al-astak*), a simple hole (*al-thaqb*), a shallow trench (*al-tahfir al-yasir*), or the likes. Such defects will not cause the price to be refunded and the house cannot be returned to the seller.

(The defect) that causes a small decrease in value will not necessarily cause the goods to be returned, if the seller admits it. What is necessary in such a case is to reduce the price because of the defect, for example the crack on the wall or what is similar to it.

As for (the defect) that causes a big reduction in value, if the seller admits it without adding or removing anything, then the buyer has an option whether to return (the house) and redeem the price or accept the transaction without any compensation.

Master-mason Muhammad says: For a permanent defect, which cannot be removed, the house should be returned and we will explain that.

The judgment is based on the practice of blocking the milk in the udder of camels and cows where The Prophet said: "Do not block the milk of camels and cows (to cheat in sale). If one does this, then the buyer has two options, either to keep it or to return it along with a *Sa'* of dates."[122]

33- Discourse On A Minor And Major Defect And The Evaluation Of Its Price.

Master-mason Muhammad says: The assessment on the defect is subject to different opinions; al-Qadi Abu al-Walid bin Rushd said: I do not know from our predecessors the limit of a minor defect that will not oblige the buyer to return back the house to the seller. I looked at Ibn 'Itab's opinion: He was asked about a

---

[122] Narrated by al-Bukhari, 4:361.

defect, which decreased a quarter of the house's price. He replied: That is too much and the house ought to be returned.

Ibn al-Qattan said: If the value of the defect is worth two *mithqal* then it is a small matter and the buyer can return to the seller (to ask for compensation), but the transaction cannot be rescinded. If the value of the defect is worth ten *mathaqil,* then it is a large amount and must be refunded. Ibn 'Itab said: Ten *mathaqil* is a lot, but it is not explained out of how much; however, in my opinion: Ten *mathaqil* out of one hundred *mithqal* is a large amount and it ought to be refunded.

Master-mason Muhammad says: In *al-Ahkam* of al-Qadi Abu Ishaq Ibn 'Abd al-Rafi', he said: From al-Ahkam of Ibn Jadir: The defect is minor when it is equivalent to one tenth of the price of the house or close to it. For example, when some parts of the house are made of reed (*maqsab*) or when a house that should have two water points, but has only one. Indeed, the opinion of our scholars differed on that; some said: The purchaser has an option, if he wishes he can return the house or he can claim the price of the defect; others said: He has no choice except to return the house or accept the defect. Such a case happened to a man who bought a house worth seven hundred *dinars*; he found defects therein worth a hundred *mithqal*. Ibn ᶜItab said: He should demand for the price to be reduced, while Ibn al-Qattan said: He should return the house and nothing else. Thereupon another similar case occurred and Ibn ᶜItab said: The contemporary jurists disagreed (on that); some said: The purchaser should return the house while some others said: He should claim for a price deduction because of the defect, and either judgment is right.

Master-mason Muhammad says: In *al-Ahkam* of *al-Faqih al-Qadi* Abu Ishaq bin 'Abd al-Rafi' he said: Ibn 'Itab said: If the defect decreases a quarter of the house value, then it is too much and the house should be returned. Abu Bakr bin 'Abd al-Rahman[123] said: Once the value of the defect reaches one third of the original price, or more than that, then the purchaser should return the house.

---

[123] He is Abu Bakr Ahmad b. 'Abd Rahman b. 'Abd Allah al-Khulani (d.432/1041) from Qayrawan. 'Iyad, *Tartib al-madarik*, 2:700.

Thereof Master-mason Muhammad says: Al-Shaykh Abu Muhammad bin Abi Zayd said: There are three kinds of defects in the house: -

Firstly, a dangerous defect reducing a huge amount of the value, such as when the purchaser fears that the wall of the house will collapse. In such or similar cases, the buyer should return the house and demand reimbursement.

Secondly, a simple defect that does not decrease the value: This kind of defect does not cause the house to be returned, but because of it, the reduction of its value should be demanded. An example is a small crack on the wall or something similar to that.

As for the third kind of defect, the price should be reduced, but the house should not be returned. It depends on the value of the defective part. Master-mason Muhammad says: This opinion is similar to what he said in *al-Mudawwanah*. Muhammad bin al-Mawwaz said in his book: The house should not be returned; rather the price should be reduced.

Thereof Master-mason Muhammad says: In *al-Mudawwanah*, Ibn al-Qasim said: For a man who buys a house and finds a crack in the house; if he fears the consequences of the crack then the house should be returned to the seller.

Al-Lakhmi has a similar view in *al-Tabsirah*.

Thereof Master-mason Muhammad says: There is a disagreement concerning a small crack, should the house be returned or should the price be reduced? Based on the previous opinion in *al-Mudawwanah* and the opinion of al-Lakhmi, Ibn al-Mawwaz and Ibn Abu Zayd said: The house should not be returned; rather the price should be reduced.

Ibn al-Baji said in *al-Muntaqa*: Some of our Andalusian scholars say that the house should be returned.

Master-mason Muhammad says: Our practice and ruling is that the price should be reduced. Such cases occurred to us often, so I reduced the price.

Abu al-Hasan al-Lakhmi said in *al-Tabsirah*: A crack in one wall should not cause the house to be rejected, even though there is fear that the house may collapse; for, if that wall is reclaimed (by someone else), the house is not returned (to the seller); and if that wall is contiguous to the seller's house, returning the house to him can benefit him while the price is deducted according to it's value.

The author says: Sahnun said in *al-Ahkam* of Abu Zimnin: Ibn al-Qasim said: Whoever buys a house and finds a crack therein, and he (Ibn al-Qasim) continued: If the crack may cause the house to collapse, then it is a defect. Perhaps the crack in the wall has been there since a long time ago, and I do not consider it a defect if nobody fears it.

Thereof Master-mason Muhammad says: In *al-Ahkam* of al-Qadi Abu Ishaq bin 'Abd al-Rafi', he said: I was asked about a man who sold a shop, with a water channel of his house passing through it. He did not inform the buyer about that and then when he wanted to clean up the channel, the buyer prevented him saying: You sold the shop including its entire rights, so your right on the channel becomes void. Hence, Abu 'Umar al-Ashbiliy[124] issued a *fatwa*: The buyer has an option either to keep the shop with the defect or to return it, while Ibn Zarb and others issued a *fatwa*: The selling of the shop has ended his right to the water channel. Compared that to a problem discussed by Asbagh in *Jami' al-Buyu'*: For somebody who sold his lower floor, through which the supply of water of his upper floor must pass, and he (the seller) does not inform (the buyer) about it; and the buyer prevents him (from utilizing the water channel), he (the buyer) has the right to do so and he (the seller) cannot compel him (the buyer) unless it is a well known matter which the purchaser also knows about. Since the water flows through the lower floor, check if it is really like that, then the purchaser can take possession over it and if not, he should not do so.

Thereof Master mason says: This case happened to us. A man who had bought a house found out that there is a water channel passing through it. Following that, both men brought their case to be judged before the judge Abu Ishaq Ibn 'Abd al-Rafi', and he said to the buyer: You have the option whether to keep it and accept the defect, or if not, take back your money.

Another case I was involved in was when a man who had purchased a house found out that his neighbor's water channel was located behind the house. The wall became wet from the water flowing through the channel. He asked us about it and we told him that the condition would damage the wall and the defect

---

[124] He is Ahmad b. 'Abd al- Malik al-Ashbiliyy (d.401/1011). Ibn Bashkawal, 1: 22.

cannot be removed. The judge said to the purchaser: You have the option whether to take your money back or be satisfied with the defect, and the purchaser said: I will take the money back and thus the seller must refund and repossess the house.

Master-mason Muhammad says: Often cases like this happen and the buyer either returns the house or is satisfied with the defect. Likewise, for every defect, which could not be repaired like dampness or something similar to that, the house ought to be returned since the defect cannot be valued.

Master-mason Muhammad says: Regarding the leaning wall (off its original perpendicular alignment) of a house, it is considered to be a defect as narrated by Ibn al-Qasim concerning the cracked wall. If the leaning could cause the house to collapse, then the house should be returned, if there is no fear of the house collapsing, then it should not be returned.

Master-mason Muhammad says: Regarding the leaning wall, opinions differed depending on the quality of construction. If the wall is properly built, and is anchored to the roof or there are supporting beams behind it or something similar to that, and if the leaning wall is not dangerous, such a wall is possible to remain, based on proof, for a long time.

If the wall itself is poorly built and its construction is defective; and it is slanted, it ought to be demolished even though it is not unbalanced. This is because it is weak and its construction is defective. In that case, the house should be returned and the price should be refunded, depending on the condition of the wall, its length, and the dimensions of the interior of the house, and its value. In contrast, a low quality wall costs less, as has been discussed previously and opinions differed.

Thereof Master-mason Muhammad says: This case happened to a man who had bought a house and later on found out that the house was defective, with its wall slanting. Then both (the buyer and the seller) brought their case to *al-Faqih al-Qadi* Abu Ishaq bin 'Abd al-Rafi', the *Qadi al-Jama'ah* of Tunis. The judge ordered them to seek the opinion of the experts (*ahl al-ma'rifah*). Then I went to the house together with other experts. Thereupon I saw a huge, slanted wall, imbalanced and out of its perpendicular alignment. Its construction was not so strong and seemed horrifyingly about to fall. We also saw ten beams belonging to the adjacent neighbor inserted into the wall; small cracks also appeared on other walls. The buyer said: The seller did not mention to me that the wall was about to fall, rather he mentioned that the wall was slanting but still strong.

Master-mason Muhammad says: I wrote to him (the judge) a letter saying: What has been mentioned to the buyer is that the wall, together with its front door, is slanting (out of balance). He (the buyer) has agreed to that on the assumption that the wall is strong and will last long; this was the statement of the buyer. Below the (buyer's) statement, we wrote: He who testified after examining the said wall: The wall is slanting and is about to fall and it is impossible to stand much longer because of the said condition. Then we said after that in the document: Beams have been inserted into the wall. These (the inserted beams) together with the slanting condition and cracks in other walls. All the said defects have been there before the transaction. These additional defects plus the already mentioned reduce the value of the house by forty *dinars*. We completed the document according to what ought to be and we attested it together with both of them standing before the judge where the purchaser submitted the said document. The judge decreed that the seller should give back to the buyer forty *dinars* for the value of the defect. Thereupon the seller refunded the money to the buyer and we were dismissed.

Afterwards the seller returned to the previous owner again complaining about the same defect, saying that the defect had been there earlier than the time he bought the property, so both of them stood before the judge to seek a solution. The judge said to the one who had paid the value of the defect: You have no reason for doing that, so demand your *dirham* from whom you paid and take it; for you have mentioned in the sales contract about the wall being in a slanting position, which also means that it may fall down. This is a mistake from the experts who differentiate between slanting and falling; slanting means falling. Consequently, the seller who had paid the price of the defect returned to the buyer and they argued. The judge said: Return to him (the seller) what he has given you for the price of the defect; for he has told you that the wall is slanting (wall) which also means it is falling down. However he (the buyer) said to the judge that the experts said: The slanting sometimes can last longer and sometimes will cause the wall to fall?

Then he commanded us to appear before him whilst he was in the court, saying: What's your opinion on the wall, which is out of balance, will the wall last long or not? We replied: The slanting wall is possible to last long if the quality of the construction is good, but it will not last long if the quality is poor. In this case we do not have any other opinion. (He said): Take these men to the prison; and then he pushes us toward the prison and says to us: What do you say about the wall that is out of balance, can the wall collapse or not? We replied: Sometimes it will collapse and sometimes it can last longer depending on the structure of the wall and its defect. He asked me: Any other opinion? I said to him: This is what we know and I have nothing except what I have told you and then you may judge on that. After that, the first verdict was nullified and it was decreed that the buyer must give back what he had taken from the seller, which was the value of the defect on the wall on the view that the word slanting also implied the meaning of falling down, different from what we had said earlier. Some of the expert masons are in the opinion that the wall that is out of balance sometimes can last longer and sometimes cannot. We saw so many slanted walls that last long. We are going to mention the characteristics of the wall that will fall down in the book of the falling of the wall that is forthcoming.

Thereof: In his book al-Qadi Abu Ishaq bin 'Abd al-Rafi' said: If water from the well of a house is bitter (*zi'aqa*), then the house is considered defective and should be returned if the occupant dislikes its bitterness. Likewise, if the wall plaster of the well is falling down, then it should be rejected with the condition that the buyer is not able to repair it unless the entire wall plaster is removed.

Thereof Master-mason says: From *Wathaiq* of Ibn al-Qasim, al-Qadi Abu al-Hasan said: If the buyer claims defect during the sale and the contract includes a clause for a closer examination (*taqlib*)**,** the seller should take an oath that it is unknown to him during the inspection, and if such a deal lacks in the contract, the seller should take an oath based on the external condition and he should do that on what is unknown to him, if the buyer claims that he showed him the defect.

Thereof: The difference between houses and other goods. Master-mason Muhammad says: The house is not refundable for a simple defect unlike other goods. Scholars disagreed on its justification. Some said: The difference between these two is that: The house is not intended as a valuable asset to be used (*al-athman*) in a normal condition for trade. Thus a minor defect is not considered as something that can cause the house to be rejected.

Master-mason Muhammad says: Ibn Muhriz[125] in his *Tabsirah* opposed that justification, saying: This justification is baseless; for, it will cause the buyer to lose his right to claim the cost of a defect. The same goes to the one who makes a justification that a house is reliable.

Some of them said: The value of the house does not diminish because of its defects. Animals have more defects, but their value does not drop, the same with slaves, who conceal their defects, but are not returnable even though the buyer finds out about the defects later.

Al-Shaykh Abu Muhammad 'Abd Allah bin Abi Zayd said: What makes the house different from any other goods is that the house is hardly free from defects.

Ibn Muhriz said: This opinion has no ground; for sometimes the house has no defect. Some of them adduced (*'allala)* that a house has many components. So if one component is defective, then the reduced value only applies to that component alone. So the buyer has the right to claim according to the value of the defective part.

Ibn Muhriz said in *al-Tabsirah*: This is also baseless; what is correct in my opinion is that: The defect in the house is possible to repair as long as it is not permanent. Whereas goods and other things are not repairable, for after being repaired those things are still not perfect. Therefore the purchaser has no right on the house except the cost of the defect, for the cost of a defect will complete its entire value. Muhammad said: This justification is like a simple defect on a boat: The boat should not be returned, but any defect should be repaired.

Thereof Master-mason Muhammad says: Intermediate defects (*al-'uyub al-mutawassitah*) are like:

A simple crack, that will not cause the wall to fall apart, or a simple slanting that will not cause the wall to fall down, if the cost (of repair) can be rightly estimated; A collapsing well but not in danger of being totally destroyed; The stone buttress, which supports the wall concealing the defect; A broken cistern, if the crack is still repairable; An abandoned underground store which is repairable; A broken small window (recess) that

---

[125] He is Abu al-Qasim 'Abd al-Rahman b. Muhriz al-Qayrawani (d.450/1058).

exposes the inside of the adjacent house, once it is unable to protect the exposed house; The plank and reeds of the roof that has decayed; The head of the beam that has decayed; A broken water channel; The underground store that is damaged and the surrounding soil is not properly entrenched; A structure built alternately with baked bricks and mud bricks; Plastering the wall with *al-bughli*[126] and dressing it with lime and gypsum; Applying plaster ceiling (*al-akhal*) in the middle of the house and the likes. All the above are examples considered as intermediate defects, which can be compensated in the form of value, if it is not clearly stated in the sales agreement. Such things happened to us often and the judge ordered according to the value of the defective parts without having to return the house.

The defects, which cause the house to be rejected, are many: - A total defect which is not included in the agreement; such as a leaking water channel which causes water to leak through some parts of its wall or located behind a wall which can cause obvious harm; an irreparable well and cistern; A small window that cannot possibly protect overlooking; A large part of the wall that has broken down; Smoke that damages residents; Unpleasant smell originating from a wastewater channel that comes from a neighboring house; A stable (*arwa*), located behind the house that causes the wall to vibrate and prevents the occupants from sleeping, or upsetting the owner of the upper or lower floors.

All of the above defects are the grounds for the house to be returned, if they are not properly mentioned to the buyer. Such cases happened to us and we nullified the transaction. The house, if it is famous for *al-Shu'um*[127], should also be rejected.

Thereof Master-mason Muhammad says: The above provisions are applicable if the seller pledges that he has not made any addition or reduction; if the seller claims any shortage in the selling such as something in the house is ruined, when it is already in the possession of the buyer, then it must be decided whether what is broken down is minor or major. If the damage is major and it is a clear defect that will cause the house to be returned, the buyer must not return the house but rather he should receive the value of the major damage that he has suffered on the

---

[126] A material produced by mixing sand and lime.
[127] Haunted house or causing bad luck to the occupant.

house. If what is damaged is minor and the buyer protests about the defect which will cause the house to be returned, then the buyer has the right to return the house and he should evaluate the damage. As for the seller, he has to bear the price (of the damage) and the house. That is also the practice on any extension done to the house.

A case happened to us in Tunis where a man who had purchased a house found a defect therein. Then both the buyer and the seller brought their case to the judge Abu 'Abd Allah al-Ghammaz, who was *Qadi al-Jama'ah* at that time. He asked our view on that and we wrote that the defect was enough for the house to be returned. His ruling was that the house should be returned. Then the seller claimed from the buyer the cost of damage to the house after he had bought it. Both argued in front of the said judge. The judge said: The experts should check whether the damage is big or small. We wrote a report and the text was as follows: All praise be to Allah. He who stands as a witness said afterward: I had examined the said defect when I saw it and I confirmed that it was earlier than the period of the said transaction and that it ought to be returned. Thereupon he asked me to determine the damage in the house after it was sold. It was a major damage that was not refundable since it occurred after the sale was completed. The value of the defect was such and such. Master mason says: Then we testified and judged on the cost and the house could not be returned with the defect because of the expiration of sale caused by the big damage.

Master-mason Muhammad says: Then I came back to the judge and said to him: O! My master, specify to me regarding the problem that I attested on the many defects (that would cause the house to be returned) the seller claimed against the buyer on another big damage (that occurred in the house) after the sale was completed. I decreed that the extensive defect should be compensated with a price instead of returning the house (to the original seller). He (the judge) said: Yes. I said to him: If it is only a small damage, then how does one judge it. He replied: To begin with, the house should be returned as attested since the defect caused the house to be returned. Afterwards, he assessed any damage to the house (at the hand of the buyer) and the buyer must pay the price (of the damage) to the seller; I said to the judge: Is that the practice regarding any renovation to the house whether it is big or small? He said: Yes, similar to the previous discussion on damaged houses.

Thereof the author says: A case happened to a man who had sold a house to another man and he (the buyer) stayed for some period of time. One day his backside neighbor came and said to him: Create for me a passageway so I can open my water channels which passes through your house. The man said to his neighbor: I did not buy the property that has a water channel passing through it, and he prevented access to the channel. Thus, they brought their case to the judge, al-Qadi Abu Ishaq bin 'Abd al-Rafi' and he asked the man to allow his neighbor to clean his water channel and to determine the defect. After determining that the channel was running through the man's house, the judge gave his verdict on the case that the buyer was given the option whether to accept the defect or to return the house (to the original seller). The buyer said: I would return the house, and the judge commanded the seller to refund the money to the buyer.

Likewise, another case happened to a man who had bought a house, and he found out later that behind his house there was a wastewater channel carrying human filth. The judge decided on their case; the buyer was given the option to either accept the defect or to take back his money. Such cases occurred very often and the judgment was as we stated.

34- Discourse On The Disagreement Of The Experts On Defects And Harm, And The Testimony (*Shahadah*) On It.

Master-mason Muhammad says: In the book of *Mu'in al-Hukkam 'ala al-Qadaya wa al-Ahkam* Al Qadi Abu Ishaq Ibn 'Abd al-Rafi' said: If the buyer verifies that the wall of the house is cracked and about to collapse, and the defect will greatly reduce the value, and it is already there before the transaction; but the seller claims that the house is safe and will not collapse, for the wall is only leaning and the cracks are harmless, even though the defect is obviously visible, Ibn ʿItab said: The verdict on that depends on the reports of both sides (of those who examine the condition of the house). Ibn al-Qattan said: The decision should favour the buyer who confirms the defect of the house according to the rule stated in *al-Mudawwanah* and *al-Mustakhrajah*. What Ibn al-Qattan referred to is in *Kitab al-Sirqat* about the disagreements of evaluators on the theft. Some of them said: The price does not reach three *dirhams,* and the others said: The price is three *dirhams*. He said: If two-trusted experts are in agreement on a certain price, then ignore the opinion of those against them.

Thereof Master-mason Muhammad says: From *Mukhtasar Nawazil* of al-Qadi Ibn Rushd, written by al-Qadi Abu Ishaq Ibn 'Abd al-Rafi': If two witnesses testify that the judge or the legal guardian (*al-wasi*) has settled the price while the other two witnesses deny that, (and say the price is higher) then the testament goes to those who testified the payment.

Thereof he said: If there is a testimony that this property belongs to a person while others deny it, the contradiction of testament must be justified by seeking the most upright testament from them. If they are in equal status, each testimony is also equal.

In the book of Ibn Hisham and the book of al-Qadi Abu Ishaq, both authors said: If the age of the harm is unknown, whether it is old or new, Master-mason Muhammad explained that it raises two opinions:

First Opinion: It is recent until there is proof indicating that it is an old one. This opinion was stated by Ibn al-Hindi in his *Wathaiq* and Ibn Ziyad[128] in his *Ahkam*. Some writers of *al-muwatthiqin*[129] including Ibn Hisham said: The judgment and practice is based on this opinion.

Second Opinion: Taken from the book of Ibn Sahnun: If the age of the harm is uncertain, whether old or recent, then it should be considered old until it is proven to be recent. This opinion is not practiced.

Thereof Master-mason Muhammad says: From *Ahkam* of *al-Faqih al-Qadi* Abu Ishaq Ibn 'Abd al-Rafi': If the statement saying the harm is recent is not decisive except they say: In our opinion it is something that clearly indicates that it is recent and it is harmful; then the harm has to be prevented by the oath of the petitioner that it is recent; unless if there is a counter-statement from the owner saying that the harm is old.

From the same book: If there is an oral testimony testifying that it is damaging while another testifies the contrary, the former must be preferred. Abu al-Hasan Ibn al-Qasim added in his

---

[128] He is Ahmad b Muhammad b. Ziyad al-Lakhmi (d. 312/924) one of the judges of Cardova. He authored a book entitle *al-Akhdiah wa al-ahkam.* al-Khasani, *Qudat Qurtubah*, 98-100.

[129] Document or report writers.

Wathiqah: Do not consider the testimony stating that there is no harm, for those who confirm the harm are more knowledgeable.

Thereof: Master-mason Muhammad says: From *Nawazil al-Qadi Ibn Rushd*: If witnesses attest that a man appropriated a part of the street for 20 years, and he has maintained the road by himself and with their consent, the appropriated part is considered his property.

Master-mason Muhammad says: Opinions differed on getting evidence from a person about the defects of houses, mills, and in the case of a physician; is his saying to be considered a testimony or a report? They also differed on the number of persons, how many should be considered, one or two? Are his words to be trusted as from a just man, or is he being angry? Ibn Kinanah said in *al-'Utbiyah*: I asked Malik regarding a person who is responsible for determining the defect and whether it is sufficient with only one person or two? Malik replied: If two are available, then that is better and in case of one witness, the condition is he must be a reliable person. So that the judge may pass the judgment based on the man's saying. Ibn Habib said: The judge will give the verdict based on one witness in case of defect, and in case of a woman on what she sees, and the saying of a non-Muslim physician; because his testimony is not an oral evidence (*shahadat*) but a report (*akhbar*) to the judge by which the judge will use it in his judgment.

35- Discourse On The Rented House, When It Is Completely Or Partly Destroyed, Should The Owner Be Forced To Rebuild It Or Not?

Master-mason Muhammad says: In *al-Wadihah*, 'Abd al-Malik said: If a man has rented a house for one month or one year, and either the leasing period has expired or not, then the house or a part of its wall is destroyed, the owner will not be forced to build it or the part which is destroyed. However the owner has a choice to do it, if he is able to rebuild and let the tenant complete the rental, unless the condition is not suitable for occupancy, hence the tenant has the right to terminate the contract. If the property owner has repaired the house and the period of occupancy is yet to expire, then it is not necessary for the tenant to return after being asked to move out. When the owner refuses to rebuild, and if the tenant says: I will repair it using the rental fees that I will have used to pay you with, it is not permitted except by the consent of the owner. The tenant should move out of the house when it is unsafe, or he can reduce the period of tenancy on the rented house.

If we examine his saying that "or he can reduce the period of tenancy on the rented house", the matter becomes clear, because if the condition is not harmful to the tenant, he should not vacate. This is what Ibn al-Qasim said in *al-Mudawwanah* as 'Abd al-Jabbar[130] and Ibn Abi Sulayman [131] informed us from Sahnun. However, the above report is not mentioned in the narration of Yahya Ibn 'Umar but from Abi Zayd through Ibn al-Qasim in which what Ibn Habib meant with his saying: 'When something from the house collapses and is harmful to the tenant', 'such as when the screen of the house collapsed' and his saying: 'or reducing the rental period' or 'the broken part is dangerous to the tenant'.

'Abd al-Malik[132] commented about the previous problem: Reducing the fee is based on the time the tenant has lived there before the damage occurs. The rental charges can be fixed according to the decreasing benefit due to the destruction of the house, unless what is destroyed has no effect on the tenant, and he does not reduce the period of the tenancy, so no revision of the rental rates can be considered.

Master-mason Muhammad says: According to Ibn al-Qasim in *al-Mudawwanah*: 'If the tenant does not protest at all until the period of rental is over, he has to pay all the rent whether the damage is minor or major.

'Isa bin Dinar said about it in *al-'Utbiyah*: If the tenant says that: 'I have spent some money to fix the damage, the proprietor has no reason to prevent him. For by preventing it is harmful to the tenant compared to the proprietor who is not exposed to the harm. This opinion was attributed to Malik and it was clearly clarified to me by his companions.

The author says: In *al-Mudawwanah*, Ibn al-Qasim said: Whoever offers his house for rental is free to fix the rate, either higher or lower than a similar house. If one has leased a shop to a

---

[130] He is 'Abd al- Jabbar b. Khalid b 'Umran al-Serti (d. 281/894), among the close companions of Sahnun. 'Iyad, *Tartib al-madarik*, 2:260.

[131] He is Abu Ja'far Ahmad b Abu Sulayman b. Daud (d. 291/904). 'Iyad, *Tartib al-madarik*, 2: 242.

[132] That is 'Abd al-Malik b. Habib the author of *al-Wadihah*.

tailor, he is also entitled to charge the same amount of rental fee to a blacksmith, or a baker, unless (the trade) is extremely harmful to the building, then he should not charge the same fee unless its impact is not severe.

The author says: From *al-Mudawwanah* also: If a tenant has leased a building (that is not his) to another person and this person causes damage to the building, he (the second tenant) will be accountable for that. The first tenant will not be blamed for he has done what is allowed for him to do.

The author (of *Mudawwanah*) also said: If the tenant ties an animal in front of the door and then the animal destroys the door, he is not liable for that. (This case) is similar to a person who steps down from his animal at the door of a mosque or the door of an Emir (ruler) or the door of a shop, because of some necessity, then whatever happens to him is fate.

In the *Wathaiq* of Abu al-Hasan Ibn al-Qasim, he said: The owner (of a rented) house is not obliged to repair the leaking roof. Others disputed this opinion, and obliged the owner to repair it. Sahnun also has the same opinion and it is followed in practice and judgment.

Ibn al-Qasim in *al-Mudawwanah* was of the opinion that: If the leaking is obvious, the owner of the house will not be forced to repair it unless he wishes to. On this case Ibn al-Qasim's opinion is similar to his opinion on other defects.

The other said in *al-Tarar*: The owner is not responsible to repair any damaged toilet unless he wishes to, and this also applies to other similar things.

Master-mason Muhammad says: In *al-Ahkam* of Ibn Abi Zimnin, Sahnun said: Ibn al-Qasim said: If someone rents a house, and then the roof leaks during the winter and it damages him while the owner refuses to repair, the tenant has the right to move out. If the owner repairs the house, then the rental fee is ought to be paid, however, the owner cannot be forced to repair the damage. Again Ibn-Qasim said: The tenant is not responsible to repair the damage by using the rental fee while he stays in residence. This was the opinion of Malik.

Once the damage is harmful, the tenant should be asked: If you wish, you may remain, or you may leave. If the tenant leaves and the owner rebuilds the destroyed part within the remaining rental period, the tenant is not obliged to reoccupy the house to complete his rental duration.

He (Ibn al-Qasim) also said: If the damaged part is not harmful to the occupant of the house and the owner refuses to rebuild it, the tenant should remain there and he should not move out. Furthermore, there should be no revision of the rental fee.

Ibn Abi Zimnin said: According to some reports in *al-Mudawwanah*: Except when the (damage) is a necessary house utility, then a certain amount should be reduced from the rental fee based on the value of that utility.

Master-mason Muhammad says: If the tenant rebuilds the damaged part, he will not get anything (for compensation), for he does it voluntarily, as Ibn al-Qasim said. He also said that: If the house collapses or it is feared that it will collapse while the owner is not around, then the tenant should testify and move out if he desires to.

Master-mason Muhammad says: In the book of 'Isa bin Dinar, he said: Ibn al-Qasim was asked about a man who rented a two storey house. He requested the owner: Make a ladder to the above floor, for we cannot reach it without a ladder. The owner neglected it and the tenant could not benefit from the above floor for one year. Ibn al-Qasim said: Estimate the value of the upper floor and then deduct it from the rental fee. Abi Zimnin in his Ahkam also reported that opinion.

Thereof Master-mason Muhammad says: 'Isa said that Ibn al-Qasim was asked about a man who had leased his house to another man. The tenant did not stay in the house except for two months and then suddenly the house collapsed. So the tenant rebuilt the house while the owner was away. After one year the owner returned to ask for the rent. According to Ibn al-Qasim the owner has the right over the rent before the house collapsed and the rent of the open space after the house collapsed. The tenant had no right to demolish what he built if he is given the compensation for rebuilding it.

Master-mason Muhammad says: 'Abd al-Malik interpreted the word *al-darar* (harm) in the house that is dilapidated, if the landlord wants to repair but the tenant prefers to terminate the rent. Another meaning is: if the house is partly or completely destroyed, and the tenant is forced to move out, then the rental contract is void.

As for the *hammam* (bath): The damage to a *Hammam*, either big or small that prevents the tenant from using it, will not invalidate the rent if the landlord asks the tenant to repair it since the repair can be carried out within several days or a month when the rental is for a year.

So too concerning the mill or the quern, if its base is destroyed or its rampart breaks down or some of its tools broke, and repair is needed to be done; If he has started repairing it, the tenant should pay the rent as long as the work does not take longer than the rental period. If the process of repair takes too long, the remaining period of the lease should be voided between both parties.

If the tenant is a miller who relies on water, whether it is little or much, such condition does not nullify the rent between the two parties. Once the water flows back in abundance, the rental agreement should be continued for the remaining period. The landlord is entitled for the rental fee and the tenant is entitled to complete his tenancy. This is according to Malik's opinion regarding a worker who gets sick after he is hired for a year: If he, the worker, recovers within the remaining of the year, he gets the right to stay, and the employer has to complete hiring him for the rest of the duration. He (the worker) is not entitled to any payment during the period of his sickness.

Master-mason Muhammad says: Others than Ibn al-Qasim said: The contract is binding as long as both parties do not nullify their agreement.

'Abd al-Malik said: The rental fees is to be deducted as a compensation for the period of an unworkable mill.

Master-mason Muhammad says: In *Wathaiq* of Ibn al-Qasim: If the well of a house or the water channel to the *Hammam* dries up, the rent is considered void during the time it dries up and there should be no rental charge according to the well-known view relating to drought cases. But if the water flows again within the remaining period, then the tenant has the right to lease it again, unless both of them have nullified the contract by mutual understanding. The leasing contract is not void for being without water.

Thereof Master-mason Muhammad says: In *al-Wathaiq*, Abu al-Hasan Ibn al-Qasim said: If someone leases a room and the owner specifies that the tenant cannot share it with others and should not keep heavy objects in the room for fear of the durability of the wooden floor. He (the landlord) has the right on that condition, and if the tenant does not abide by it, he should be held liable for any damage incurred.

In *al-Mudawwanah* Ibn al-Qasim said: If a man leases a house with the condition that he has to stay alone, but then he gets married or takes a slave, he should not be prevented if it is not harmful to the owner, and if otherwise, he should be prevented. Perhaps the floor of the room is not structurally durable, and other things similar to this should be noted.

36- Discourse On A Tenant Who After Completing His Leasing Contract, Claims That Part Of The House Is Built By Him But It Is Denied By The Landlord.

The author says: 'Abd al-Malik said: If a man rents a house and then after completing his leasing contract claims that some parts of the buildings have been built or repaired by him for his own benefit, and he wishes to demolish it; however the landlord repudiated the claim and says that nothing has been added from the first day of occupancy, the statement of the landlord is considered valid and accepted with his oath on what has already been constructed in the house and in its surroundings such as whether the wall is made of stone or wood or others. As for what has been cast and assembled such as stones placed in the courtyard of the house or a pillar placed (somewhere) or wood or bricks or unbaked bricks assembled together or a door placed in the courtyard of the house or something similar, the tenant's statement is accepted with his oath.

Section: Ibn al-Qasim said about a dispute over the period of (using) the *hammam*: The statement of the owner of the *hammam* should be accepted as true because he is the determinant (*muthbit*) in the case.

'Abd al-Malik said: If someone rents a house and he is granted by the owner the right to repair and restore the house as part of the rent; when the leasing contract is completed, and the renter then says: I have spent such and such; and the owner replies saying: You did not spend anything at all, then the statement of the renter will be accepted with his oath; for the landlord has entrusted his house to the renter. And if the landlord says: I have given you my permission to spend on the repair but you have done nothing and you have not built anything, and the renter replies: I have renovated this house or I have repaired (the roof) or I had built this wall, examine whether the construction is seen as recent and the repair is clear. If it is so, the statement of the renter is accepted; but if the effect is not seen as being recently made, then the statement of the landlord is accepted; for whether he is sincere or he is lying can be discovered. If there is a doubt on what has been repaired or constructed a long time ago such as since one or two years ago, then the structure should be examined. People should recognize that. Then the statement of the renter is accepted with his oath until his lie is discovered (if he has lied), since the landlord has confirmed that he has ordered and entrusted the renter to repair it.

Section, Sahnun said: Others (except Ibn Qasim) said: The renter has to give written evidence (*bayyinah*); for the rent is a debt upon him and it will not be discharged except by written evidence.

37- Discourse About Two Floors That Are Owned By Different Persons, To Whom Does The Roof Belongs?

Master-mason Muhammad says: Maliki scholars and their followers agree that the roof belongs to the owner of the lower floor.

That is basically drawn from the Quran and saying of the Prophet. From the Quran: "And were it not that mankind would be one nation, We would have appointed for those who disbelieve in the All-merciful roofs of silver to their houses, and stairs whereon to mount".[133]

The roof is a necessity of the house. If one owns a lower floor and another person owns the upper floor then the roof is in the possession of the owner of the lower floor and he ought to repair it, once dilapidated, until the roof becomes workable. This is the opinion of Malik.

From the Quran: "And We set up the heaven as a roof well protected"[134] the sky is the roof of the world. God's saying signifies that whatever is higher than the earth is the roof of those below.

From the Prophet's sayings: If man goes out from under his house's roof he will see his deeds, if benevolent, then he is fine, if malevolent then he is bad.[135] Such evidence are numerous and

---

[133] Al-Qur'an, *al-Zuhruf*: 33.
[134] Al-Qur'an, *al-Anbiya'*: 32.
[135] Both editors failed to find the above so called *hadith*.

what we have mentioned are proofs of Malik and his followers' opinion that the roof belongs to the owner of the lower floor.

Master-mason Muhammad says: If a house belongs to a man and the upper floor belongs to another; and the wall of the house collapses and its roof beams decay: The possibilities are whether the damage on the house and the roof are caused by the act of the upper floor's owner or by the weakness of the wall; if it is caused by the act of the upper floor's owner, such as from the flow of water or others, then the upper floor's owner ought to repair the wall of the lower floor and the roof.

al-Lakhmi said in *al-Tabsirah*: If the damage is due to the weakness of the wall or initially not due to the actions of the upper floor's owner, then the lower floor's owner has to rebuild it, according to what Malik said in *al-Mudawwanah* and *al-'Utbiyah*.

Master-mason Muhammad says: It is upon the owner of the lower floor to provide wood, trunks, reeds (*al-dis*)[136], soil and other roofing materials. It is impossible for a house to not have a roof. The roof of the lower floor is the floorboards of the upper floor and the house roof is the responsibility of the lower floor's owner (ground floor); this was the opinion of Ibn al-Qasim, Ibn Wahb, Ibn Kinanah, al-Makhzumy, Ashhab, Ibn Nafi', Mutarraf, Ibn al-Majashun, Asbagh and the rest of al-Madaniyyin and Egyptian scholars.

Al-Shafi'i said: They (the upper and lower floors' owners) ought to share the cost and expenses of the roof, half by the lower floor's owner and half by the upper floor's owner.

Thereof, Master-mason Muhammad says: When we say: Beams, planks (*qasb*), reeds (*dis*) and soil are upon the owner of lower floor. Who should provide the waterproofing plaster (*al-Akhal*) and (*al-astak*), which preserves the roof from moisture?[137] We say: The original condition, is either the roof is still intact or is damaged, whereas *al-astak* and *al-akhal* have disintegrated because of the lack of maintenance by the owner of the upper floor. So it becomes the responsibility of the upper floor's owner to do the repairs, not the owner of the lower floor. That was how

---

[136] A kind of plant used in constructing a roof.
[137] *Al-astak* is a layer spread below *al-akhal* which seals cracks and prevents moisture from seeping through.

we saw our masters ruled and it was in accordance with what Abu al-Hasan al-Lakhmi said in *al-Tabsirah*.

If the roof is recently renovated or it is in the early stages of construction, then the opinions of our scholars in Tunis differed; some of them said that the owner of the lower floor must provide *al-astak* and *al-akhal* and likewise it was upon him to get beams, planks and soil. Since it is necessary for him to provide those things as if the house has no upper floor and for the owner of the roof to renovate his roof; the repair is considered incomplete without *al-akhal*, which makes the roof long lasting; for *al-akhal* is a must for the roof.

Al-Shaykh Abu 'Abd Allah al-Ghammaz said: The owner of the upper floor ought to provide *al-akhal*.

Master-mason Muhammad says: The aforementioned case happened to us to a man who owned a kiosk for bakery and its roof had collapsed. Because of that the upper floor, that is located above it, collapsed. The kiosk owner then rebuilt it and made a roof with a vault *(al-damus)* and put on it the soil. Then the lower owner requested the upper owner to apply *al-akhal* on the roof. The upper owner replied: You have built your roof; you must do that together with all its necessities; for *al-akhal* is one of the necessities for a roof, so both of them raised their case before us for judgment. I asked some of our scholars how both of them should be judged? Some of them said the lower floor's owner ought to do that; for it was part of the roof; their opinion was also my opinion.

Our master *al-Faqih* Abu 'Abd Allah bin al-Ghammaz said that the upper floor's owner ought to apply *al-akhal*; I said to him: Why is he ought to do so, is it because it is part of the roof? He replied: The lower floor's owner is responsible for the beams, planks *(qasb)* and soil, while *al-akhal* is the responsibility of the upper floor's owner. I said to him: If the lower floor's owner builds the roof for him without applying *al-akhal* on it, then the owner of the upper floor will say: I will not apply it this time', and after that the roof remains exposed to the rain causing damage. He (Abu 'Abd Allah al-Ghammaz) said: Tell the owner of the upper floor: Apply *al-akhal* on the roof; for it is your responsibility to do so; If he disobeys, then the owner of the lower floor should put *al-akhal* on the roof and he can prevent the upper floor's owner from the building until he pays him the cost of *al-akhal*.

Master-mason Muhammad says: This is not clear to me; for *al-akhal* is compulsory and a basic component of the roof; for it is not to be called a roof unless it consists of four things: First, the beams, then what is put on it of planks and stems, then soil and then *al-akhal* and *al-astak,* or covered with stones and others. If it only consists of beams, soil and *al-Akhal* without the planks, then it is not a roof, it does nothing; for nothing can uphold soil except planks or stems. If it is only made of beams and planks, but without soil, then the roof is not perfect and none will dare to walk on it. Likewise, if it is only of beams, planks and soil without *al-akhal* then nothing will be actualized from what has been done and will not be complete until the roof is made durable and protective to those residing under it. As it is part of the elements of the roof.

Malik said that: The beams and planks are the responsibilities of the owner of the lower floor until it becomes habitable to those living inside the house; for it is the roof of his house and the roof is associated with him once it has been raised up, that was what Malik said.

Master-mason Muhammad says: This is clear from his sayings that implies *al-akhal* and others.

Thereof, Master-mason Muhammad says: Al-Shaykh Abu al-Hasan al-Lakhmi said: And as for the beam for the shelf boards (*khashhab al-ajnihah*); it is a buttress which is used for shelf boards towards the public road or inside the house; who should do the repair if some parts of it are damaged? For us it is whether the owner of the upper floor is the one who built the buttress or it has already been present during the ownerships of both levels. If the upper owner is the one who built the buttress including its covering (*fursh*) and (*zinar*), then the upper floor's owner alone ought to repair what is broken. If the buttress has been built when both floors were owned by one owner, it will be either: The remaining buttress is beneath the roof of the lower floor or it is a part of the roof beams of the lower floor. If it is a part of the roof beams of the lower floor then it is his beam and what is outside belongs to the upper floor's owner, while what is inside belongs to the lower floor's owner; If it extends from under the roof or on the wall, then the upper floor's owner ought to do the repair, whether the buttress is in the house or outside the house. That was as narrated by Abu al-Hasan al-Lakhmi in *al-Tabsirah*.

Thereof, Master-mason Muhammad says: The owner of the upper floor is prevented from punching (nails) on the wall of the lower floor, for it will harm and push the wall unless it has already been on the wall. However, no written evidence can be shown on that since it is according to my own opinion based on the harm caused by it.

Thereof: If a man owns the upper floor and the lower floor owned by another man, then who should repair the stairs if it has collapsed? There were two opinions:

First, Ibn al-Qasim said in the book of Ibn 'Abd al-Hakam: The upper floor's owner must build the stairs to reach up; If there is another upper floor then the owner of that higher floor must build it to that floor; this is the famous opinion.

Abu 'Abd Allah bin Abi Zayd said in *al-Nawadir* (from some of his companions), the lower floor's owner must build the stairs up to the first floor, then the first floor's owner must build the stairs to the other upper level (that is higher than him).

Master-mason Muhammad says: If there are objects below the stairs such as a room or something useful to the owner of the lower floor and his roof collapses then the lower floor's owner must rebuild the roof in order for the upper floor's owner to build the stairs whether the roof is built of wood or soil, half moon shaped or sickle shaped *(damus* or *minjal)*; for it is like the roof, thus it is the roof for the owner of the lower floor, but it is to the upper floor's owner a foundation to build his stairs. If what is under the stairs is not useful to the lower floor's owner then opinions differed: According to the famous opinion the lower floor's owner is not obliged to re-build it; while another weak opinion states that the lower owner has to do it

If the stairs are outside of the lower owner's structure, and if the stairs are owned by the owner of the upper level, the stepladder also belongs to him: But if the beams are curving (*mujannabah/mahniyah*) then the beams necessarily belong to the owner of the lower level.

Thereof, the author says: If the lower floor belongs to a man and there is an upper floor belonging to another man, and the owner of the upper floor wishes to turn his roof terrace into a mosque or other use, then he has no right to do so as Abu Muhammad said in *al-Nawadir,* and others also had the same opinion.

The aforementioned case happened to us in Tunis regarding a man who had a stable while a second man had an air space half of which belonged to a third person staying on the upper floor. The upper floor's owner donated (*habasa*) a place, which belonged to him, above his neighbor's stable to build a mesjid (prayer space). The owner of the stable asked my opinion regarding the case; should his stable's walls be used as the foundation of the above mesjid; and was it permitted for his neighbor to use the air space above his stable or not? I replied to him: If the lower floor does not belong to him, then he is not allowed to. However, I wrote a letter asking a *fatwa* to *al-Qadi al-Jamaᶜah* 'Abd Allah bin al-Ghammaz, *Qadi al-Jama'ah* at that time: Praise only be to God, my dear master, what do you say on the rights of the upper floor's owner above a *stable* connected to his floor, the door of his roof terrace and an air space of the stable belongs to another upper floor's owner (second owner) adjacent to the said property. Thereupon the second owner of the upper floor who owns the air space of the stable donated that for building a mesjid without the consent of the stable owner, and there is harm related to that manner particularly to the stable owner (*ruwa'*), so should he be prevented or not? May you bestow us with answers and may you be rewarded. Following that, *al-Qadi* replied with his own writing: "Praise be to God, one who owns an air space has no right to build the prayer place by donating (*habasa*) it when the lower floor belongs to another person, Allah the guider, no God but Him and only Him be worshipped".

38- Discourse On The Obligation Of The Owner Of The Lower Floor To Rebuild And Renovate, And Can The Owner Of The Upper Floor Build An Extra Structure In His Airspace.

Master-mason Muhammad says: In Ibn Sahnun's book, Ashhab said: The owner of the lower floor has no right to demolish his ceiling except for necessity (*darurah*). By demolishing his ceiling it effects the upper floor's owner and thereby it can destroy the bricks (*tubah*), and will demolish it.

Master-mason Muhammad says: If the ground floor belongs to a man, and the first floor belongs to a second person and there is a third floor belonging to a third person and then the ground floor collapses causing the other two levels to follow suit. So, is it possible to compel the owner of the ground floor to rebuild? According to Ibn al-Qasim from Malik as stated in *al-ᶜUtbiyah*:

The ground floor's owner can be obliged to rebuild followed by the first floor so that the owner of the top floor can also rebuild if he desires and if not he may not do so. Ibn 'Abd al-Hakam said the same from Malik and Sahnun also said it in the book of his son. Sahnun narrated the same view via Ashhab. Ibn Wahb also had the same opinion and he narrated that from Malik, who said: The owner of the lower floor is obliged to rebuild or hire someone else to rebuild it.

Sahnun said: In this case it is permitted to sell as an emergency if he has no money, but if he has money, he is not allowed to sell it unless with the condition to rebuild; what is meant here is (the owner) is obliged to rebuild.

Ibn al-Qattan said: The ground floor's owner is forced to rebuild his floor unless the upper floor's owner chooses to rebuild it with his own money. So the owner of the ground floor will be prevented from using it until he pays him the cost.

Al-Shaykh Abu al-Hasan al-Lakhmi said: My opinion is that the ground floor's owner can opt either to rebuild it or hire someone else to do so. It is also possible for the upper floor's owner to rebuild it, if he wishes, then both can share the ground floor based on the rental fee of the space, or on the rental fee of the building unless he, the owner of the lower floor, pays the owner of the upper floor the cost of rebuilding on the day of taking it over.

Thereof Master-mason Muhammad says: Abu al-Hasan al-Lakhmi said in *al-Tabsirah*: If the upper floor collapses and damages the lower level, the possibilities are that whether the lower floor's owner was present and has realized (that the building is not in good condition) or he is absent. If he is present and has realized it, and does not warn (the upper level's owner) about it, he (the upper level's owner) is not liable.

A dispute arises when the lower floor's owner is absent and the structural condition of the upper level is not that bad (not in danger of collapsing). In this situation, is the upper level's owner liable or not? Some people of this school (Maliki) were in the opinion that: He is accountable because the collapse is due to bad maintenance and it is as if he has exploited the other person's wealth, so he is responsible. Some said: The compensation is valid if a proper complaint has been lodged. If he (the owner of the lower floor) has forwarded the case to the judge and the judge has orderd him (the owner of the upper floor) to prevent the harm but he refuses, he is responsible. But if the case has never been brought forward to the judge then he is not liable.

Master-mason Muhammad says: If the lower floor belongs to a man and the floor above him belongs to another, and the upper floor's owner wants to make an extension to his top floor, the opinions differed on this issue. Ibn 'Abd al-Hakam stated in his book from Ibn al-Qasim: He cannot do that except for what has already existed, which he can renovate and rebuild as it was before. Ashhab had two opinions; He said in Ibn Sahnun's book: The top floor's owner has no right to build something which has not existed before – in agreement with Ibn al-Qasim – adding that if the beam of the top floor's roof has cracked, a newly inserted beam is heavier and threatens to collapse harming the lower floor's owner, he should be prevented from doing so. Meanwhile in *al-Nawadir* he (Ashhab) said: He has the right to increase the height even up to the sky as long as no harm will occur to the owner of the lower level. Shaykh Abu Muhammad said, and followed by Abu Thawr and what is the famous opinion as we mentioned earlier: The owner of the top floor is not permitted to build any extra structure that has not existed earlier. Another opinion in *al-Nawadir* (except for Ashhab): If the top floor collapses, he (the owner) can only rebuild with the same weight as before.

Master-mason Muhammad says: If the lower floor's owner desires to do something to the wall such as to make a door or to open a small window (*kuwa*), or to move the wall to the front or to the back: There are two different opinions on this; Shaykh Abu Muhammad 'Abd Allah bin Abi Zayd said in *al-Nawadir*: He has no right to open a door or a small window (*kuwa*) nor can he put in beams even if it will not harm the top floor's owner, except with his permission.

(Second opinion) It is narrated from some of our companions: The owner of the lower floor has the right to do whatever he likes because it belongs to him, such as to open a door or a small window (*kuwa*) or such other thing as long as no harm occurs to the owner of the upper floor.

Master-mason Muhammad says: Cases like this happened to us many times. I examine whether it is harmful to the upper floor's owner or not, and if it is not harmful we allowed it; since to prevent him from his rights is harmful to him, as the Prophet said: *La darar wa la dirar*.

The author says: In *al-Nawadir*, Ibn 'Abdus narrated from Ibn al-Qasim: The lower floor's owner has no right to construct any extra structure on his floor except for what has already been built, if his action harms the upper floor's owner.

Thereof Master-mason Muhammad says: If the ground floor belongs to a man and the upper floor belongs to another, while the door for the upper floor is located within the entrance vestibule of the lower floor, then the door of the lower floor collapses, who has to rebuild it? There were two opinions on this: First, Ibn al-Qasim and Ashhab said in *al-'Utbiyah*: The owner of the ground floor has to repair the door of his house and also the upper floor's door because he is the owner; Asbagh also had the same opinion.

Ibn Sha'ban said in his book: Both of them should undertake the repairs, because the entrance and exit doors belongs to them. Ibn Zayd said: With that we judge; so too some of our masters, as they also have the same opinion.

39- Discourse On Who Is Responsible For Building The Supports Of The Upper Floor, And Who Is Responsible If The Supports Fall and Destroys Other Structures.

Master-mason Muhammad says: If the lower floor belongs to a man and the upper floor belongs to another, when the lower floor weakens, who should build the supports? Three different opinions were expressed:

The first opinion: Ibn al-Qasim said in two different books, in *al-'Utbiyah* and the book of Ibn 'Abd al-Hakam, from Malik: The cost of the support (buttress) should be imposed on the owner of the ground floor until he strengthens his ground floor. He is responsible to support the upper floor: Both the building and the supports; this is the famous opinion and the judgment is based upon it.

The second opinion: In *al-Nawadir*: Asbagh and Abu Ja'far al-Dimyati[138] said from Ibn al-Qasim: The cost of the buttresses is the responsibility of the upper floor's owner; Abu al-Hasan al-Lakhmi also subscribed to this opinion because the contract between them is for the safety, and that the upper floor building is supported by certain structures. They (as two different owners)

---

[138] He is 'Abd al-Rahman b Abi Ja'far al-Dimyati (d. 216/ 831).

do not know what the ruling would be applicable to during the time of damage. As soon as a certain part becomes unsteady the owner of the lower floor should not be held responsible to hold the upper floor with a beam, but instead he ought to rebuild a new structure to hold the upper level.

The third opinion: Ibn Shaʿban said in his book: It is the responsibility of the upper floor's owner and he has to build the buttress, unless the owner of the lower floor without any reason destroys it. Then he should be held responsible to build the support for the upper floor.

Master-mason Muhammad says: The different opinions cited above are applicable to the cases when there is damage to the wall of the ground floor, but if the damage happens to the wall on the upper floor only, then it is unanimously agreed that it is the responsibility of the upper floor's owner to strengthen the supports.

Master-mason Muhammad says: If both floors collapse and the supports are totally damaged, who should bear the cost of pulling out the pillars from under the rubble, is it the owner of the pillars or the owner of the house? This case was brought to us, and our scholars differed on this, some said: It is on the owner of the pillars. Others said that it was on the owner of the house, and this opinion prevailed.

Thereof the author says: If one desires to attach a room to his house using his neighbor's wall, he is allowed to do so if it does not cause any harm to the neighbor. The neighbor cannot prevent him from attaching the beam onto the wall as long as it does not cause any harm. Refer to the book of *al-Tarar* by Ibn ʿAt. It is said: In the last part of the second chapter of Ibn Sahl's book: I Ibn 'At wrote a letter in Shaʿban of the year 456 A.H. (1064 C.E.) to the scholars of Qurtuba asking them: Is it possible to strengthen the structure of a shop by attaching (its beams) to the wall of the mosque since the shop(s) are a donation from the mosque or should it be left unattached? Can neighboring people insert their beams onto the walls of the mosques or Jamiʿ as into the neighbor's wall (since one is permitted to insert a beam onto a neighbor's wall)?

Ibn ʿItab replied: Our masters did not prevent the people from using the mosque's wall as a supporting structure if it would not be harmful to the mosque, just like the case of affixing it to (a neighboring) house. To those who were in such places they had the right to insert their beams into the mosque's wall. If it is not harmful, they should not be prevented.

The author says: Among the arguments of the scholars on this is the saying of the Prophet regarding inserting a beam onto the neighbor's wall as mentioned before. This tradition also applies to the *mesjid* (local mosque) as well. If one's house is adjacent to a mosque, then the rule of inserting a beam applies to him, and if it is not a neighbor to the mosque, then nothing can be attached to its wall.

The masters do not mention about *Jami'* (grand mosque), it is indeed my opinion (*ijtihad*) based on their opinions. Ibn al-Qattan wrote that it was not permitted to insert a beam onto the wall of a mesjid while Ibn Malik[139] said that the beams of the shops were not allowed to be inserted onto a mesjid's wall.

40- Discourse On The Cleaning Of The Restroom Between The Upper And Lower Floors, And Who Is Responsible For Building It?

Master-mason Muhammad says: If the lower floor belongs to one man and the upper floor to another while the filth (*al-atfal*) is collected in the lower floor's cesspool, then in our opinion: The possibility is whether the cesspool is owned jointly by them or it belongs to the lower floor's owner.

If the cesspool is jointly owned, then the responsibility should be based on the number of occupants on each floor. This view was reported by al-Lakhmi in *al-Tabsirah* and stated by Shaykh Abu Muhammad bin Abi Zayd in *al-Nawadir* from Muhammad bin 'Abd al-Hakam.

If the cesspool belongs solely to the owner of the lower floor, then there are two different opinions:

Ibn al-Qasim said in the book of Ibn al-Hakam: The owner of the lower floor must clean the cesspool up to its roof. Master-mason Muhammad says: What Ibn al-Qasim meant is that the owner of the ground floor must clean the cesspool up to the inlet from the upper floor.

The other opinion is by Ibn Wahb who said: Both of them have to clean it based on the number of occupants of each floor, few

---

[139] He is 'Abd Allah b. Muhammad b. Malik from Cordova (d. 460/1068). Ibn Bashkawal, *al-Silah*, 1:303.

or many. This opinion applies and is considered the best. Yahya Ibn 'Umar also had the same opinion.

Thereof: If the toilet, which is jointly owned, becomes faulty, which of them has to fix it? Ibn al-Qasim said in the book of Ibn 'Abd al-Hakam that: The owner of the lower floor has to fix and clean it. Ibn al-Qasim was asked why the owner of the lower floor has to clean it. He, Ibn al-Hakam said, because the owner of the upper floor would say to the owner of the lower floor: You are responsible to build for me so as to dispose of my filth into the cesspool and you also have to clear it once it is full.

41- Discourse On The Cleaning Of The House's Water Channel Between Two Partners.

Master-mason Muhammad says: If two people share a house and its restroom *(al-kanif)* or its cesspool needs to be cleaned, two opinions were cited in such cases:

Ibn Habib said in *al-Wadihah*: I asked Mutarrif on how to organize the responsibility and cost between them; by what measure to be counted, by the house or by the number of occupants. Mutarrif explained to me: By the number of occupants because perhaps there are many people in one house and they have only one restroom; or there is a man with a servant or with his wife living in the other house. If it is to be counted based on the size of the property owned by each person, then this man with his wife or servant has to provide more than the other house that has many occupants. And to clean the restroom is like to clean the rubbish gathered in their houses as well. It is necessary that each person has to clean his house and their surroundings from rubbish.

Second opinion: 'Isa Bin Dinar said: The cost is to be based according to the size of the property of each person, regardless of the number of people in those properties, few or many.

42- Discourse On The Grievance Between A Landlord And A Tenant On the Cleaning Of The Water Channel.

Master-mason Muhammad says: This case is related to a previous discussion about the cesspool between two partners.

From *Kitab al-Nawadir* of Ibn Abi Zayd al-Qurawiy: If a man asks his partner to sell the cesspool or to divide it, and his co-partner refuses, then the one who refuses cannot be compelled to sell or to divide it. The shared ownership is similar to a jointly owned courtyard or entrance hall, which is indivisible, or what is similar to that. It should be left undivided for them to share.

ᶜIsa bin Dinar said: Muhammad bin Talid – *Qadi al-Jama'ah* – was asked about that, and he explained: None of them can be forced to sell or to divide and it remains as a shared property.

Thereof: Master-mason Muhammad says: If a man rents a house and then finds the wastewater channel clogged with human excrement (*tifl*) and waste water from washing; It should be determined whether the clogging occurred before the rental agreement or after the agreement. If it occurred before the agreement, then it is upon the landlord to clean it by unanimous opinion. If the house is uninhabitable because of the clogged channel, then the owner should be forced to clean it. If the channel becomes clogged after the contract and the tenant has already occupied the house, then two different opinions were cited, both from Ibn al-Qasim. He said in *al-Mudawwanah*: The landlord ought to clean the toilet and improve its channel until it becomes suitable for living.

Master-mason Muhammad says: Ibn Habib narrated in *al-Wadihah* that Ibn al-Qasim said: The cleaning of the restroom and the house is on the tenant whether the landlord stipulated that or not.

Ibn Habib said: Mutarrif and Ibn al-Majishun told me: Both ought to follow the custom and practice of the place and I prefer this opinion.

'Abd al-Malik said: The custom (practice) here in al-Andalus is: The tenant ought to clean the house and the landlord ought to clean the toilet.

Master-mason Muhammad says: Al-Qadi Abu Ishaq bin 'Abd al-Rafi' adopted the Andalusian custom. He told me one day to impose on the people this practice when he asked me to clean a street.

Someone other than Ibn al-Qasim said: The resident ought to clean the toilet except if it is part of an inn; when the landlord ought to clean it.

Master-mason Muhammad says: Abu al-Hasan preferred this opinion when he said in his *Wathaiq*: The cleaning up has to be upon the tenant while it is upon the landlord to clean the inn's toilet. Then he said: This is the most accepted opinion; although the old practice of cleaning the toilet was the responsibility of the owner.

Master-mason Muhammad says: Ibn Habib and Asbagh reported from Ibn al-Qasim and Ashhab that both said: The tenant has to clean the restroom; while the inn's landlord has to do it, not the lodger.

If the occupant is not asked to clean the restroom, then the occupant is also not responsible to clean it up upon leaving. Likewise in the Inn: The condition there is that the occupant is not responsible to clean the toilet. But the opinions differed concerning the tenant who accepts the conditions stipulated by the owner during the tenancy, as in the case with the bath (*hammam*), if he accepts the conditions stipulated by the landlord (*hammam* operator), is he responsible to clean it up or is it still the responsibility of the landlord? The answer regarding the channel is the same as the answer regarding the toilet.

A tenant resides in a house that has a recently cleaned channel and he had made a contract that requires him to clean up the channel when needed. A dispute arises when it is time to do that: Should the landlord or the tenant clean it? Master-mason Muhammad says: What is obvious to me is that the occupant should do it because it is his trash, and it does not matter if the channel is full of wastewater or human excrement.

Shaykh Abu al-Hasan al-Lakhmi said: If the channel was not cleaned and his stay is short, he should not be held responsible; he should be treated like the lodger in an inn.

Thereof Master-mason Muhammad says: Ibn Habib said in *al-Wadihah*: If the owner stipulates that the tenant cleans whatever is in the channel when the contract is made, Ibn al-Qasim said: It is acceptable, whereas Ibn Habib said: The consent is disputed; if he is required in the contract (to clean) the toilet before his tenancy, then the condition is considered unacceptable. For it could be dangerous, since he does not know what kind of waste and filth was flushed down into the cesspool. If the condition stipulates for a new or clean toilet prior to the residency, then it is permitted because such a condition is well known and is widely practiced.

Master-mason Muhammad says: Sahnun said that Ibn al-Qasim mentioned in *al-Mudawwanah*: If the tenant specifies as a condition to the landlord or the operator of the public bath (*hammam*) to clean the toilet, the house, and the *hammam*, it is permitted because such practice has been recognized and well known among the people.

43- Discourse On Cleaning the Filth And Wastewater Of Residential Channels That Are In Lanes And The Main Road.

Master-mason Muhammad says: Two different opinions were cited regarding the cleaning of residential channels.

Sahnun said: The owner of the first house has to clean it up to the second house and then both the first and the second owner have to clean it up to the third house. The third then together with the first and the second have to do so up to the fourth and it goes on with the following residents until the last; for the first has benefited most from the channel and his wastewater flows through it all.

Second opinion: Yahya bin 'Umar said of those who have a wastewater channel running through where wastewater flows from one channel through the adjacent channel and through the next one and so on all the way to the main sewer. Then one of the channels clogs, so the first owner cleans it. However the water still clogs at his neighbor's channel. He says to his neighbor: Clean your channel until my wastewater flows; likewise (he asks) the succeeding owners downstream. Yahya said: If a person's channel is clogged, he should clean it until the neighbor's water flows. By this method they are required to clean the channel until the water flows out to the main channel and then to the sewer line (*al-khandaq*). If it is rainwater, then the cleaning should be done according to the number of the houses; if the water channel contains human filth then it should be based on the number of persons in each family. Abu al-Hasan al-Lakhmi said: Yahya's view is not quite clear because cleansing the channel together is only applicable in the case of a water channel that carries water from a river to farms.

Master-mason Muhammad says: We are going to explain about rivers later. What happens to the first house on the lane and in the fourth are similar to what happens to the second and the third. Then the second says to the first: If it is not because of the waste from your house, it will not have accumulated onto me this much; the third says: If it is not because of the waste from both of your houses it will not have accumulated onto me this much. What Yahya implies is that the residents of the lanes and alleys do not have to join the residents of the main street in carrying out the cleaning of the channel adjacent to it. This is unfair (*zulm*); for each of them says that if it is not because of the waste from the other house, then his house and the following house would not have collected so much filth, but only as much as accumulated by the first house in the lane.

Abu al-Hasan al-Lakhmi said: I am not impressed by Sahnun's view that each person should carry out the work up to the main sewer line equaly because each person does not know what is discharged that affected his channel and the degree of harm that was created.

Master-mason Muhammad says: In my opinion the responsibility of cleaning the wastewater channel should be based on the numbers of persons in each family, for the owner of the first house on the lane or alley will say: We have to do as much as the owner of the last house on the lane will do. For our responsibility regarding the content of the filth in the channel is equal. No one can determine whom this dirt belongs to. Thus, I (the first house owner) will do as what you have done. Likewise, the second, the third, and the rest of the owners will say the same. We say: The channel has two possibilities; whether the land is descending in such a way that nothing inside the channel is trapped except when it is caused by something from the outside; or its land is flat where its content hardly moves except by a small amount. If the land is flat and the water flows very slowly or not at all, then to me it is like the restroom. The responsibility to clean it is the same as the opinions of Ibn Wahb and Asbagh, which is per number of occupants whether it is a small or large family, regardless of whether the house is the first or the last on the lane.

If the channel is located on sloping land, where the content is not trapped due to its incline, then it should be decided whether the channel overflows from the beginning to the end or overflows only at the beginning while it is empty at the end, or overflows at the end and empty at the beginning.

If the channel overflows all the way up to the end, then it is the obligation of the residents, based on the number of occupants in each house. If the channel overflows at the beginning, but empty at the end, then it is also the responsibility of all residents based on the number of occupants in each house.

If it overflows at the end while empty at the beginning, then the obligation goes to the first and last houses; for the last can say: If it is not from your houses, we will not have this much, but the waste that comes from your house has caused our part of the channel to clog. Therefore, all of them (the occupants) ought to carry out the duty of cleaning up equally. This should be done according to the number of people not the number of houses because perhaps there are ten people in one house and only two people in another. Thus, if it is based on the number of houses, then the house with two people will have to do more work than the house with ten occupants.

If the channel which is on the main road overflows while the lane's channel is empty, we have to see whether the lane's empty channel is without any human excrement, then they (the lane's residents) must be obliged to clean with the residents of the main road equally, as per head. This is because all their filth is collected in the main channel adjacent to the public road. Therefore, they have to help the residents of the main road to clear their channel. If there is something of the filth in their (lane) channel, then they must clear it up. If the (main) channel becomes full then they must hold back the amount that comes out from their channel and release only a small amount to the main channel; if they wish they can open it themselves (to clear the clogging part).

If the water channel of a lane or an alley overflows while the water channel of the public road is functioning well, then the residents of the lane or the alley have to open it themselves (to clear the clogging part) while the residents of the public road are exempted. They have to clean up their channel up to the boundary of the main channel.

Master-mason Muhammad says: It was stated in *al-Mustakhrajah* that if the channel is clogged at its beginning, people who live at the beginning of the channel have to clean it without the help of the others living downstream. If the channel gets clogged at its end, then people who live both at the beginning and at the end of the lane ought to clear it together. This is legally applicable to the case of the wastewater channel; for if it overflows only at the beginning, then the harm only occurs to the people who live at the beginning of the channel as their wastewater and filth cannot be emptied. As for the rest of the people, if their part of the channel does not overflow, then there is no harm to them. However, if the overflow occurs at the end of the channel, then it will harm all of them; because if the overflow occurs at the end, then the congestion will also affect the beginning of the channel and it will harm them all.

44- Discourse On The Maintenance Of Waterways In Farms.

Master-mason Muhammad says: Abu al-Hasan al-Lakhmi said in *al-Tabsirah*: Damage to the water channel occurs in three different places:

First, the damage occurs before it reaches the farms after leaving the water source (*al-ain*). Second, the damage occurs between the farms. Third, the damage occurs after it has come out of the farms due to excess water.

If the damage occurs between the water source and the first lock (*awwal mughlaq*), the consensus is that all of them must do the maintenance work. However, there is a disagreement on how to calculate the cost (*al-qadr*). There were two different views: Ibn al-Qasim said it should be based on the number of farms while Asbagh said it should be based on the calculation of the share. If the blockage occurs between the first and the second locks, then the first must do the maintenance, because of their opening and closing of the channel where soil is unintentionally deposited by the gushing water.

Disagreement arises when the blockage occurs at the end of the channel. There are two opinions:

Al-Lakhmi said in *al-Tabsirah*: The people located first have to bear the cost together with all of them (other farmers along the channel). Likewise, the second and the third, each of them has to bear the cost up to the last owner.

Yahya Ibn 'Umar was of the opinion that each owner (with a blocked waterway) is responsible for the cost, including for the channels after them, but they are not responsible for the ones before them.

If the congestion happens at areas outside the farms, then the responsibility falls on all of them to clear it. If the cause comes from a farm and the water source is a spring (*al-'ayn*) then it is the obligation of those residing adjacent to the clogged channel together with the people after them, and none of the people before them should take part since the channel passing through their area is not clogged.

Abu al-Hasan al-Lakhmi said: In my opinion, if the congestion is caused by them because of their opening and locking, then the cost, by a fair amount should be divided among them. The amount should be assessed according to what is the practice of the people. If one of them receives more water during the day of distribution or on alternate days while others receive only one day after five days of opening and closing, (so the financial responsibility) should be based on how much water each person is entitled to. Likewise, if the blockage is caused by factors that are external to the farms, then it is upon all of them as mentioned before; since it is outside of their control. Except when the blockage is not caused by excess water, it is acceptable to say that the responsibility is divided based on the numbers of farms, and when it happens between the spring (*al-'ayn*) and the first lock, then Ibn al-Qasim's view that (the cost) should be based on the number (of people) is applicable.

45- Discourse On The Construction Of A Channel On The Main Road Between Residences And How The Financial Responsibility Should Be Determined.

Master-mason Muhammad says: If a channel of a residential street is damaged, and they want to rebuild it, how is the cost to be arranged between them? There are two different opinions on this:

Sahnun said in the book of Muhammad replying to a question from Ibn Habib, regarding a water channel passing through four houses that is in need of repair, should each owner repairs it individually or should they share the cost? Ibn Habib said: Sahnun said: The owner of the first house must repair his channel alone, then he helps the owner of the second, then the first and the second help the third; then all of them should help the fourth.

In *al-'Utbiyah*, in the discussion with Ibn al-Qasim regarding a damaged water channel in need of repair that passes through a residential lane; what if some of them want to repair it while others refuse to do so? Ibn al-Qasim said: Those refusing should be forced to work on a shift basis with those requesting to rebuild it based on the number of shares.

Master-mason Muhammad says: Since Sahnun's opinion is widely accepted, thereby I believe the owners of the water channel are obliged to repair their parts of the channel based on the approach described by Sahnun.

46- Discourse On A House Which Has No Water Channel And The Owner Wishes To Build One.

Master-mason Muhammad says: If a house that belongs to a man has no water channel, and he wants to build a new one and connects it to the channel in the lane, the possibilities are either; the channel passes through the lane until it reaches the main sewer line (*khandaq*), or it passes through someone else's house; if it passes through someone else's house then no one can add another channel to the existing one except by the permission of the owner of the house. All the scholars agree on this. If it does not pass through any of the houses, then there are two opinions;

First, Sahnun said in the book of his son Muhammad: That should not be permitted and can even be prevented if he insists on doing so.

Second, Abu al-Qasim Khalaf bin Abi al-Firas al-Qurawiy said: That has to be prevented unless he pays them the cost of constructing the pre-existing channel that precedes his channel. When he has paid his due and the pre-existing channel is in the public road and does not pass through anyone else's house, then he should not be prevented, on the condition that he has been with them when they constructed the earlier channel. This condition is applicable if he has no right of utilizing the water channel with them.

If he has the right to utilize the water channel with them, then they cannot prevent him, unless they can prove, with the testimony of an expert that such action will damage or clog their channel.

Thereof Master-mason Muhammad says: If a channel belongs to a man passing through a lane, then the man wishes to shift the channel to another lane which is more convenient to him, Sahnun said in the book of his son: The channel should not be removed from its original place; he (Sahnun) was asked: If it has already been removed and has been in the other lane for the past three years, can the house owners of the lane demand its removal? Sahnun said: Yes, for three or four years is very short. They can do so. Master-mason Muhammad says: This case is contrary to the earlier case.

47- Discourse On Someone Who Wants To Discharge His Rainwater Onto The Street.

Master-mason Muhammad says: In *Nawazil* of Ibn Rushd which was summarized by al-Qadi Abu Ishaq bin 'Abd al-Rafi', Ibn Rushd said: If a man builds a house and wishes to discharge rainwater onto the lane (zuqaq), but is prevented by his neighbor; but if an expert attests that he has no other possible outlet for the rainwater except that one, then he should not be prevented from doing so.

Thereof: Al-Qadi Ibn Rushd also said: If a water channel of a house owned by a man passes through his neighbor's house and he wishes to replace it with a larger channel, he should not do so except with his neighbor's consent.

Master-mason Muhammad says: A problem occurs when a man who has two houses. One of the houses is small and the other is large; the channel of his small house goes through his neighbor's house and he wanted to reroute the channel of his larger house to replace the channel of his small house. The neighbor has the right to prevent him from doing so.

Master-mason Muhammad says: The reason is because of the mounting burden and the increasing filth caused by the drainage of the big house. A big drainage is not comparable to a small one. Furthermore, the channel needs to be opened more often and this increases the harm resulting to the house that the channel passes through; so the neighbor has the right to prevent him.

48- Discourse On An Old Channel That Causes Harm To The Neighbor.

Master-mason Muhammad says: If an old channel causes harm to the neighbors, then it should not be removed from its place, Ibn al-Qasim said: This is because it existed earlier. He narrated this from Malik.

In the book of Ibn Sahnun, Muhammad said: Habib asked Sahnun about an old channel that was close to the neighbor's wall which caused harm to the neighbor. So the neighbor asked the owner to relocate it. Sahnun said: An old channel should not be relocated even though it causes harm to the neighbor.

Master-mason Muhammad says: This happened to a judge, who worked elsewhere, and he had a house in Tunis. The house had a well attached to a wall and adjacent to that wall was a channel belonging to the neighbor. The water from the channel seeped through the wall (into the well). Consequently, both of them brought their case to al-Qadi Ibn 'Abd al-Rafi' and the Qadi assigned us to examine the condition that caused the dispute. Thereupon I could see that the water from the channel was seeping into the well and was damaging it. Certainly, the channel was causing harm to the well. *Al-Faqih al-Qadi* told the owner of the well: Repair your well. As for the owner of the channel, he was asked to clean up his channel, especially from the filth (human excrement) and he was not ordered to change its location. The ruling is correct.

Master-mason Muhammad says: From *Nawazil* of Ibn Rushd, summarized by Abu Ishaq bin 'Abd al-Rafi', Ibn Rushd said: If a spring flows out inside a man's house and he wishes to make a channel for it through the courtyard of a neighbor until it can be accessible for drinking. If the spring poured out naturally then he can do that; but if he generated its flow it by digging, then he has no right to channel it through his neighbor's property except by the neighbor's consent.

49- Discourse On A Man Whose Rooftop Water Flows Down To His Neighbor's House, And He Wants To Cut It Off.

Master mason Muhammad said: 'Isa bin Musa said: I was told that my grandfather 'Umar bin Yusuf [140] said: I asked Muhammad bin Talid about a man who had a water spout directed toward the neighbor's house. The man wanted to heighten his house, onto which the rain water flowed and to build a room on it. The neighbor protested, he said: If your house is heightened and the water is flowing towards my house (from that hight), it would create damage, but you can point the spout towards your property. If the builder said: I will put a shelf board at the level of where the spout was, so the water will be shed from the earlier location, and the water flows down to you as it was before. Do you see whether this is alright or not? Then, he answered me: The man, who pointed his rain water spout

---

[140] He is 'Umar bin Yusuf bin Musa (d. 337/949) from Tudela (located in northeast Spain). He has a wide knowledge on jurisprudence especially on building rules (*Ahkam al-Bunyan*). See *Tarikh 'Ulama' al-Andalus* by Ibn al-Faradi 1: 323. and 'Iyad, *Tartib al-Madarik* vol 2:276.

towards the neighbor's house, and placed it higher than before due to the increase in the height of his building, he is ordered to remove it, because it is harmful. That, for me is justified. And if he says: I will put a shelf board in its previous location, the harm created will not be eliminated

Master-mason Muhammad said: *Muhraq* is a gutter through which water flows. If one's gutter that sheds water down to his neighbor's house, is nearer to the ground, then it is less harmful, but the higher it is, the more harmful it is because of its stronger splash.

50- Discourse On Water Spouts Pointed Towards Neighbors Houses.

Master mason Muhammad said: Asbagh (Ibn al-Faraj) said in *al-'Utbiyah*: I asked Ibn Nafi': What is your opinion about water that flows from one's rooftop down to his neighbor's house, and the situation existed for a long time (*qadim*), recognized by his neighbor, but harmful to the neighbor's property because of the spillage. His neighbor wanted to divert the rain flow from his property by building a high channel (*qanat*) near the roof of the house from which the rainwater originated. But the owner was reluctant to allow that. Ibn Nafi' said that the man could not divert the water unless the owner of the house from which the rainwater originates allowes it.

Master mason Muhammad said: This is a good answer, because if the man built a high channel adjacent to his neighbor's wall, it will be harmful to the wall because it will make it damp.

Asbagh answered the first question, which I asked him: If the owner of the property receiving the rainwater wants to build a channel attached to the wall of the owner of the property from which the rainwater originates, (what is your opinion?). He said: He has no right either to attach it to that building, or to build onto the passage of the waterway, but can build below that if the owner of the property from which rainwater originates gives him permission.

Master mason Muhammad said: A similar case occurred in Qairawan. Isa b. Musa reported it, from his grandfather ('Umar b. Yusuf) regarding a man whose waterspout poured the rainwater onto his neighbor house. The neighbor wanted to put a gutter on his wall, so that it will cut off the water flow. Both of them brought the case to Muhammad b. Talid - Qadi al-Jama'ah.

The Qadi prevented such solution since one cannot divert the flow of his neighbor's rainwater from his property.

Problem: 'Umar b. Yusuf said: I asked Muhammad b. Talid about a man who disposes his rainwater from his roof onto the neighbor and he had no gutter. The neighbor kept silent in a spirit of tolerance and hospitality. But after about ten years, he (the neighbor) protested and wanted it to stop. The man said to his neighbor: The water flows on your property for a long time, you do not have any right to prevent it. Do you see whether the man is right or not? He (Muhammad b. Talid) answered: Since the man who has watched his neighbor build and direct the rainwater spouts toward his house and did not protest. And since his neighbor has spent some money on that, the man cannot demand his neighbor to redirect that, his silence is an approval of his neighbor's action. Therefore, there is no excuse for him to say: I disagree with that. There are different views about this case.

51- Discourse On A Man Who Wants To Create A Room In His House And Wants To Direct the Rainwater Towards The Neighbor's House.

Master mason Muhammad said: There are two opinions about it: First opinion: from *Kitab al-Jidar* by Isa b. Dinar, he was asked about the partition wall between two houses of different owners, the wall belonged to one of them. The owner of the wall wanted to roof his property and shed the water down to the neighbor's house. The neighbor disagreed with that. Does the neighbor have the right to prevent the man from continuing his action? Isa said: He does not have the right if the action does not harm him, but if the action will harm him, then he has the right to prevent it.

Second opinion: From *al-Wadihah*, Ibn Habib narrates from Mutarrif and Ibn al-Majashun, said: He has no right to do that unless the neighbor gives his permission on the condition that it will not harm him. Ibn Habib said: I said to him, what if the neighbor's house is large and the flows of water does not harm him? Both of them replied: Even if the neighbor's house is large, he still does not have the right unless with the permission of the neighbor. He should make a gutter to collect all his rooftop rainwater.

Thereof, Master mason Muhammad said: If the owner of the wall wants to take down his wall and rebuild it within his property, thereby creating a channel in its location for the rainwater, then there are two opinions:

Someone asked Isa b. Dinar: If the owner of the wall wants to demolish his wall, and rebuild it further within his property, and in its former location he will use it to dispose his rainwater from the rooftop, is he allowed to do that? Isa said: Yes. Second Opinion: From *al-Wadihah*, Ibn Habib narrates from Mutarrif and Ibn al-Majashun: He cannot do that; because it will harm his neighbor, because where the wall used to stand would become a channel, and will pollute his neighbor's house. The wall was separating them; but separating them with a channel, that may collect dirt, is damaging.

52- Discourse On A Land Which Its Water Flows to Another Land.

Master mason Muhammad said: Ibn 'Abdus in his book said: I asked Ibn al-Majashun about a man who owned a land, which was higher than his neighboring land owned by another person. Whenever it rains, the water overflowed from the higher ground to the lower one and both plots were cultivated. Later on, some people purchased the higher ground and they built several houses and covered their roofs with tiles. The owners wanted to channel the rain water from the roofs to the lower ground, but the owner of the lower ground protested. He said: This water that used to flow through my land is not like this. And what if the owner of the lower ground sold his land, and the buyers built it up, what is the status of the discharged water from the higher ground? He said: he cannot turn away any water from the upper ground since this has been their (the owners of upper land) right for a long time.

53- Discourse On Two Neighbors Regarding Rainwater That's Flowing From One Roof Top Onto The Other.

Master mason Muhammad said: The experts disagreed on that, in *al-Nawadir*, Abu Muhammad b. Abi Zaid narrated that some of his colleagues asked Abu Abbas al-Abyani[141] about a man whose rooftop water flowed onto his neighbor's rooftop. He wanted to

---

[141] He is Abdullah Ahmad b. Ibrahim b. Ishaq al-Abyani (d. 352/963) a faqih from Qayrawan. See *Tartib al-Madarik* 3:347-352.

divert the water to his property instead of his neighbor's, but the neighbor prevented him and said: The water benefits me. Al-Faqih Abu al-'Abbas replied: He has the right to divert the water from his rooftop, because the water harms his neighbor. The neighbor has no right to retain the situation.

Al-Sheikh Abu Muhammad b. Abi Zaid said: I think that what Abu al-'Abbas implied is that he supposed the water created more harm than benefit, assuming the water was generally harmful, but if he knew that the neighbor's need for the water was clear, that he had a cistern to catch the water, thus he may share the water with his neighbor. The man can rightfully take the water, being what is poured on him is what is to be gained. Nevertheless, if he has clear benefit from water, then he has the right to prevent the owner of the rooftop from re-directing the water away from him.

54- Discourse On Rainwater Being Contested Between Owners Of The Upper And Lower Floors.

Master mason Muhammad said: I was told by al-Qadi Abu Zayd Abd. Al-Rahman b. Uthman b. al-Qattan, he said: I read the script written by the jurist Abu Muhammad Fayyad[142] statement saying: I read the script written by jurist-Mufti Abu 'Ali al-Dhabit,[143] his statement saying: Abu Muhammad Ibn Abi Zayd was asked about a house owned by a man parts of which was higher than his neighbor's house. The water from the higher house flowed onto the roof of the lower house and down into a cistern. The owner of the higher roof wanted to divert the rain flow to his own property, and the neighbor prevented that. He (the neighbor) said: This water is a right that belongs to my house. The owner of the higher roof answered: It belongs to me and I have the right to channel it to wherever I want". In your opinion, who is right? Abu Muhammad wrote an answer: If there is no agreement stating that the water belongs to the owner of the lower roof, then the owner of the higher roof deserves to re-direct the water. The water still belongs to him even if he swore

---

[142] He is Abd al-Hamid b. Muhammad al-Harawi (d. 486/1093), a jurist from Qairawan but lived in Susa. See al-Dibaj 159.

[143] He is Uthman b. Abi Bakr b. Hamud (d. 444/1052), better known as Ibn al-Dhabit al-Safaqasi. See *Tarajim al-Muallifin al-Tunisiyin*. 3:261-263.

to channel it to the owner of the lower roof, who has no right to claim that the water belongs to him.

Ibn Shiblun[144] said: The water belongs to the owner of the lower roof, and that is his right. The owner of the higher roof has no right to re-direct the water from the owner of the lower roof because he has benefited from it.

Master mason Muhammad said: This problem is still prevalent in our place, and I was consulted about it. We consider if the situation to have existed for a long time (*qadim*), we shall order it to be maintained as it is; but if it was recently created, the owner of the higher roof is allowed to redirect the rainwater to his property.

Thereof Master-mason Muhammad said: I was told by al-Qadi Abu Zayd Abd al-Rahman b. al-Qattan that similar cases had happened in the city of al-Mahdiyah. A man passed away and the rainwater from his rooftop was collected into a cistern. One of his heirs bought the upper floor of the house with a condition that he would benefit from the cistern for 20 years. Hence the cistern remained as it was until the owner of the upper floor died, the upper floor then passed on to his heir. An outsider then bought into the ground floor, while the water agreement was still in place. The new owner nullified the agreement and prevented the owner of the top floor from benefiting from what had been agreed. The owner of top floor wanted to re-direct the water to another location owned by him but was prevented by his ground floor neighbor. The transaction agreement between both of them did not mention anything useful shared between them.

I asked the knowledgeable jurist Abu al-Qasim b. al-Barra[145] about this problem. He answered in his script with many arguments and analogies, among his answer in writing is: There is no doubt that the roof of the upper floor is owned completely by the top floor owner, and the water then belongs to him. There is no indication against that, except that the water is channeled into the cistern with the condition that it is to be used for drinking for a certain period. Whoever wishes to nullify the

---

[144] He is Abu al-Qasim Abd al-Khaliq b. Abi Said Khalaf b. Shiblun (d. 390/1000) a jurist from Qairawan. See Ibn al-Naji, *Maalim al-Iman* 3: 155-157.

[145] He is Abu al-Qassim b. Ali b. Abd al-Aziz b. al-Barra al-Tanukhi, a faqih from al-Mahdiya (d.677/1278). Appointed as qadi al-jamaah of Tunis year 657/1259. See Zarkashi, *Tarikh al-Daulatain* 35-45.

ownership must bring the evidence. An obvious indication that the top floor owner owns the water, is that it flows from his roof terrace into his cistern for the purpose of drinking. There is no reason for the owner to remove the cistern since he owns the water, and it is proper that the ownership of water is determined by its source.

55- Discourse On The Ownership Of Water Collected In A Cistern Between Tenant And Landlord.

Master-mason Muhammad said: The scholars disagreed on water collected in a cistern as indicated by two opinions; Al-Sheikh Abu Abdullah (Muhammad ibn Ali) al-Mazari[146] was asked about rainwater collected in a cistern of a rented house, did it belong to the landlord or tenant? He answered: It depends on the regulating custom of the place. Then we asked about it with respect to its judicial case. He said: Regarding the case, al-Sheikh al-Qadi Abu Muhammad held the opinion that the cistern water belonged to the landlord, whereas a group of muftis from Mahdiya such as al-Sulaimi and others said that the water belonged to the tenant. I spoke to al-Sheikh Abu Muhammad Abd al-Hamid[147] and I asked him his solution, he said: The basis is this: One does not spend his wealth unless by certainty. When he rented a house, he rents it for occupancy, and the occupancy does not include water, either legally or conventionally. Thus he has no right to use it unless it is acknowledged in an agreement or by custom. If there is a dispute, then the water belongs to the landlord. Based on this I decided that the water belonged to the landlord, but then I had put aside this view, and afterward came to me an opinion that the water belonged to the tenant, when he rented the house with all its facilities and the water was part of it, because it flowed on his rooftop and belonged to him, thus my answer was that the water belonged to the tenant, since it was beneficial to him. However, the water is part of the house facilities and it belongs to the original owner, like pigeons or locust that fell down on the rooftop, this was the text of his opinion. But after almost seven years I realized that this

---

[146] He is Muhammad b. Ali b. Umar al-Mazari [Mazar was a village in Sicily] (d. 536/1142). See Ibn Khallikan, *Wafayat al-A'yan*, 4:285.

[147] Abu Muhammad Abd al-Hamid b. Muhammad al-Qairawani, better known as Ibn al-Saigh (d. 486/1093). See *al-Dibaj* 2:25.

argument was contradictive, that was his statement: The tenant rented the house with all it's facilities, but the claim that the water was part of these utilities needed further proof. Therefore, I refer to local custom for a decision.

Master mason Muhammad said: He then revoked his statement that the water belonged to the tenant, and the problem remained as to what the Sheikh said earlier as a disputable case and it depended on local custom. Nevertheless, all is good.

56- Discourse On the Well Located In A Man's Land But The Access To It Is Located Inside Someone Else's Property.

Master mason Muhammad said: A man whose well is on his land, but the access to the well is in someone else's land; there are three opinions on that:

First Opinion: Isa b. Dinar reported from Ibn al-Qasim in *al-'Utbiyah* as well as in *al-Majmu'ah*: The well belongs to whom the access is located, because the benefit belongs to him, similar to the condition where the upper floor belongs to a person and the lower floor belongs to another, the upper has no right on the lower. Therefore, the well belongs to the person having its access location and whatsoever on it belongs to the owner of the land.

Second Opinion: He also said in *Kitab al-Itq*: Everyone who needs a well must dig in his own land and benefit from it, he must fence it between him and the neighbor, and therefore the latter does not deserve to benefit from it.

Third opinion: From *al-Nawadir* as copied by Abu Muhammad from *al-Majmu'ah*, Sahnun said: If only one well exists, and the two neighbors are dependent on each other, then the well belongs to the owner of its access location. But if he (the land owner) has another access location independent from his neighbor, then the well belongs to the owner of the higher land and not the owner of the access location.

Master mason Muhammad said: The same case happened in Tunis on a ruin site where there was a house. A man bought it and built a house, similar to the earlier one, and then he found a well and beside it was an access location for a cistern. He also found another access location in his neighbor's house. Both then went to complain to al-Fakih al-Qadi Abu Yahya al-Nuri. Both quarreled for some time. The Qadi Abu Yahya al-Nuri- Qadi *al-Jamaah* ordered some experts to investigate the access location (*al-Fam*) from which the water was derived, to check whether the owner of the house without the cistern had recently constructed it, or it was an old access location. They came down to check, but could not make any decision, so they stripped the alley where the water flowed under a small manhole. They did it in order to check whether the construction of the house was contemporary with that of the cistern or not? They found out that both were built at the same time and nothing was added later on, and the place of drawing water, the access location, was of the old cistern and not new. The cistern channel leaned toward the one who was drawing the water. Then, they informed the judge Abu Yahya al-Nuri, who decided that the well belonged to the neighbor who owned the access location, not to the man who owned the land. He also ordered the owner of the land to cover up the intake point on his side by permanent construction so it would be impossible to open it.

Master-mason Muhammad said: Our custom of constructing a cistern is to make two openings: One wide opening for accessing the interior of the well. Another narrow opening for water intake on the side of the cistern. The judge ordered the bigger opening to be covered, but not the one for water intake.

57- Discourse On An Existing Unused Channel From A House On A Private Lane, Whose Owner Wants To Reclaim It.

Ibn Sahnun said: Habib asked Sahnun about a dead end street (*cul-de sac*), surrounded by the front doors of the surrounding houses, and the back of one house without a door facing this dead-end street, and adjacent to this house was an abandoned cesspool, which was connected to the house through a channel. Both were not in use for a long time. The owner of the house wanted to reclaim and revive both, but was prevented by his neighbors. Sahnun answered: They cannot prevent him except for the location of the access of the cesspool, and if they cannot find it, he can reclaim it again based on the evidence.

He said: If it was bought from others, then he has the right on it as the previous owner had.

Master mason Muhammad said: I saw a statement of Abu al-Hasan b. al-Qasim in his *Watha'iq*: Those that claim that the toilet or channel is old must prove it. If he fails to prove it, then he can take an oath against the one who opposes him. If it is established that the restroom is an old one, and the neighbor who opposes him fails to counterclaim, then the restroom should remain with the claimant.

58- Discourse On A Man Who Owned A Water Channel Running Through The Neighboring House, Whose Owner Wants To Renovate it.

Master mason Muhammad said: Different opinions were recorded regarding a man who owned a channel running through a neighbor's house. His neighbor had to demolish his house because the street had been rendered higher. If the neighbor increases the level of the floor of his house, the action could cause harm to the owner of the channel. Does the owner of the house have a right to rebuild the house at a higher level?

Three opinions are mentioned:

Ibn 'Abdus said: He has the right to heighten and renovate his house and he can tell his neighbor (owner of the water channel): increase the height of your channel.

Second Opinion: Abu Muhammad said in *al-Nawadir* from some of his companions and was recorded by Ibn Yunus in his *Diwan*: The neighbor cannot demolish and increase the level of his house unless he gets the consent of the owner of the water channel, because if he heightens his house it will harm his neighbor.

Third opinion: *Tafarrukah*: al-Sheikh Abu Muhammad Abdullah b. Abi Zaid said: If he can relocate the water channel through the lane (*zuqaq*), with minor changes, then he has no right to heighten his house without the neighbor's (owner of the water channel) consent, but if the cost is higher he has the right to heighten his house and demolish the water channel.

Master mason Muhammad said: The provision for the case is that the water of the former flows through the latter, not running through a built channel. Because, if the latter renovates his house, the water is still flowing in the channel, then the man is not being deprived of water by his neighbor's renovation. In this case a man cannot be prevented from renovating his house if the water channel is built in his house. The owner of the water channel does not have any reason to prevent the owner of the house from renovating it, because it will cause harm to the owner of the house who wants to counteract another harm facing him.

59- Discourse On Distribution of Rainwater From Streets Between The Gardens.

Master mason Muhammad said: From *Sayl al-Awdiyah*[148] by Ibn Abi Zayd: Sahnun said regarding two gardens abutting a street among the city streets. One was higher than the other. When raining, the water accumulates on the street. Sahnun said: The higher garden deserves to collect the water until it reaches the level of a man's ankle. Then he must release it to the lower regardless if it is enough or not. If they are on the same level, they should share it equally. If parts of the lower garden faces a part of the upper, then the lower should give what is equal to a man's ankle, and the rest should be shared equally. If some gardens cultivated are older than others, then the former has the right to be irrigated first.

From *al-Ikhtisar* of al-Fakih al-Qadi Abu Ishaq b. Abd al-Rafi', he said: owners of the gardens have priority over the water, than owners of mills.

Thereof Master-mason Muhammad said: Regarding the free flow water that had for a long time been taken by both upper and lower gardens for irrigations. Then the owner of the upper garden introduced a new vegetable plot that needed a lot of water. This endangered the owner of the lower gardens. Some of them protested, saying: I irrigate my greens, but cannot irrigate the fruit trees (because of a lack of water), therefore, the owner of the higher (garden) has no right to irrigate except his existing plants and not to introduce new vegetables into his garden. However, there is no reason for the owners of the lower gardens to prevent the owners of the higher gardens when they take their share of the water and irrigate what they want.

Thereof Master mason Muhammad said: If the owner of the higher ground started planting later than the owner of the lower ground, Asbagh said: The priority of using water goes to the higher garden than the lower, although there is nothing left for him (owner of the lower ground). It was said that the lower comes earlier, except in a condition that there was a surplus from the higher that would be enough to the lower. This was the opinion of Ibn al-Qasim.

---

[148] A chapter in *al-Nawadir wa Ziyadat* of Ibn Abi Zaid al-Qayrawani.

Thereof: Master mason Muhammad said: If a man has a spring in his garden and his neighbor digs another one causing his spring to run dry or decrease its water level, if the expert says that this was caused by the newly dug well, then it should be closed up.

Thereof Master mason Muhammad said: If a man has an irrigation channel running through the land of another man who does not have access to its source, but has access to the passage of water, then he has no right for whatsoever that grows on its edges. If he owns the access to its source (*Raqabah*) then the trees that grow along its edges belongs to him; if both are claiming ownership without any evidence, then the trees belongs to the owner of the water, because the access to its source belongs to him. Nevertheless, he has no right to cultivate on the surrounding area of the channel except on the edge of the channel as long as it does not harm the owner of the land, since every owner has a zone of a protective area (*harim*).

60- Discourse On Drainage Running On The Surface And Disposing Waste Water Onto The Street.

Master mason Muhammad said: This is about a man who built a house and wants to drain his courtyard water onto the street; it is either wastewater or rainwater.

If it is wastewater, then it should be prevented. Sahnun has said that in the book of his son, and Ibn Yunus copied it in the explanation of *al-Mudawwanah*.

Master mason Muhammad said: A case happened in the city of Qairawan. Most of the houses in the city dispose their wastewater through a small outlet under the main door sill onto the street. I visited Qairawan for a reason and I saw that most of the houses dispose their waste water through the main door onto the street. I discussed this situation with the Qadi who ordered a public crier to announce the new order to all city dwellers: Whoever did not seal their water outlet that discharged into the street will be punished. Some of them shut their outlet, but some continued their habit. One day the Qadi walked the streets and found a servant washing the entry hall of the house and let the wastewater flowing onto the street. He sent to the owner of the house, and ordered that he be lashed thirty times and ordered that he be walked on the streets for his violation.

Thereof Master mason Muhammad said: What if it is rainwater running through the door sill, Sahnun said in the book of his son:

It does not matter even if it is harmful, as it is unavoidable, and a common practice.

Master mason Muhammad said: This occurred during the tenure of al-Faqih al-Salih Abu Ishaq b. Abd al-Rafi' Qadi *al-Jamaah*. There was a garden in the outskirt of the city of Tunis. The owner subdivided it into many parts, which was bought by different people. Each built a house on their individual plots. A man bought one plot, which was adjacent to an existing house neighboring the garden. He created a channel to dispose rainwater, household water and sewage. His neighbor (owner of the existing house) complained to the judge about it and said: Adjacent to my house was a garden without a water channel. The judge then ordered the channel to be removed, and to let the rainwater flow on the surface in front of the house.

Master mason Muhammad said: I narrated the case to al-Faqih al-Mufti Abu Abdullah b. al-Ghammaz whether it is right for the owner of the new house to discharge the rainwater on the surface as decided by the Qadi? He said: Yes, he can let the rainwater flow on the surface of the earth (as ordered by the Qadi) as it was before the house was built. The owner of the earlier existing house has no right to prevent him even if the rainwater may harm him.

Master Mason Muhammad said: The regulation regarding this type of case in our times refers to our opinion that the owner of a new house should not be prevented from discharging their rainwater on the surface of the earth. There is no scholar in our time, who had a different opinion.

Thereof Master mason Muhammad said: If a man built a house, and he made a gargoyle that discharged the rainwater into the street, he will face two conditions:

It will harm the opposite wall in a narrow street due to the force of evacuation of the rainwater from the gargoyle, or it would not harm the wall because the street is wide.

Al-Sheikh Ibn Abi Zaid said in *al-Nawadir* that the man should be prevented from discharging the rainwater onto the street, if his action harms his neighbor. But if it does not harm, then he is free to do that. This opinion is also held by Abu Hamid al-Ghazali[149] in *Ihya' Ulum al-Din*, and Sahnun as transmitted by Ibn Yunus.

Master mason Muhammad said: I was in the city of Susa and saw a man building a gargoyle on a narrow alley that discharged the rainwater into the street. The owner of the opposite house complained about it. Then I was asked by al-Qadi about this case. I said to him: The harm should be removed from the victim. The Qadi ordered the gargoyle to be removed. The owner of the gargoyle angrily protested and he was a man of high ranking. He said to the judge: Take my case to Tunis, and ask them whether I should remove my gargoyle or not? The judge of Susa wrote a letter to the judge of Tunis explaining the matter. The judge of Tunis replied that the gargoyle should be removed in order to prevent harm to the neighbor.

Thereof Master mason Muhammad said: If a man made a gargoyle to dispose rainwater that is discharged through his door to the street and passes by a neighbor, who protested. If the owner of the discharged water can prove that it is only rainwater, he cannot be prevented. But if it is proven that the water is household washing water, he should be prevented. If it is proven that the water is not contaminated with any other elements, then the saying of the owner of the house that the gargoyle is for rainwater can only be trusted and allowed to dispose the water if he takes the oath.

61- Discourse On Overhanging Ledge Of Houses And Usage Of Its Airspace.

Master mason Muhammad said: Sahnun said in *al-Mudawwanah*: I said to Ibn al-Qasim: If the house is divided into two parts, a different person will occupy each part. The overhanging ledge (*ajnihah*) is located on the side of one of them, is it his property? He answered: Yes, if the overhanging ledge is located on his part. I said: Why the overhanging ledge belongs to the one who owns that position, whereas it's overhanging above the *fina*. When each person took his or her part (of the house) the *fina'* between the houses is still there. And the *ajnihah* is above the *fina'*. He said: The *ajnihah*, when

---

[149] He is Muhammad b. Muhammad b. Muhammad b. Ahmad al-Tusi (d. 505/1112). See *Wafiyat al-Ayan*. 4:216-219.

purposely built is part of the house, it is not part of the *fina'*, and it belongs to the house. When the house is divided into two parts, and each one takes possession of their part, the *ajnihah* belongs to the one who took the part that has the *ajnihah*, because the *ajnihah* is part of his portion and it is not part of the *fina'*. This is my opinion.

Thereof: Master mason Muhammad said: From the book of Ibn Sahnun, Muhammad said: Habib asked Sahnun about a man who owned an overhanging ledge protruding onto a neighbor's house that was not screened, and he wanted to screen it but was prevented by his neighbor. He answered: He (the neighbor) has no right to prevent him, since the ledge can be screened by its owner.

Problem: Master mason Muhammad said: He (Habib) also asked him (Sahnun) about a man who had an overhanging ledge protruding towards the neighbor's house. Then the neighbor built a wall adjacent to his wall and he (the neighbor) wanted to heighten his structure over the overhanging ledge. He answered: He cannot build over it, because the owner of the *raff* owns its airspace.

Thereof: Master mason Muhammad said: Ibn Sahl said at the end of his book: I have posted a question to our scholars in Cordova in the year 456 A.H. (1064 C.E.) asking them about two neighboring houses that belonged to two different persons. Between these two houses, there is a wall belonging to one of them. Attached to the wall was a *raff* with its wooden support protruding towards the neighboring house. The owner of the *raff* wanted to build a wall at the edge of its supports with baked brick or other materials, so that it could be heightened in order to build a room. The neighbor prevented him, saying: The airspace is mine; because it is in front of my house, what you have is only an overhanging ledge (*raff*) protruding towards mine. Can the owner of the overhanging ledge (*raff*) remove it and heighten his wall and place the overhanging ledge (*raff*) on it as before? Ibn Itab replied saying: The owner of the *raff* has no right to build on the edge of his supports, because the airspace belongs to his neighbor, but he can heighten his wall within its own airspace and put the shelf board on it as it was before.

Ibn Qattan replied: The *raff* owner can build on the edge of his supports as he wants and he cannot be prevented from that and from heightening his wall without harming his neighbor except for fresh air and light or something similar which is regarded as not inflicting harm.

Ibn Malik wrote: The *raff* owner cannot proceed with his plan except with the permission of the neighbor.

Ibn Sahl said: The same case happened in the city of Tulaitulah (Toledo) between me and Ibn al-Saqa, the judge of Wadi al-Hijarah, and the answer of Ibn al-Qattan was similar to mine.

Thereof: Master mason Muhammad said: If the edge of the supports, the *raff,* are protruding onto the neighbor's house, and he wanted to roof it and build on it, Sahnun said: He cannot do that. He said: and the neighbor also has no right to build on it. He was asked: If the neighbor insisted to build on it, should the *raff* owner be compelled to cut it off (the protruding part) from his house? He said: Yes, he should be compelled because it is protruding onto someone else's property.

62- Discourse On Protruding Cantilevers And Ledges Onto The Street.

Master mason Muhammad said: Projections from houses toward the street are either occurring on a public street or private lane (dead-end street). If it is to occurr onto a dead-end street, then it is prohibited. This is what has been narrated by Ibn Qasim and others and it is a well known opinion in the Maliki School.

Master mason Muhammad said: Any projections onto the dead-end street are prohibited. However, one who has an old protrusion on that alley and wants to rebuild a new one above it, is also prohibited. Ibn Shaaban in *al-Nawadir* said: Even if he puts it together or under the old one, it is also prohibited.

Master mason Muhammad said: *al-Ajnihah* (plural of *Jinah*), is a protrusion from a wall towards a public street, is not prohibited. That is the opinion of Malik and Ibn al-Qasim, so too with Ibn Habib from Mutarrif and Ibn al-Majashun.

Master mason Muhammad said: I did not see any disagreement regarding the case in the Maliki School, except in al-Shafii School, that stipulates that one should not be allowed to make any protrusion onto the street.

Ibn al-Qasim in *al-'Utbiyah* said: It was practiced in Medina and nobody protested, and in fact Malik bought a house that had a protruding shelf. Ibn Shaaban said: If the door of a house is facing the street and one of the owners wants to build an overhanging ledge, he should not be prevented if he is earlier than others (residents).

Master mason Muhammad said: If two neighbors next to each other want to build cantilevers and they quarreled, Ibn Abi Zaid said in *al-Nawadir* from Ibn Shaaban that, they should divide the air space equally between them.

Thereof Master mason Muhammad said: From *al-Nawadir* Abu Abdullah b. Abi Zaid said: The height limit of any ledge or cantilever above the street surface should be the height of the largest loaded camel with sufficient space on top of the rider's head so as not to harm the rider. If it is too low and will cause harm to the rider then the structure should be demolished. This is the opinion of Ibn al-Qasim.

Thereof Master mason Muhammad said: If the protrusion fell on a man and killed him, Malik said that the owner is not responsible. Someone said to him: The scholars of Iraq, said: He is responsible; because he built something that should not be there, Malik was surprised by their opinion but maintained his position.

Fatwa: Master mason Muhammad said: I asked al-Sheikh al-Faqih al-Alim Abu Abdullah b. al-Ghammaz about a protrusion built above the street, which was too low and caused accidents because people's heads bumped into it. Should it be demolished or the surface of the street should be dug so that it does not harm passer-by? He said to me: the owner of the protrusion has options, whether to lower the street level so that no harm is caused to passers-by, or to demolish the structure and raise it sufficiently to allow free passage of pedestrians and riders.

63- Discourse On What Is Allowed And Disallowed In The Street.

Master mason Muhammad said: In *al-'Utbiyah* Sahnun was asked about a man who owned two houses facing each other; one on the right and the other on the left side of the street. He wanted to build above the street a room or balcony attached to his wall. Sahnun said: he is not prevented from doing so. He should be prevented if the structure narrows the street, but if the structure does not harm the street or passers-by then he should not be prevented.

Thereof Master mason Muhammad said: I was told by al-Faqih al-Qadi Abu Zaid b. Qattan (who said): that he was told by al-

Sheikh Abu Bakr Ali, who said: I have written to al-Dhabit asking him about a man who had two houses, one was on the right side of the street, and the other on the left. He then made a *sabat,* or a room above the street between the two houses, attached to both walls. When he passed away, the two houses were sold to two different persons, each bought one house. Then they quarreled about the wall of one of the houses. The owner of the house said: the wall belongs to me, within it are my beams, and it (the wall) is one of the four borders of my house. The owner of the other house with the *sabat* said: the wall is shared between us, because my roof structure rests on it and its arch reaches over the wall by about one and half hand-spans. Al-Dhabit answered: if the construction of the arches is not bonded with the other wall that supports the beam of the other house; and if the bond and construction of protective covering (ceiling of the arc) are not bonded to the disputed wall, the owner of the *sabat* cannot claim ownership of that wall. He is still entitled to fix his beams to the wall. Since the wall is connected to the house on the eastern side, of the owner that does not own the *sabat*, they do not jointly own it. The wall belongs solely to the owner of the house on the eastern side who has his beams properly inserted and bonded to the wall. So the owner of the *sabat* has no right on the said wall except only for inserting his beams. If the expert testifies that the base of the arch is properly fixed (well bonded) to the wall, then they jointly own the wall.

64- Discourse On Building Columns And Benches In The Street.

Master mason Muhammad said: Ibn Wahb was asked about a man who owned a house abutting a street. He wanted to build a row of columns alongside his wall that faces the street to use it for support. Ibn Wahb said: He has the right to build it with the condition that it does not harm anybody. Ibn Wahb added: so too with the small steps that do not harm anybody.

Master mason Muhammad said: The small steps are sometimes used to place various types of loads. I do not see why any should be demolished as long as it does not harm or narrows the street. Thereof Master mason Muhammad said: The benches that are used for sitting which are built in front of a neighbor's house should be demolished even if they do not harm passers-by.

Master mason Muhammad said: Sahnun was asked about a man who built a bench next to his front door abutting an alley, which did not harm anybody on that alley. But the bench was facing his opposite neighbor's door and it's harmful to the neighbor, because he used to sit on it, so too his friends. Sahnun said: He should be prevented from creating the bench since it harms the other. This is also his answer to Habib in the book of his son.

65- Discourse On What Is Disallowed And Allowed In The Street.

Master mason Muhammad said: Abu Hamid al-Ghazali in his *Ihya' Ulum al-Din* mentioned about what is prohibited in the streets: among the prohibited things are: building columns and benches connected to private buildings, planting trees, protruding ledge and cantilevers, placing of woods, food or various loads on the street. All these are prohibited if it narrowes the street and harms the passers-by, but if it does not create harm because the road is wide, then there is no prohibition. It is however lawful to unload woods, food or various loads for a short period before they are transferred to the houses, with the intention to quickly complete services to the houses.

It is also prohibited to tie animals of burden on the street since it will narrow it and pollute the street with its excrement. But mounting and dismounting on the street is allowed. This is because the street is shared among the public, nobody has an exclusive right except to fulfill his needs. Passers-by need the street primarily for access according to custom without any exception.

Also to herd a group of animals that are carrying thorns that rip people's clothes is clearly prohibited, and the thorns should be tied up in order to prevent them from tearing up people's clothes. The animals should also be gathered in an empty place. If not, the animals can be allowed in the street provided that the safety of the masses is taken care off. The loads on the animals should not be left on the street for too long, except for removal. Animals of burden should not be forced to carry something that they are not capable of, so too with slaughtering animals in front of a butchers shop and polluting the street with animal blood. Slaughtering of animals should be done within the butcher's premise. All those things should be prevented because it will narrow the road, whereas the excrement is harmful to people.

Other things that need to be prevented on the street: throwing garbage (or) watermelon skin and excessive spraying of water, which might cause people to slip on the street.

The people should be prevented from disposing water from their gargoyle onto narrow streets since it will contaminate passers-by clothes. But if the street is wide, then it is allowed since people can avoid it. Rainwater and snow should not be left on the street without sweeping. But (the sweeping) is not the responsibility of a particular person. However, if the snow or water came from any particular house, then the owner of that property should be responsible for sweeping it from the street. As for rainwater, it is the duty of the surrounding residents and is supervised by the authority.

66- Discourse On The Wall And Room Feared To Collapse If It Is A Shared Property Or Under the Trustee Of A Legal Guardian.

Master mason Muhammad said: There are two different opinions on a slanted wall;

Ibn al-Qasim narrated from Malik in *al-Majmu'ah* and also in the book of Ibn al-Mawwaz: If there is a testimony against the owner, he is responsible for what might happen, but if there is no testimony, then he is not responsible.

Second Opinion: Ashhab said in two books[150]: If the slanting is getting worse and the owner does not demolish it, then he would be responsible for what may happen regardless whether there is a testimony or not; because he is considered as a careless person (for not demolishing it), he is like the one who tied his animal in a prohibited place. If the case is not as we mentioned, then the owner is not responsible whether there is testimony against him or not. Because leaving the testimony does not dismiss his obligation, and it is not imposed on him except what is obligatory such as tying the animal at the wrong place; but if he is ordered by the authority, he has to demolish it. This is a responsibility according to the case, but protest by people is not necessarily followed by the necessary act.

Master mason Muhammad said: The accepted opinion is as what was said by Ibn al-Qasim. The testimony is not applied on those

---

[150] The two are *al-'Utbiyah* and Kitab Ibn 'Abd al-Hakam.

whose house is in their charge by mortgage or rent when the owner is present; if the owner is absent, the case should be brought to the *imam* (representing the local authority). This is the view of Ibn al-Qasim. Asshab said: The owner is free, so are those who take it for mortgage or rent when there is no fear about the presence of the owner. If he disappears and such incidence happens, the owner is responsible not the tenant or creditor, even if the authority already advised them (the tenant or creditor) to demolish.

Thereof Master mason Muhammad said: If the wall is shared among some people and is leaning and about to fall, and they have been advised to demolish it but ignore it until it falls down on something and destroys it. The damage should be shared among them equally and they should be forced to compensate that. I do not look at either bigger or smaller share, but all should be liable because the wall belongs to them. This is the opinion of Muhammad b. Abd al-Hakam in *al-Majmu'ah*, though there is some debate about that.

Thereof Master mason Muhammad said: Ibn Abd al-Hakam said: If the wall is about to fall, the judge should notify the owner immediately to demolish it. If the owner is absent, the judge can order the wall to be demolished. He should compensate the one who will demolish it, if he found out that they are poor or the owners could not be traced, or if he is worried that the wall will soon fall.

Thereof Master mason Muhammad said: With this directive, al-Sheikh al-Faqih al-Qadi Abu Ishaq b. Abd al-Rafi' ordered that if the owner is absent, the wall is to be demolished and the judge compensates the one who demolished it. If the house belonged to an orphan who has not matured, then the order should be forwarded to the legal guardian. If the order were given and no action is taken by the legal guardian, and the wall collapses, causing death or destruction of property, then the orphan is not to be held responsible. In my opinion, the legal guardian should be held responsible and pay the damage with their own money since they had the opportunity to act but ignored that. Muhammad b. Abd al-Hakam also had the same opinion. Ibn Kinanah said experts should be sent to investigate the wall. If, in their opinion, the wall will fall, they can order the owner to repair it. If the owner is poor or destitute, he should be forced to sell his property, whether he likes it or not.

Thereof Master mason Muhammad said: Ibn Sahnun said in *al-Majmu'ah*: The Qadi Shajarah asked Sahnun about a man who complained to the Judge about his neighbor who had a leaning room or wall. He said: if it is clearly dangerous, then the potential damage to the public must be eliminated regardless whether the owner is present or not.

Master mason Muhammad said: Al-Sheikh al-Faqih al-Qadhi Abu Ishaq b. Abd al-Rafi' once ordered me to walk the streets of the city to check on any leaning wall and to demolish it. Whenever I found any leaning wall I demolished it. One late evening I found a tilting wall about to collapse. So I said to the owner: demolish it, he replied: let me demolish it tomorrow, since the time is late, it is difficult to find a worker in the late evening to demolish it. I said to him: I will allow you if the judge gives his permission. Then we came to al-Qadi Ibn 'Abd al-Rafi' and he was in the court. I told him: he has a leaning wall, which I am afraid is about to fall. He (the Judge) said: go and demolish it. The wall's owner said: let me demolish it tomorrow, because the time is too late, and it is difficult to find a worker in the late evening to demolish it. He said: no way, demolish it right now and continue into the night. The judge disgraced the man and did not accept any excuse from him.

I came one day to him, and said: I found a leaning wall about to fall and I could not find the owner, the house was empty. He ordered me to demolish it and we did and sold it's spoil to pay the workers. Thus, whenever he heard about or saw a leaning wall, he would notify the owner, and could not accept any excuse until it was demolished. Most of the time he would say to me: I have seen in so and so place a leaning wall, and I am afraid it will fall on people. He feels responsible for the safety people.

67- Discourse On A Man Who's Building Is Slanting Toward The Neighboring Airspace.

Isa b. Dinar said in *al-'Utbiyah*: Ibn al-Qasim was asked about a man who built a high building and its structure was protruding toward his neighbor's airspace. This neighbor then built something within his property and airspace, but the owner of the adjacent slanting building prevented him to complete his construction. Ibn al-Qasim said: everything that protrudes towards a neighbor's air space should be demolished, even if it will cost a lot, or a little.

Master mason Muhammad said: Similar cases occurred in Tunis several times. A building was first built but protruded into the neighbor's airspace by the width of two fingers, but then they added another floor. On it a second level was built. Then a third level was built on it, and it became impossible to describe because so much had been spent to build it. They later occupied the building when it was completed. After a while, a neighbor built a wall next to the protruding structure. He heightened his building until it could not go up further because of his neighbor's slanting structure. He protested this slanting condition and said to his neighbor: mend your building because it protrudes into my airspace. The neighbor answered: it is impossible to mend it except to demolish it completely. Both then brought their case to the judge Ibn 'Abd al-Rafi'. The judge ordered the owner of the slanting building to demolish all the slanting parts to enable his neighbor to continue his construction and complete it as he liked. Thus, every slanting structure that protrudes into a neighboring air space must be demolished to enable the neighbor to heighten his building within his airspace.

68- Discourse On A Ruin In A Residential Area With Huge Garbage And Harmful To The Neighboring Houses.

Master mason Muhammad said: The garbage is either: on someone's property or on the public street, both are harmful. If it is in someone else's property, then three different views are expressed:

First opinion: It is the responsibility of the owner of the ruined property. This is the opinion of Sahnun from a question by Habib.

Second Opinion: The neighboring houses are responsible for it. The nearest is the most responsible to solve the problem, followed by the next neighbor and so on.

Third opinion: An alternative view as proposed by some contemporaries is: If the owner of the ruin prevents anyone from removing the garbage, and they collect it for themselves, they are obliged to sweep it and to protect the public from any harm. Whereas, if they do not collect it and do not prevent others from cleaning it, then the responsibility is on the neighbors to sweep it. This opinion is narrated by Ibn Hisham in his *Mufid al-Hukkam*. If the garbage is on a public street and it does not belong to anybody, then the responsibility for sweeping is on the neighbors as mentioned by Sahnun. Al-Sheikh Abu Muhammad Abdullah b. Abi Zayd said: What Sahnun meant is that usually it is the neighboring people who are responsible for disposing their garbage over there.

Thereof: From *Nawazil* written by al-Sheikh al-Faqih Abi Zaid b. Uthman al-Susi- Qadi al-Jama'ah in Tunis, I found a question addressed to Ibn Ziyadat Allah al-Qabisi, and his answer: I was asked about a man who owned a property adjacent to another person's property which was in ruin. After sometime, the man built a wall adjacent to the ruined property and he built it from the foundation up and inserted wooden beams in it. After a long time, the owner of the ruin asked him to remove the garbage that was amassed in it, which was close to his wall, and he said that the trash would be harmful if it remained. The owner of the ruined property said to the owner of the wall: most of the garbage is from you and the rest belongs to other neighbors. The owner of the property used to operate a bakery, and most of the surrounding neighbors disposed the garbage out there. He (owner of the ruined property) said: and you in the process of repairing your property dumped a lot of soil, you removed some but others remained. The owner of the wall said: the dirt on the wall is not harmful and it is old. He issued a testimony as evidence, that others had sworn that this person was not the one who threw garbage on someone else's property.

The owner of the ruined property said: 'your testimony is meaningless, because you clearly have built and repaired your property adjacent to my ruined property. The testimony is also unreliable, unless they witnessed that you removed all of your garbage from my property after completing your work. And they're saying that: Whatever is harmful to Muslims is prohibited, therefore, take the oath in front of me, that you never threw anything and nothing is left of your dirt inside my ruined property, so that I will not hold you responsible.

Thus, what is your opinion? Is he freed from the oath or should he swear and the owner of the ruined property should remove any harm from the wall, explain to us, please!

Then Ziyadat Allah al-Qabisi answered: the evidence could be deduced from their saying: If they said: we did not see it legitimately, then their testimony is useless, because the Muslim, as has been mentioned, never considers something prohibited as permissible. If they say: What we meant is that he does not approve such action and he should not swear except when asked for it, unless it is known who the person is who said that he saw him throwing the rubbish on the said ruin. In this instance he should take the oath to clear his name.

69- Discourse On Dirt From A Man's Property Brought By Rainwater To Neighboring Doors Or Someone Else's Door That Blocked The Water Channel.

Master mason Muhammad said: There are two opinions about the dirt that was moved by rainwater from a man's door to a neighbor's door.

Yahya b. 'Umar said: To the owner of the original dirt, it can be said: Take the dirt if you like, but if he does not do that, then tell the owner of the clogged channel: remove the dirt from your channel if you like. He also said: the owner of the property where dirt originates cannot be forced to remove it from other's property. Al-Sheikh Abu Muhammad said in *al-Nawadir*: the owner should be held responsible.

Master mason Muhammad said: if the owner lets the dirt accumulate on the street and he ignores it, then rain fell and swept the dirt to the neighbor's door, then he can be forced to remove it without any excuse because he is the one who let the dirt accumulate in the first place. But if the dirt came from his renovation work and he is busy, but not ignoring it, then the rain fell and swept it onto someone else's door, this can be forgiven. It is a kind of misfortune fallen on someone else. To the victim can be said: remove the dirt if you like, but the original owner is not obliged to remove it for you.

Sahnun said about the dirt of renovation work: If the dirt is swept into the street, the owner is forgiven because he could not avoid it, but the owner is also responsible to remove it without excuse. All judges whom I have consulted ordered me to force whoever left the dirt, without any excuse, to remove it immediately.

70- Discourse On The Ground Floor Belongs To A Man And Upper Floor Belongs To Another And The Road Was Heightened Making The Door On The Ground Floor Shorter.

Master mason Muhammad said: Ibn 'Abdus said in *al-Nawadir* about a man who owned a ground floor and the other man owned the upper floor. The owner of the ground floor wanted to raise his level to be equal to the street level, because the street level increased in height and his front door opening became shorter. The owner of the top floor is obliged to let the owner of ground floor to heighten his level (which includes using some of the former's airspace) with compensation.

71- Discourse On A Shared Well And House Between Two Persons, Both Properties Collapsed But One Of The Partners Refused To Participate In Rebuilding and They Quarreled About That.

Master mason Muhammad said: From *al-'Utbiyah*: Yahya b. Yahya narrated from Ibn al-Qasim, that Malik said: As for the house or something which can be divided, then it should be divided. The one who wanted to build can do so within his newly divided area. But for the well and other properties that cannot be divided, then to the one who does not want to participate can be given options: either to join your partner to rebuild or oppose him, or hire someone to do so for you, or we sell your part at the right price so that you cannot prevent your partner from benefiting from his portion.

Thereof Master mason Muhammad said: If there is a well shared by two persons, one of them irrigates his farm, which diminishes the water. When his partner wants to upgrade the well, but the owner refuses, saying, 'I am afraid (that it will damage the well). If the expert testifies that the upgrade would damage the well, he has no right to do that. This is the opinion of Ibn Abd al-Hakam in his book, since the Prophet said: *La Darar Wa La Dirar.*

Thereof Master-mason Muhammad said: If a shared well between two people is collapsing or depleting and one of them wants to repair, but the other refuses; the one who refuses will not receive any water from that well even if there is a surplus, unless he compensates his partner half of the total cost of repairs.

If a shared waterway or well used for orchard irrigation needs to be cleaned, but one of them refuses, when the lack of maintenance of the waterway is harmful and decreases the flow of water, the water shall not be enough for both of them. Then, the one who cleanes it gets the first priority over the other who refused to clean. He (the one who refused to participate) will get back his share after paying half of the maintenance cost to his partner.

The same is applied to a ranch well. If the flow of water decreases and some of them want to clean, but others refuse, then it is judged like the orchard well. If some of them clean it, they all share the quantity of water before cleaning, therefore the increase in quantity should be solely utilized by the groups who cleaned the well. The group that cleaned the well should water their animals first, and then the quantity that is left should be shared with the others equally. Once the others pay the cost of cleaning, then they should share the water equally as before. This is the opinion of Malik.

Thereof Master mason Muhammad said on a well or water spring shared by two persons, when the water level shrinks and one of them wants to repair, but the other refuses, to the one who refuses can be said: either you join him or hire someone else to do it for you. The third option is to tell the one who wants to repair: do your job and whatever increases in the water level belongs to you until the other one pays his half of the cost. This is the opinion of Mutarrif, Ibn al-Majashun in the book of Ibn Habib. This is also the opinion of Malik.

72- Discourse On A Shared Vacant Lot Between Two Men One Of Them Wants To Build.

Master mason Muhammad said: There is a vacant lot shared by two persons and one of them wants to build, he cannot force his partner to join him if he refuses. He can say to him: either you join me in developing this lot or we divide it. This is the opinion of Malik in the book of Ibn Abd al-Hakam. We have discussed this in a previous chapter about a dilapidated wall, which is shared by two persons, one of them refuses to repair when it collapses.

73- Discourse On A Jointly Owned Grapevine Wall That Is Falling.

Master mason Muhammad said about a grapevine shared between partners with its wall falling. This will damage the trees and some of them want to repair the wall but others refused. If each share in the grapevine is well divided and partners knew their lot, then the one who refused cannot be forced to repair. And who wants to save their grapevine should do so.

On the other hand, if the grapevine is randomly divided and they differed in the work, then the one who refused can be forced to join the work, after that each can protect their own portion. If the grapevine has fruits that could not be divided and without the restoration work the fruit will spoil and the trees destroyed, and if the grapes are ripening, to the one who refuses restoration can be said: fence them up or sell your fruits to them for compensation.

If the grapes are not ripe, this can be said to the one who want to restore fencing: Fence up if you like, take the share of those who refused to participate until they compensate you for your expenses. If the cost is higher than the price of the grapes, he will not get more than the price of the grapes. All these were taken from the report of Yahya b. Yahya in *al-'Utbiyah* and *al-Majmu'ah*. Ibn Abi Zaid and some of our contemporaries have the same opinion.

Thereof: Regarding a garden belonging to two men that has no wall around it. One of them wants to start planting and asked his partner to fence the garden with him. According to Ashhab based on Malik's opinion in *al-Majmu'ah*: he has no right to force his partner to join him.

74- Discourse On Somebody Who Alters The Boundary.

Master mason Muhammad said: Ibn Wahb narrated from Malik (the *hadith* linked to Said b. Zayd) as he said: I heard the Messenger of God say: Whoever steals a hand span of land, he would be submerged to the seventh layer of the earth.

He said: Abdullah b. 'Umar told me that Marwan b. al-Hakam sent some people to Said b. Zayd b. Amru (b. Naufal) asking about Urwa bint Uwais who did some injustice, he said: Urwa did injustice upon us, and I heard the Prophet say: Whoever steals a hand span of land, Allah would submerge him to the seventh layer of the earth.[151]

I was told by 'Umar b. b. Zaid b. Abdullah b. 'Umar b. al-Khattab, from his father from Said b. Zaid, as he said: I was told by Yunus b. Yazid, from Ibn Shihab and Abu Bakr b. Hazm, and I was told by al-Layth from Yahya, all of them have told me a similar story about Urwa bint Uwais. Yunus said: Ibn Hazm said: When we were young we heard people telling others, "may Allah

---

[151] Sahih Muslim hadith no. 1610 V 3:1230-1231.

blind you as He made Urwa blind", we assumed that al-Urwa is a kind of wild animal, whereas what caused her to suffer is because of supplication by Said b. Zaid. He said: I was told by Usamah b. Zayd al-Laythi that Abdullah, the slave of Ummu Salmah (the wife of the Prophet), informed them something about two men quarrelling about a land which its boundary was changed whereas the person who knew about it had died. The Prophet said to both of them: 'I will judge between you based on what I have heard from you; which of you is better than the other in the argument I will decide for him and I see the right is for him. But if in fact, the right is for his brother, then my judgment to the former comes with a piece of fire encircled on his neck in hereafter from the seventh layer of the earth. When they heard this, they cried and said, 'O the Messenger of Allah, give my portion to him'. The Prophet then said: 'Go and do *ijtihad* on dividing your land into two portions. When each of you has taken his portion, the other has to legitimize his brother's portion'.

Ibn Wahb said: I was told by Bukayr b. al-Ashujj that Abu Ishaq Maula of Bani Hashim told him, that Ali b. al-Husayn and Abu Salmah b. Abd al-Rahman were quarrelling adjacent to the room of Aishah. She asked to investigate what they are saying and what the dispute was about. Surely the Messenger of Allah said: Whoever took a hand span of land illegally, Allah will submerge him to the seventh layer of earth in the hereafter.

He said: Ibn Luhay'ah told me, from Ubaydullah b. Abu Jaafar, from Abu Abd al-Rahman from Abdullah b. Mas'ud, who said: I said, O Messenger of Allah, what is the greatest oppression? He said: a cubit of land taken from the property of his brother. Not a portion taken except it would submerge him in the hereafter into the bottom of the earth, and nobody knows the bottom of the earth except the One who created it.

Ibn Wahb said: The *hadith* is referenced to Abu Hurayrah, that the Messenger of Allah said: The greatest oppressor is the one who takes a hand span of land of others into his own. I asked: how is it O Prophet?' He said: You find two neighboring men sharing one house, one of them takes a portion of his brother's right to himself, there is not a portion taken from his brother unless it will repress him into the bottom of the earth. No one knows its bottom except the One who knows the bottom of Hell, and no one knows its bottom except the One who created it.

He said: Hafs b. Maysarah told me, from Zayd b. Aslam, that the Prophet said: cursed to the one who curses his parents, cursed to the one who alters the land boundary and takes something that is not his right, cursed who misleads the blind from the street.

Ibn Wahb said: I heard from Abd al-Rahman b. Abi al-Mawali said that Yazid b. Abi Ziyad, narrated from Muhammad b. Ali from his father, that he said: it was found at the base of the Prophet's sword a page written on it: Cursed cursed who misleads the blind from the street, cursed cursed to the one who steals from the boundary, cursed cursed who obeyed not his Lord or denied the grace of Allah which had been given to him. But Ibn Abi al-Mawali doubted this. Ibn Wahb said: This tradition is attributed to Abdullah b. 'Umar that the Prophet said: Allah has cursed whoever alters the land boundary.

75- Discourse On Disagreement On Land Boundary.

Master-mason Muhammad said: Land boundary falls into these conditions: Either the land surface is equal or one of them is higher than the other. If the surface is equal, it should be judged as judging the wall between two men: it belongs to the one who takes oath that it is his property. If both of them take the oath, then the disputed land is divided between them equally. If one's land is higher than the other, and they both claim ownership: there are different opinions among experts on this.

Ibn al-Qasim said: it belongs to the owner of the higher land; this has been mentioned in *Mufid al-Hukkam* of Ibn al-Qasim. Abu al-Hasan Ali b. Yahya Ibn al-Qasim said in his *Wathiqah*: the location of the land is not taken into consideration in determining one's land boundary against the other.

It is also quoted from Abu al-Hasan in another topic of his *Wathiqah*: the land boundary belongs to the owner of the higher land. He said: this is a good statement, because the boundary marker determines the boundary in case parts of the land slides onto the lower land.

Master mason Muhammad said: The owner of the lower land gains more advantage than the higher because the higher land slides every year toward the lower. Thus the boundary marker belongs to the higher, whether it was built up or not, because the owner of the higher land will not build if he knows that part of his land would slide.

Master-mason Muhammad said: If we say the boundary marker belongs to the owner of higher land, is he allowed to change its location? Two opinions:

Some said: He has the right to change its location. And others said: He has no right to change it, and this is preferable, for the Prophet said: Cursed to the one who changes the boundary marker.

76- Discourse On The Protective Area (*harim*) Of The Well.

Master mason Muhammad said: Ibn Nafi' reported from Malik in *al-Majmu'ah* as well as in *al-'Utbiyah* that Asshab heard from Malik: he was asked about the protective area (*harim*) of the well, he said: the protective area in open wilderness that are not owned.

Ibn Nafi' said: Ibn Abi Dhi'b told me from Ibn Shihab from Ibn Abi al-Musayyab from the Prophet that he said: The protective area of a *badiyy* well (used by livestock) is 25 cubits while that of farmland is 500 cubits.[152]

Ibn Shihab said: I do not know about the Harim for the well of farmland whether it is from tradition (*Hadith*) or from the saying of Said. But Ibn Wahb mentioned that the tradition was narrated from Yunus from Ibn Shihab, from Ibn al-Musayyab. He mentioned that the saying of Ibn al-Musayyab regarding the *'adiyah* and *badiyy* well like what is mentioned by Ibn Shihab. He (Ibn Shihab) added: I heard people say: The protective area of a spring is 500 cubits. And it was said that: The protective area of a river is 1000 cubits.

Master mason Muhammad said: In another tradition by Ibn Wahb, from 'Umar b. al-Khattab, the protective area of *'adiyah* well is 50 cubits, and *badiyy* well is 25 cubits, and that of a farm is 300 cubits and for a spring is 500 cubits.

Al-Sheikh Abu Muhammad Abdullah b. Abi Zayd said: Some scholars said: The protective area of a well, according to Malik, is relative to the place and there is no definite border for that. Nevertheless, the border that was narrated by Ibn Shihab cannot be ignored, unless there is an analogy, of which the Prophet has determined, that must be followed.

---

[152] Narrated by al-Daraqutni 3/4:220, Baihaqi Sunan 6:155, and Abu Ubaid in *Kitab al-Amwal*, p.369-371.

Malik said: The *Harim* of a well for grasing and a farm well has no definite border, and neither of a spring, because of the difference of both lands. The former is a well in soft soil, and the latter in solid soil or in an unpolluted area, there is a difference; however, the prohibited area is not affected by that. The owner of the well has the right to prevent others from digging another well or something similar within his protective area. Because it is the right of his well, and a new well might harm it. Even if the digging of another does not harm the first well when the soil is solid, the first owner still has the right to prevent others because the area is for him to kneel his camel down and to rest his sheep and cattle.

Ibn Wahb narrated the tradition from Yunus, from Ibn Shihab from Ibn Musayyab. He also mentioned that the narration of Ibn al-Musayyab about the *adiyah* well and *badiyy* well is exactly similar to the previous one.

77- Discourse On A Man Who Prevents Others To Benefit From The Surplus Of His Well Water.

Master mason Muhammad said: Malik narrated a tradition in al-Muwatta': From Abu al-Rijal Muhammad b. Abd al-Rahman, from his mother Amra that the Prophet told her 'the surplus of well water should not be prevented from others'.[153] Abu al-Rijal Muhammad b. Abd al-Rahman also narrated from his mother Amra from Aishah that the Prophet said: the surplus of well water and the accumulated still water should not be prevented from others.[154]

Master mason Muhammad said: Abd al-Malik said in *al-Wadihah*: Al-Uwaisi narrated to me that the son of Abu al-Rijal heard his father say about *Naq'* and *Rahw*: It is still water that is not used for watering.

Master mason Muhammad said: The owner of the well has either a partner in the ownership of the well, and he prevents his partner benefiting from the surplus of the water; or he fully owns the well and prohibits others from benefiting the surplus.

If he has a partner who during his turn only occasionally watered his camels or his trees or when he does not water at all on a

---

[153] Narrated by Malik in *Muwatta* 2:745
[154] Narrated by Ahmad in *Musnad* 6:112,139,252,268

certain day. His other partner wants to utilize his portion, but the other wants to prevent it, saying: my turn still remains so the water is my right, I will do watering when I need, if not then I will preserve it and not going to give it to you'. Abdul al-Malik said from Mutarrif from Malik: He cannot prevent his partner from utilizing the water when he does not want to utilize it, and it does not harm him if he let his partner utilize it. This is the explanation for the tradition which say, 'the surplus of well water and still water should not be prevented from others'.

Master mason Muhammad said: as far as we know, there is no dispute about this.

Whereas there are three different opinions on whether people are to be prevented or not benefiting from the water from a privately owned well:

First Opinion: Ibn Habib said in *al-Wadihah*: I said to Mutarrif: How about a man who owned a well privately in the corner of his garden, and his neighbor who had no share in it wanted to utilize the man's surplus water for his own garden. Mutarrif said: I heard Malik say: he has no right on that, except if his own well is destroyed. Then he is allowed to use his neighbor's surplus water until he repairs his well. He (Malik) judged on that and that is part of the interpretation of *the Hadith*, which is, 'the surplus water of a well should not be prevented from others'. However, he should not delay to repair his well, indeed he should be asked to repair his well without any delay. Malik said: This is applicable to palm trees and cultivation, if without a functioning well, it would destroy the trees and cultivation. But he has no right to utilize his neighbor's surplus water if he wants to use it for new seedlings. Abd al-Malik said: I have asked Ibn al-Majashun about the matter and he said to me the same thing as Mutarrif said.

Master-mason Muhammad said: Ibn Abd al-Hakam and Asbagh reported from Ibn Wahb and Ibn al-Qasim the same opinion as what was said by Ibn Habib from Mutarrif and Ibn al-Majashun.

Second Opinion: There is a well between two adjacent farms and it is owned by one of them and he waters his garden using it. He has surplus water. The owner of the adjacent farm is in need of water for irrigation. He can utilize the surplus water, even if he does not have a share in it, and he does not have to ask for permission.

Third opinion: Ibn Nafi' and Isa b. Dinar said: He (owner of the well) must be commanded, and exhorted to give the surplus water so that the neighbor may use it for watering. But if he is reluctant to obey no action should be taken to force him to give his surplus water.

Master mason Muhammad said: There are four different opinions on whether the surplus water should be charged or not:

Malik said: These are about two persons; one of them owned a well in his garden. His neighbor who has no share in the well wants to utilize the surplus water from the well. Malik said: He has no right except to buy it from him. If his own well is broken, then he has the right to that surplus without paying anything. At the same time he has to repair his well. If there is no surplus water, then the neighbor will have nothing. This is also the opinion of Asbagh and Ibn Abd al-Hakam.

Master mason Muhammad said: This is the second opinion (of Malik): It is narrated in *al-Nawadir* from Malik: He may take the surplus with a price.

Third opinion: Ashhab said: If the neighbor, who needs the surplus water, is a rich man, he can be charged; but if he is a poor man, he can utilize the surplus without paying anything.

Fourth opinion: Abu Zayd said from Ibn al-Qasim: the neighbor may take the surplus with no charge except in a place where the water is valued there, he might be charged, and if not, then he is free to take it. Sahnun said: He must be charged for the water.

Master mason Muhammad said: The opinion of Ibn al-Qasim is more prominent and closer to the tradition when he said: if the water is valued then he must be charged, this is based on another tradition: 'taking the property of a Muslim is not lawful without his benevolance'.

78- Discourse On A Man Who Sells His Pasture.

Master mason Muhammad said: Ibn al-Qasim commented on the tradition of the Prophet: 'If you deny excess water, you will deny the benefits of pasture', and on another *hadith*, 'The surplus water should not be prevented from others'. He (Ibn al-Qasim) said: that applies to the wilderness, but it is allowed to cultivate grass in villages or stony areas, a man has a right to the pasture of his land when he needs it, if not he can leave it for others. This is the opinion of Malik. He said in another chapter: If he wants, he can sell it (the pasture). He said in another chapter: Malik said: It is allowed for a man to sell pasture from his land which is planted for a year, then after the new seedling grow and mature he would not sell it for two years. There is dispute on this, and we will elaborate on it soon.

Abdul al- Malik said: I was told by Mutarrif that he heard Malik say in his commentary on 'If you deny excess water, you will deny the benefits of pasture', that this applies on the well of animals in the desert, which are neither traded nor inherited. Nonetheless, those who dug or inherited it have priority over water than others. After they take their water, they may let others take the surplus. They do not have any right to prevent people from taking the surplus water. If they prevent it, it also prevents the growth of pasture, because people make use of pasture that grows around their well for their livestock. If they were prevented from taking the water, they were also prevented from taking the pasture. Ibn al-Majashun also has the same opinion.

Abd Al- Malik said: I asked Asbagh, and Ibn Abd al-Hakkam, and they both said: this is our opinion and the opinion of all our colleagues, and they narrated it from Malik. Ibn al-Qasim said: The (water) well for livestock and irrigation located in wasteland are originally not for sale. The surplus is also not for sale even if the need is there. However, surrounding people who used it have the right for watering and for their livestock, but they have no right to prevent people from taking the surplus. Peoples have the same right on it; whereas, the water from farm's well can be sold, because it is on private land. He said: Whoever has a well in his house or land he has the right to prevent others (from using it) or he can sell its water, or to prevent passers-by taking the water except with a price. If some people are really in need of water and without it they will perish, they cannot be prevented from taking the water, and they have a right to fight for it if prevented. He said: whatever well they dug for livestock or watering, which is not in their own land, cannot be prevented. They can fight for whoever prevents them. If the caravan is unable to defend themselves until they die because of thirst, then those who prevented them should pay the compensation.

79- Discourse On A Well Shared Between Two Neighbors Is Feared to Collapse.

Master mason Muhammad said: If there is a well shared between two persons and part of it collapses, and one of them wants to repair it but the other one refuses to join. There are two different opinions from Malik.

Yahya b. Yahya narrated in *al-'Utbiyah* from Ibn al-Qasim from Malik that he said: this is to say to the one who refuses, either you join your partner, compensate him or hire someone else to do the repair, or we buy your share and you cannot prevent your partner from benefiting on what he does to solve this damage'.

Second opinion: Malik said: He cannot be forced to join his partner to prevent the damage, but he can be forced to compensate if the well risks to collapse. Thereof the author said: from the book of Abdullah b. Abd al-Hakam: if there is a well shared between two people; one of them uses it for farming and then the water decreases, the other intends to dig another well, but was prevented by his partner saying: I am worried about the other one, and if in the opinion of the expert that the second well will harm the first one, then he has no right to do so, because the prophet said: *'la darar wa la dirar'*.

Malik said: If there is a well shared by two persons collapsing or clogging, and one of them wanted to repair it, but the other refuses; he who refuses would not get any water at all, even if there is a surplus, until he compensates his partner half of the total cost. Ibn Abd Al-Hakam reported this.

80- Discourse On A Well Shared Between Two Persons With Decreased Water, Shall One Of Them Be Forced To Repair It Or Not?

Master mason Muhammad said: Regarding the well or spring that is shared by two persons and the water decreases and one of them wants to repair it, but the other refuses; Malik in *al-'Utbiyah* said: this is to say to the one who refuses, either you join the work or you hire someone to do it, if not we would say to your partner, continue your work and the increase in the water that comes because of your work is completely yours, until your partner compensates half of your expenses.

Mutarrif and Ibn al-Majashun in *al-Wadihah* have the same opinion as reported by Ibn Habib. Ibn Habib also said: If a shared channel (*qanat*) or well used to water the land needs to be cleaned because the water is decreasing, some want to clean, but the others refuse since the water is enough for them but not for those who want to clean. The group who cleaned the channel (*qanat*) or well will get priority on any increase in the quantity of water over the others who refuse until they get compensated for their work. If they are compensated, then the distribution of water will be equal. 'Abdullah b. 'Abd al-Hakam has the same opinion. Master mason Muhammad said: I did not see any difference of opinion about it.

81- Discourse On The Method Of Digging A Well And Its Preparation.

Master mason Muhammad b. Ibrahim al-Rami said: Allah said in the Holy Quran: 'And We sent down out of heaven water blessed, and caused to grow thereby gardens and grain of harvest'[155], and in another He said, 'And We sent down out of heaven water in measure and lodged it in the earth; and We are able to take it away'[156]

Malik was asked about the interpretation of these verses, it was said to him: Does that refer to autumn? He answered: No, by the name of God! But that is in autumn and winter, and whenever Allah sends the water down from the sky as He will, and He is able to drain it off. He sends down all water on the earth from the sky and He allows it to remain, but He is also able to remove it.

Master mason Muhammad said: It is proven that all water is from the sky except four kinds of water which we will mention. Every kind of water from the earth is pure, but some is bitter, salty, or changes occur to its taste and color, and it varies according to different kinds of soil; because there are good and bad soil, Allah said: 'From the land that is clean and good, by the will of its creator, springs up produce, (rich) after its kind; But from the land that is bad springs up nothing but that which is scantily; Thus We explain the signs by various (symbols) to those who are grateful'[157].

This is our argument: Land with its loose rocky soil, whether it is white, red or yellow, and when we dig it to make a well until the water pours out, will produce sweet water (fresh water). Whereas a clayish soil, whether it is yellow, black or white when we dig a well in it and the soil does not change, will produce a water that

---

[155] Qaf: 9
[156] Al-Mu'minun: 18
[157] Al-Araaf, 58.

is salty, bitter and tingle depending on the composition of the soil that produced it.

If a well is dug in a clay soil, and the soil below changes into a loose type, it will produce sweet water depending on the amount of modification to the type of soil. If it is free from clay or anything of its kind then the water is pure. But, if it is mixed with clay, its nature will change according to the mixture of the soil. As for the sandy soil, if its soil is salty, then the water from it is bitter. But if it is a well located far from the salty area, it will produce fresh water. However, there is diversity in sandy soil. If the first stratum of the soil is sandy but the lower level is clay, it will produce pure water. That is all what I understood, experimented and consulted the expert on it.

Malik narrated: There are four rivers from heaven in the world: The Nile, Euphrates, the Sihan and the Jihan (the latter two, according to Arabic sources, are located in Anatolia).

Master mason Muhammad said: The places of water sources are varied in this world and the conditions also differ, for the experts have different opinions on its nature. And he also said: If a man wants to dig a well in his house, he will either deplete the well of his neighbor or does not affect it at all. If his well does not deplete the water of his neighbor's well and does not harm him, he could not be prevented from digging his well. If it does deplete the water of his neighbor's well, there are different opinions:

Malik in *al-'Utbiyah* said: A man has the right to dig a well in his house, except if it harms the neighbor with clear evidence that his well depletes the water of his neighbor.

Ibn Kinanah said: He has the right to dig a well on his property even if it harms his neighbor's well.

Ashhab said: If it is a newly created well, but not really needed, then he is prevented from digging. But if he really needs the well, he is allowed to dig even if it harms his neighbor's well.

Master mason Muhammad said: All can be summed up into four different opinions:

1. He can dig a well, even if his action harms his neighbor's well.
2. He has no right to dig if his action can cause harm to the neighbor's well.
3. The main differentiation is whether his well will sap the water from the neighboring well, or it will not.

4. The other differentiation is whether he has other options instead of digging a new one or not.

Al-Mutiti said: if a man wants to dig a well in his house, and his neighbor objected and said; you sap the water in my well by digging a new well. If the soil is solid, the expert said that there is no harm at all and he cannot be prevented. But if the soil is soft, and there is harm to his neighbor's well, then he should be prevented.

82- Discourse On A Man Digging A Well In His House, Whether He Should Be Prevented Or Not?

Master mason Muhammad said: If a man digs a well in his house he will either harm his neighbor's wall or his neighbor's well. If the digging causes harm to a neighbor's wall, he is definitely prohibited from doing so. But if it harms the neighbor's well, this was discussed before with several different opinions.

Digging well in a house, in my opinion, is different from that in a garden or farming area. Because garden and farming land need a lot of watering for trees and greens. When a person starts seedling or something like that, he needs extra water. If he has little water, he will seek other resources until his water supply becomes sufficient for seeding or planting. If another person digging a well nearby and causes his water level to decrease, insufficient for seedling and planting, this is a clear damage. To the one who digs a new well can be said, fill up your well and dig another one far away to avoid harming others. This is the argument for those who deal with gardening and farming.

Regarding a well for a ranch and farm, the owner needs sufficient water from the well for he has to provide drinks for his sheep and cows and watering the plants and so on. And when another person causes his water to decrease that is a big harm to him.

On the other hand, houses need little water. Houses only need a small quantity of fresh water for drinking. Asshab said about this: A man has no right to dig a well in his property that causes a problem to his neighbor. If he has another option, he should go for that. But if he cannot avoid it, then he has a right to dig a well even if this will harm his neighbor. This is the case because prohibition will harm him, as digging will harm the neighbor. It is better to ask his neighbor not to prevent him from digging a new well because it is on his own property.

Ibn Kinanah also said: He may dig a new well within his house, even though it will harm his neighbor. The Prophet said: *"La Darar Wa la Dirar"*. The majority of scholars conclude: If there are two harms, allowing the lesser is better. The person, who is prevented from digging a well in his house that does not harm the wall of his neighbor, is in a problem, since he cannot supply water for him and his family; whereas, the neighbor whose well water could decrease has less harm than him. The water only decreases a little since underground water still flows between them.

Ibn al-Qasim said regarding the close proximity of Houses: If a neighbor digs a well or latrine in their house and this causes harm to the older well, he should be prevented and the well should be filled up.

Thereof Master mason Muhammad said: Ibn al-Qasim said in *al-Nawadir*: Whoever digs a well far away from the neighbor's well, but still causes the water of the neighbor's well to stop running, and if it is proven that the new one is the cause then it must be filled up and destroyed.

Ibn al-Qasim also said in *al-Nawadir*: He who digs a well in others property or in the public street or in another person's land without the owner's permission or beside a well for livestock without prior permission from the owner and causes harm to it, is prohibited to do so. If a man or animal is injured or perishes because of it, the one who dug it must be responsible. Malik said: whoever digs a well illegally, is responsible for whatever mishap caused by it.

Master mason Muhammad said: It is said in *Mufid al-Hukkam* by Ibn Hisham that: Asbagh mentioned about a man who digs a well in his house that harms the neighbor's house and the neighbor claimed that the new well caused harm to his well. According to Asbagh the new well should not be closed until the evidence is clear that the water of the neighbor's well has been sapped into his well. Al-Mutiti said in *al-Mutitiyah*: If the soil is soft, he is prohibited, but if the soil is hard, then he is allowed to dig a well. Thereof: Ibn al Hakam said in his book: If a man digs a well in his house adjacent to the wall of his neighbor, but it is harmless to the wall, he should be allowed to do that. Thereof: Asbagh said regarding wells in houses: If a man digs a well and his neighbor digs another well that saps the water from the former, the latter should be prevented, because it creates harm. Whereas if they both started at the same time and it is clearly done in a good manner with a lot of expenses, I do not think one of them should be prevented to save the other. However, if the location of both wells are too close to each other and there is clear harm, such as one of the wells is not functioning, then both wells have to be covered. The reason is both cause harm to each other, until they move away from each other in a good manner.

Master mason Muhammad said: A case happened in Tunis when a man dug a well in his house adjacent to his wall. Behind his wall is a cistern belonging to his neighbor. The owner of the cistern said: Your well harms my cistern because it is too close to the wall of the cistern. Both of them brought their case to al-Sheikh al-Qadi Abu Ishaq 'Abd al-Rafi'. He then ordered us to investigate whether there is harm or not. We saw that the cistern is very close to the well or almost touching it. We reported the matter to the Judge and we told him: if the cistern was left alone (without the well), it would remain strong and safer, we are worried that the cistern will break down because it is too close to the well. Thus, he ordered the well to be filled up and covered firmly with a heavy stone to make its closure permanent.

Master mason Muhammad said: Ibn Kinanah said about a man who digs a well in his house and another one has a water tank nearby. The owner of the well told the owner of water tank:

I will dig for you a well in your house, but remove your water tank from my side. Ibn Kinanah said: He has no right to do that except if the owner agrees on that, with the assumption that the well might harm his (owner of the water tank) house.

83- Discourse On The Water Spring That Belongs To A Man and Its Water Leaks Into A Neighboring Plot.

Master mason Muhammad said: Asbagh said in *al-Nawadir* written by al-Sheikh Abu Muhammad 'Abdullah b. Abu Zayd about a water spring belonging to a man in his plot and adjacent to him was his neighbor's land. A secondary spring flowed through his neighbor's property and he wanted to cut it off, fearing that his water level will decrease. If the neighbor did not create it intentionally or did not dig it to allow the water to flow toward him, the owner of the spring does not have any right to prevent the water from his neighbor since this is a gift from God and no one can deny it to him. Whereas, if he intentionally digs it up and intended to channel the water toward his land with his own effort, he should be prevented, and the owner of the spring can prevent his neighbor from benefiting from it and shut the flow of water from his land.

Master mason Muhammad said: This is what Ibn al-Qasim and others said, and I do not see differing opinions about this case.

84- Discourse On A Man Who Wants To Channel His Water Through Neighboring Land To His Other Property.

Master mason Muhammad said: Asbagh said in *al-Nawadir*: A man owned a land, which had water, and he had another land far from the first one. A land belonged to another person, stood between his two properties. The man wanted to channel his water from the first property to the second through his neighbor's land. The neighbor refused to let this happen. Malik has two opinions on this:

Ibn al-Qasim narrated from Malik: The neighbor has the right to prevent him. Malik's opinion did not take into account a tradition narrated by Omar al-Khattab regarding an open channel belonging to 'Abd Al-Rahman and another tradition regarding a tributary belonging to al-Dahhak. Malik feared that people might take for granted that they have total right to channel their water through others' land. He said: If people in our time behaved like their forefathers during 'Umar's time, they can do that. This opinion is based upon the tradition, that is based on the Prophet who said: 'Taking the property of a Muslim person is not lawful without his consultative consent'.

Second opinion: Ibn Nafi from Malik: He has the right.

Master mason Muhammad said: This kind of arrangement usually happened between Bedouins. They run their water through each other's land. None of them prevent their neighbors from channeling water through their land, if theirs is not fully utilized. But if their land is fully planted and well irrigated, I do not think it will happen. It is inappropriate for someone with a vacant land to deny his neighbor from channeling the water through his land, since it will not harm him and will benefit his neighbor. But he cannot be forced to give his permission. Two trusted Bedouins who are expert in agriculture and irrigation told me that: the flow of water through empty land will harm it especially the area nearer to the channel. It will make the land salty, especially after one year. But if the water flows through planted land, it will improve the quality of the land especially around the channel.

Opinions also differed on a water channel belonging to a man flowing through his neighbor's land. The owner of the water channel wanted to alter the route to be nearer to his land or to improve the flow of water. In this case, the opinion also differed in two as cited by al-Sheikh Abu 'Abdullah b. Abi Zaid in *al-Nawadir*.

The citation for the first opinion of *al-Majmu'ah* Ashhab narrated from Malik: let people decide according to their custom on water channels, and it should be referred to an expert. If our community affairs are as harmonious (straight forward) as during the time of 'Umar b. Al-Khattab, I would let him channel his water through the other's land; because there is no trickery and harm is not inflicted, but people have changed and like to claim benefits for themselves, and I am afraid that when time passes by, people will forget the custom of passing water through their land, and they will claim others' property as theirs. Ibn Kinanah said the same thing; he ignored the tradition about Dahhak; because people are getting more corrupted.

Master-mason Muhammad said: Ziyad narrated from Malik regarding 'Abdul Rahman b. Auf's water channel that passed through the land of Amru b. Yahya al-Mazini's grandparent.

Abdul al-Rahman wanted to relocate his water channel to be nearer to his land, but the landowner refused to give his permission. Omar al-Khattab decided to let the water channel course be changed.[158]

Malik said: If the water channel does not harm the land, then it should be allowed to run through, but if it's harmful to the land then it should be prevented from changing its course.

As regards to the tradition of Dahhak b. Khalifah who wanted to run a stream through the land of Muhammad b. Maslamah, and Omar al-Khattab decided that Dahhak had the right to do that.

Thereof master mason Muhammad said: In *al-'Utbiyah* Asshab was asked: If I have a land, and next to it is a land that belongs to another. Beyond his land is my spring and I have no access to it except through his land, but he prevented me the right of passage to the spring. Ashhab answered: if your neighbor's land was

---

[158] This tradition (*athar*) is narrated by Malik in his *Muwatta*, hadith no 34 2:746

revived after reviving your land and the spring, then you have the right to pass through. But if his land was revived before your land and spring, then you have no right of passage to your spring through his land, and also you cannot create a channel through his land to draw the water.

Thereof master mason Muhammad said: From *al-Majmu'ah* Ashhab narrated from Malik regarding a person who died and left behind an idle land without any cultivation. He had no other property except this one. So the land was subdivided by his heirs and they sold it. The buyers then cultivated it; some of them irrigated it and some of them leased it. Things went on for almost forty years until they had forgotten the earlier arrangement. Later on some of them sold their land, then, the new buyer said to the one who channeled their water through his land: I will not let your channel pass through my land. The other one said: This water channel passed through this land for the last forty years, Malik said: They should bring their case to the judge and let him examine the original division and then they should abide by that. If there is no evidence of any change that took place they should stay with the original arrangement, and the new owner cannot prevent the other one from drawing the water through his land.

85- Discourse On What Is Essential On *Ijarah*[159] And *Ju'l*[160] In Digging A Well.

Master mason Muhammad said: From *al-Tabsirah* of al-Lakhmi, he said: Digging a well can be done through three kinds of contracts: *Ujrah* (Hiring), *Muqata'a* (piece work)[161] and *Ji'alah* (reward). As for *Ijarah* and *Muqata'a*, it has to be agreed to a contract and it should be mentioned whether the land belongs to an owner or not.

As for the *ji'alah*, it does not need a contract. Yet one, who is given a job (*Maajul alaih*), has an option according to the famous opinion of the Maliki School and in addition *ji'alah* is allowed on land not owned by *Jail*. Whereas it is disputed when

---

[159] The contract of hire
[160] A contract in which the entitlement to wages depends upon the completion of the task, that is, the contract entered into by independent contractors.
[161] A contract in which the worker will be paid according to the work he finishes. See N. Ghattas, *A Dictionary of Economic, Business and Finance*. Librairie du Liban, 1985. p.417

the *Jail* owned the land; Ibn al-Qasim allowed to apply the contract of *ji'alah* in agricultural land whereby the landlord retained the ownership. Also applies to digging a well. Hiring for digging a well is different according to the different types of soil; it is either hard or soft, distance of water and the skills of the digger on soil conditions.

Master mason said: from *al-Mudawwanah*, Ibn al-Qasim said as Malik said: *Ijarah* (hiring) is accepted for well digging (by specifying) the place and how deep it should be. Yahya said: Ibn al-Qasim said: If both of them are familiar with the type of soil; its softness, hardness, or both were not familiar with it at all, then (the contract of hiring) is allowed. If one of them is familiar but not the other, then hiring is not allowed.

Abu al-Zanad[162] said in *al-Mudawwanah*: It is a duty of the well digger to draw off the water. Rabia'h[163] said: It is applicable to the place where water is easily available; however, if the water is difficult to dig up, then I prefer the (contract of) *muzaraah*[164]. Ibn Yunus said: It is allowed to dig a well and compensated by the number of days of (hiring).

Master-mason Muhammad said: Ibn Hisham mentioned in his *Ahkam*: When the hirer says to the hired person: I hire you to dig a well at this site, and he did not add anything (additional conditions) to that, it is allowed except if the custom differed on the size (of the well), then he should mention the size. If both are familiar with the features of the soil but disagreed on how accessible is the water, then this should not be allowed. If they differed on the features of the soil, but agreed on how deep it should be to get the water, it is allowed on the condition that both agree on any increase in payment due to the hardship in digging that well. Compensation is based on the type of soil

Master mason said: This is contrary to what Ibn Habib has said in *al-Wadihah* that: It is not allowed unless the worker is made aware of the land's hardness and how deep to get the water.

---

[162] He is Abdullah b. Zakuan al-Qarashi Abu Abd al-Rahman al-Madani (d. 130/748) one of the Muhaddithin of Madinah. See al-Suyuti, Tabaqat al-Huffaz 54-56.

[163] Rabiah b. Abd Rahman.

[164] Share-cropping; an agreement between two parties in which one agrees to allow a portion of his land to be used by the other in return for a part of the produce of the land.

Ibn Hisham said in his *Ahkam*: If he works under the contract of *Ju'l* (reward) and after completing the job, the well cracks; the digger still has a right to his reward. If the cracks appeared before the job was finished, he gets nothing. If he digs the well and then he leaves it, he gets nothing. If the hirer (reward giver) fixed a reward to a worker (*ajir*) and then he accomplishes it, the first worker should return to the one who assigned him to claim his reward on the day when the second worker finishes his work; whether the value is based on present work or fixed by contract (*musamma*), regardless less or more. Ibn Hisham said: This is according to the opinion of Malik and Ibn Kinanah.

Ibn Habib said in *al-Wadihah*: If the well cracks before the completion, then in the guaranteed reward (*Ji'l al-Madhmun*), he gets nothing unless he finishes his work. But if he worked under contract of hiring, he will get the payment according to what he did as long as the well is not broken due to his bad workmanship. If the well is destroyed after the completion, the digger will get full payment and the trouble is upon the landowner except when the well is destroyed by his bad workmanship and thus he gets nothing.

Master-mason Muhammad said: He should compensate what the landowner has spent on the tools and others if the destruction is caused by his bad workmanship. And according to our custom in well digging: hiring and piece job (*Muqata'a*) is the preferred choice, whereas by *Jiaala* (reward) I do not know anyone who assigns his well by way of reward, so too in building. According to our custom, the (depth of) well digging is measured by way of a man's height (*qama*) in a manner that both agree, such as five or ten, or more or less with such and such according to the width of such well. So the worker begins digging and whatever ground he cuts or bores using axes to complete his job is in accordance to the agreed depth of the well. The worker has no right to complain of the hardness of the ground he digs, whereas the employer has no right to protest about the softness of the ground that makes digging easy. If a rock is causing an obstacle to the worker in achieving the desired depth as agreed by both parties, this depends on whether the difficult part is one hand-span wide, or what is approximate to that, and can be done using an axe. It is a duty of the digger to continue digging the well, with no obligation on the well owner to hire (someone else) for help. If the difficulty is more than that, then it is the responsibility of the well owner. That is according to our custom, and this is how we resolve such disputes between the hirer and the hired person when the judge refers such a case to us, or when both come to us without a judge.

Master-mason Muhammad said: From Ibn Hisham's book: The guaranteed (*daman*) in the contract of digging a well is that the worker deals with the well owner to dig the well until it reaches the water, assuring that the wages and the tools are upon him (well owner). Additionally, he the digger should not abandon the job. If the well owner dies, he could take the money from his estate. Ibn Hisham also said: Likewise, if he works on the well shaft, the assurance is on him (the worker) when he (the hirer) describes the rock and the cost of the well.

Master-mason Muhammad said: The contract of *Muajalah* in the digging of the well is: If you reached such and such, you would get a wage such and such; however, if you did less, you would get nothing and you may relinquish the work whenever you wish and the tools are on the reward giver (*ja'il*). Consequently, the digger is not forced to finish the burrowing and could not take anything for his work.

Ibn al-Majashun said: If a rock is an obstacle that prevents the digger from digging the well, then he should not receive any reward or guarantee unless the well owner might benefit from the work of the digger (for instance) for a toilet or other purposes; so he should give the digger according to what he benefited from his work, whereas in case of *ijarah* (hiring): he is paid in accordance to what he does until the rock prevents him to continue. Ibn Habib said: That is also the explanation given to me by the companions of Malik.

Hiring (*muajarah*) in the well digging: The contract is: I hire you for digging this well, excluding its inner casing (*tayy*) or with its inner casing until you finish those entire things or you should do that within ten days. The tools and the workers (*ujara*), if needed while constructing inner casing, are on the well owner, so too with the contract to build a house or the like. In case, if the digger passes away before completing the digging, he has the right to receive (for the next of kin?) according to what he worked in contrary to the contract of *mujaa'lah*.

181

86- Discourse On A Man Hiring Two Men To Dig A Well For Him, One Of Them Fell Sick After Starting Their Work.

Master mason Muhammad said: Regarding a man who hired two laborers to dig a well, after starting their work for some time, one of them fell sick so the other one completed the job. However, it was disputed whether he could get paid for work done that was supposed to be done by the other laborer?

Ibn al-Qasim said in *al-Mudawwanah*: It is said to the sick person: Compensate the digger who completed your work, but if he refuses no judgment can be passed over him if the other's work is regarded as being volunteered. Sahnun said in other than *al-Mudawwanah*: The digger's work is volunteered to the owner, not to the sick laborer.

Master-mason Muhammad said: Some scholars from Qairawan quoted Ibn al-Qasim by saying that: If both are partners, it is an obligation on the other partner towards the disability of the other. If both are not partners, then each one has to dig his portion. If one of them digs what was not assigned to him, it is not necessary for the owner to pay wages; it is like a man who sews another person's cloth or he who cultivates a land voluntarily (without the owner's consent), he will receive nothing.

Master-mason Muhammad said: The opinion of Sahnun was that when the worker got sick, the contract of hiring is automatically voided; for, it is a matter that could not be mitigated such as the death of a beast of burden during traveling. If the cancellation is compulsory with his sickness, and if a judge does not consider it as necessary (*darura*) the dug ground reverts to the landowner and thus his partner has no right to dig the ground that belonged to the other partner when he was sick.

Master-mason Muhammad said: Ibn Hisham said in his book *al-Ahkam*: The opinion of Ibn al-Qasim probably stands for guaranteed hiring (*al-Ijarah ala az-zimmah*) whereas the opinion of Sahnun probably stands for the hiring that is upon the ability of both (to finish the job). If it is a guaranteed hiring and the correct digging occurs at the early sickness of his partner, the opinion of Ibn al-Qasim is valid to the extent that it is a voluntary job. Because the sick partner may say: What is between you and me is that you should be patient until I can dig with you. If (the sick partner) continued his work after a long period of illness, then he is entitled to get the minimum payment for the fixed contract or similar payment that the other worker received. If the time of his hiring is short, he has no right except for the equal wage, but if the hiring of the other is less because of the quality of the work done. The sick partner can say: I have a right to come with someone who will make less than you are making and the well owner has no right over me when there is no defect in the well because of me, nor the right because of the sickness being short or long; for his work is assured but rather it is his duty on what is between two workers. If the hiring is on the ability of both to complete the job, the sick partner does not deserve a wage from his partner's digging; whether his partner dug during the earlier part of his sickness or later.

87- Discourse On Hiring (*Ijarah*) And Wage (*Ju'l*) In A Construction Work.

Master mason Muhammad said: From *al-Mudawwanah*, Ibn al-Qasim said: Whoever is hired to construct a house, the construction tools, axes, a large bucket, water, leather bucket are according to the custom of local people. If they do not have any tradition on that, all the construction tools are upon the owner of the house, together with the stone chisel. He who was employed by the house owner to erect a wall as described by the owner and he built half of it, then the wall falls down, he should be paid the sum for what he has built; for, he is entitled to what he has built; and he should not have to build it for a second time; whether the brick and soiis from you (the owner) or on him. Others said: He should be held responsible until he completes the work.

Ibn Yunus said: This is also stated in *al-Ummahat*, narrated by Abu Muhammad: and others said: This is the work of the man himself and he must be responsible until he completes the work. Based on al-*Ummahat*, others have different opinions of Ibn al-Qasim's saying on an appointed (hired) man; whereas based on a report narrated by Abi Muhammad others were in agreement. Sahnun said: I would refer back the problem to the problem of the wall.

Master mason Muhammad said: Ibn Yunus transmitted from some of the scholars from Qairawan, they said: it is possible what Ibn al-Qasim meant is that the wall owner should erect the portion that was damaged, then the hired man should build the rest to complete the building. Thus the hiring contract is still valid for the rest of the job, if it is possible for him to build what was damaged for him (the owner). Or he finds a place similar to the previous one to build for the owner, except if he asks to be excused, then the rest of the contract is null and void. As to what Ashhab said if he (owner) hired someone to harvest for him on a plot of land, then it spoils: the appointment is null and void, in contrary to Ibn al-Qassim opinion: that it is not void.

Master mason Muhammad said: so too if it was damaged due to an act of God, that was not caused by bad workmanship; if the damage is caused by bad workmanship, then the hiring is not void, and the builder is obliged to rebuild and be held responsible on what was spent from the wages and tools.

Ibn Habib said in *al-Wadihah*: It does not matter to build based on *mujaalah* or *muaajirah* on the condition that it is guaranteed. So too with digging a well. If the worker observed the condition of the land and the water is easy to get, and if the structure is damaged and the well broke down before it was completed; on the assured contract, there is nothing to him until he accomplishes his work. However, if he is hired on a fee basis he should be paid according to what he did as long as the damage is not caused by his bad workmanship. And if it was totally destroyed after the completion, then he has the right for his whole wage. The owner of the land should absorb the consequences of the destruction, but if the damage is due to bad workmanship, then he gets nothing.

88- Discourse On Dividing The House By *Muzaraah* And On Dividing Building And Courtyard And What Is Necessary To Be Included.

Master mason said: From the book of *al-Tanbihat* by al-Qadhi I'yad: the division (is defined as) to fairly set apart a right according to our *madhhab* and opinion of our *imam*, even though Malik considers it just like a sale. The opinion of Ibn al-Qasim and Sahnun were confusing (on what we had mentioned) of the two foundations; is *Qismah* a separation of the right or a sale. There is no binding disagreement when it happens according to the correct feature. It falls into four categories: -

Division by judgment and force (*Qismah hukm wa Ijbar*), it is division by shares and lots. It must be based on equalization (*ta'dil*), valuation (*taqwim*) and adjustment (*taswiyah*), on things that cannot be weighted and measured. The partition of lots is not to be adjusted by adding *dirhams* or *dinars* (money) or anything that is different from what is being divided by both sides.

Division by consent and valuation (*Qismah muradat wa taqwim*) of different or similar categories, is not permissible by lots. Whereas Ibn al-Qasim and others did not permit it by lots; for, because ballot casting denies consent. Thereupon a partition into lots is not permitted according to Ibn al-Qasim when the category is not similar, whereas Ashhab allowed it. Ibn al-Qassim's opinion on the permissibility of the division is deduced from his answer to the problem regarding the tree and olives.

As for division by consent without equalization, the rule is like the rule on sale in every aspect. The division is not to be revoked because of cheating as it is not to be revoked because of cheating in a sale.

Revocation is allowed in case of cheating in the first two categories; however simple fraud is excusable in the matter of division of consent. However, there is a disagreement in simple fraud in dividing through the drawings of lots such as one dinar or two dinars from a larger sum.

Abu Muhammad Bin Abu Zaid and others thought: that is excusable while others declined. They said: the division is annulled; because the judgment is incorrect, it must be nullified, since there is no difference between simple (fraud) and big (fraud). This opinion is clear in *al-Mudawwanah* and it is the opinion of Ashhab and Ibn Habib, the same opinion is also narrated in *al-Mabsut*.[165]

It was said: division of the divisor is like the judgment of the judge, which cannot be revoked except by a clear mistake.

Division of *Muhaya'ah*: it is a division of the benefits by consent and not by force through partitions into lots. It was said by *a nun (muhana'ah)*; because everyone is happy to own what he prefers. It was said with *ya (muhaya'ah)*, for every one tries to facilitate what the other requested from him. This type has two categories; division based over time and division (by the use of) the things itself. It is generally permissible, but they differed in their subdivisions such as yields (*al-ghillah*) or services or residence in a house, the house, the slave, and the land, and other than that as inferred in our principles and books of our masters.

---

[165] *Al-Mabsut* is a famous book in the Maliki School written by al-Qadhi Ismail b. Ishaq b. Ismail al-Azdari, from Iraq (d. 282/895). See *Tartib al-Madarik* 2:179.

Thereof Master mason Muhammad said: the text as in *al-Mudawwanah* from Ibn al-Qassim: if they divided a house by measurement and then partitioned into lots, and if each part of the house is of similar quality, it is permissible. If some parts are better than the others, or everything is equal except one side has more than the other, then it is not permissible.

Master mason Muhammad said: this, if the division is by measurement and partition into lots, on the other hand, if the division is without partition into lots; which some of the divisions are better than the other, or each of the divisions is equal except one side has more than the others, and they are consenting to that, then it is allowable; all these are the opinion of Ibn al-Qasim in *al-Mudawwanah*.

He also said: It does not matter to divide the building by valuation, and the courtyard by measurement, if it is equal in value and measure and it (courtyard) is divisible, but if it would become unequal, then it is not allowed.

Ibn al-Qasim said: If they wished to divide both the building and courtyard, and if each of them would take benefit from the division of the courtyard, such as for the entrance and exit and a place to tie animals and others, then the division of the courtyard could be done together with the building. If the benefit would belong to some of them and the other, who has a less share, would not benefit except for the entrance and exit only, then the building can be divided among them but the courtyard should be left undivided for both to benefit. So the one who has a smaller share among them has the same right in the courtyard as well as the one who possess more, either he (who possess a smaller share) lives with them or not.

89- Discourse Between Partners In Utilizing The Courtyard.

Master mason Muhammad said: When they divided a house by consent without distribution of lots with the condition that they should leave the courtyard for their benefit. And each of them possessed the house while some of them wished to build in the courtyard nearer to his house that would be beneficial to him. Hence, Ibn al-Qasim said: He has no right to do that and his partner has the right to prevent him.

Master mason Muhammad said: If a quarrel occurred regarding the usage of the courtyard, and the one with bigger share says: I utilize it as per my share, and the owner of the smaller share said:

we should use it equally, then there are two opinions regarding this problem:

Ibn al-Qasim said: They should use it equally, not to be based on the size of the share. Others said: According to the size of the shares, this opinion is not practiced whereas the well-known practice is what we have previously mentioned.

Ibn al-Qasim said: each one has priority on what is in front of his house and the division cannot be forced on the one who refused to divide until both of them can benefit from the houses and open spaces, and each one benefits from what belongs to him.

Ibn al-Qasim also said in *al-Mudawwanah*: If some of them wished to discharge the fodder (*al-I'lf*) and firewood in front of the door of others, then they should not do so, even if the area is wide.

90- Discourse On Dividing A Double Storey House And What Is Necessary For That.

Master mason Muhammad said: If there is a house (*dar*)[166] with an upper floor and they wish to divide it into lots; Ibn al-Qasim said in *al-Mudawwanah*: when a house belong to people and consisted of chambers (*buyut*) and courtyard with rooms and roof terrace; then they divided the building based on the value and the courtyard remaines undivided, while the roof terrace attached to the building and the room remains as facilities. The owner of the upper floor has the right to utilize the courtyard of the lower floor as the owner of the lower floor can utilize the higher roof terrace because it is not considered as *fina'*. Ibn al-Qasim adds the value of the roof terrace's beams and the room together with the price of the chambers, which are below that.

Master mason Muhammad said: what I meant by the room's beams are the beams of the lower floor's room. (The owner of lower floor should repair it) what is broken or decayed from the beams of the upper floor, which is the floor of the upper room and roof terrace, because he owns it, so it is for him to repair, this is a unanimous opinion among the scholars. The dispute about the beam, whose door of the lower and upper floor are owned by a different person was discussed earlier (see Discourse # 37).

---

[166] Dar: according to the Hanafite School, is bigger than Manzil and Bait.

Master mason Muhammad said: as for what have been mentioned on dividing the house, that one of them takes the upper while another man takes the lower, scholars differed in their opinion as follows:

Al-Sheikh Abu 'Imran[167] and other scholars from Qairawan said: the division must be by consent; this is based on his answer, referred to in the book of division in *al-Mudawwanah*. As by partition into lots: there is dispute whether it is permitted or not? Some scholars from Qairawan said that division by partition into lots is not permissible: the upper in my opinion is not similar to the courtyard, and it is only useful because of its air space. How can a man take the foundation and the other takes the utilities without anything from the courtyard except he considers the staircase to the upper floor as part of the courtyard, even though it reduces its size. It is also reported from Abu 'Imran that it is permissible, even if the division is by partition into lots.

Master mason Muhammad said: the opinion of Ibn al-Majashun from his book: if the division is without partition into lots, then it is permissible. But if it is with the intention of dividing to equalize with necessary adjustments, then it is not permissible. Ibn Sha'ban said: That is not permissible except by consent, and it is not permitted by partitioning into lots.

Thereof: the author said: Likewise, if both of them wished to divide on the condition that the entrance belongs to one of them and for the other the right of passage, then it is not permitted. This is the view of Sahnun; but if both of them agreed, then it is permitted.

Master mason Muhammad said: from al-*Mutitiyah*: if they divided and one of them gets the upper floor while the other gets the lower floor of the house and both did not clarify to the owner of the upper floor regarding the entrance and water channel, then the upper floor resident has the right to use the old entrance and water channel. This is on the condition that it also can be used by the lower owner, whereas the owner of upper floor can swerve that to such a direction that he would be able to use it, and he should not be prevented from that (see the interpretation in the following Discourse # 91).

---

[167] He is Abu Imran Musa bin Isa bin Abi Hajjaj al-Ghafjumi, from Fez, but lived in Qairawan and became their leading scholar. Died in the year 430/1039. See *Tartib al-Madarik* 4:702-706

91- Discourse On Division Of The House And The Silence About The Entrance, Water Channel, And Screen, And What Is Necessary For That.

Master mason Muhammad said: if two men divided a house, saying nothing about the entrance, exit and water channel. The entrance, exit and the outer channel happened to belong to one of them, and the owner prevented the other from using those facilities, then there are three opinions about that:

First opinion: Ibn al-Qasim said in *al-Mudawwanah*: the subdivision is valid and both of them share the entrance, exit and water channel that links to its original location, and its access belongs to the person who owns it.

Second opinion: Ibn Habib said: the division is void until they clarify a way out for each to share its entrance and exit.

Third opinion: Isa bin Dinar said: if the shareholder who owned the portion that has no door and no waste water channel, if he opens a door and discharges his waste water without causing damage to himself, then the division remains as it is.

Thereof master mason Muhammad said: As for the screen, if both said nothing about that, and if one of them wants to build a screen while the other refuses; the one who refuses cannot be forced. It is said to the other: screen equally, if the owner of the smaller share disputes after he has made the hall and the building as per his share, but the other refuses except for sharing it equally, the latter is right. The owner of the smaller share is obliged to bear the cost as much as the owner of the bigger share, because, both are equal in screening until the building is well screened. Master mason Muhammad said: I did not find any limitation as far as I know about that, or any disagreement on the equality of (sharing) the screen. Master mason Muhammad said: if both divided so that one of them has the exit to the upper floor while another has the exit at lower floor of the house. If both did not build for the owner of the upper floor (a new) entrance and water channel, then the upper floor resident has the right to use the old entrance and water channel on the condition that it also can be used by the owner of the lower floor. In the meantime, the owner of upper floor can swerve to such a direction that he would be able to utilize it. He is not to be prevented from that.

92- Discourse On Unacceptable Conditions In Division Due to Its Harm.

Master mason Muhammad said: From *al-Mudawwanah*, Ibn al-Qasim said that Malik said: if two men divided a building by consent; one of them obtained the rear side of the building while the other acquired the front side with the condition that the owner of the rear building has no access to the outside, it is permitted if both of them are satisfied and if he (owner of the rear building) has a space to create an access door, if not then it is not permitted.

Master mason Muhammad said: Likewise, if they divided a house on condition that one of them took a room without a right to utilize an exit through the lower floor; and if the owner of the room has a space to build an access door to his room, then it is permitted and if not, it is not permissible.

The author said: likewise if both of them divided a land on condition that none of them can create a lane on the other's property, and one of them has no entrance, then the division is not permitted. This is not a Muslim's way of dividing a property, and this is the opinion of Ibn al-Qasim in *al-Mudawwanah*.

Master mason Muhammad said: In *al-Mudawwanah*, Ibn al-Qasim also said from Malik: if they divided a spacious house which each of them can use its ancillaries, but they have no exit except for the (only) main door of the house. They disagreed over the width of the lane; some of them said: make it three cubits wide, others said: more than that, I would make it (the lane) sufficient for a loaded camel and their porters to pass through. Ibn al-Qasim was asked: should it be left to them to decide according to the width of the door? He said: I do not know Malik's opinion about this.

Master mason Muhammad said: Our custom regarding the doors is that it is narrower than the street. Hence, one walks in the street in convenience without being tired and it does not harm him when passing through the door due to its narrowness when what is before and after is spacious. If the street is similar to the width of the door, then it is harmful to many passers by due to the narrowness and length of the passage. This problem happened to us in a rural area, where I divided a building between them and they disagreed on the width of the road. Then I decided on a measurement of eight hand-spans that allows a camel to pass through and it should not be less than that.

93- Discourse On The Litigation Between Two Partners On A Chamber (Of The House) After Division.

Master mason Muhammad said: in *al-Mudawwanah* Ibn al-Qasim said: Two men divided a house, but the contract was delayed. Later both of them disagreed on a chamber of the house and each one claimed it for himself, but both had no proof. Such a matter calls for a careful study; if one of them possessed it, then he has a right to it after taking an oath. But if he abstained and the other takes the oath, then it is his. If it was not in the possession of one of them, both of them should take an oath, and then the division is canceled.

Master mason Muhammad said: Likewise, if two men disagreed on the boundary of the building's courtyard, with each of them encroaching upon each other's side without any proof. If both of them divided the house and the courtyard separately, both of them should take the oath for the courtyard and the courtyard should be redivided. However, if the division of the courtyard and the house was in one negotiation, then both should take an oath and the division should be entirely nullified.

94- Discourse On All Divisions And What Is Necessary For That.

Master mason Muhammad said: The basis of division is God's saying: ...whether the property is small or large, a legal share[168]. Malik established his opinion on this problem and it was narrated that he said: the bathroom, cistern (*al-majil*), the land, the small house and the small shop in the market can be divided even if it does not benefit them. Malik also said in *al-Majmu'ah*: the people of Medina followed this principle even if some of them got what was useless to them.

Ibn al-Qasim said: I believe that everything which is indivisible and is not useful be it a house or a land or a bathhouse should not be divided, but it should be sold and its proceeds can be divided; as the Prophet said: *"La Darar Wa la Dirar"* Do not harm others or yourself, and others should not harm you or themselves. So

---

[168] Al-Nisa: 7, the full text is: From what is left by parents and those nearest related there is a share for men and a share for women, whether the property be small or large, a determinate share.

too with the cistern except when each one has an individual cistern, which is beneficial, then it could be divided.

Master mason Muhammad said: In *al-Wadihah* of Ibn Habib from Mutarrif from Malik: the land could be divided, even though it is small and each one does not get (anything) except as little as a stick (*marwad*). Ibn Habib narrated from Abu Hanifah like what Malik said.

Master mason Muhammad said: This opinion is unusual because no one of Malik's companions agreed except Ibn Kinanah, and the rest of his companions from Medina and Egypt disagreed with him. They said the meaning of God's saying: whether the property be small or large, a legal share, it's meaning is to demarcate it, little or much, and then divide it according to the Prophet's tradition, and to rule out any damage; for the Prophet said: *"La Darar Wa la Dirar"* Do not harm others or yourself, and others should not harm you or themselves; and of the biggest harm is to divide what is useless for them, but it should be sold and the proceeds should be divided.

Mutarrif said and what I believe: when some of them would benefit because of his larger share, while it narrows the others' share due to its small size, then according to Malik it can be divided. But if the division does not benefit either one of them because of its smaller share, then it should be sold and the proceeds divided. Ibn al-Majashun said: whether both have small shares or one of them will have a small share, even if one of them will own a smaller portion then it should not be divided. But if the smaller portion is still beneficial compared to the larger one, and it does not cause any damage to the holder of the smaller share, the division is valid.

95- Discourse On Indivisible Things, And How To Divide Water.

Master mason Muhammad said: In *al-Mudawwanah*, Ibn al-Qasim said: Springs and wells are indivisible, but the drinking water can be divided with a kettle. A water channel is also indivisible and I do not know anyone who allowed it (i.e. to be divided).

Master mason Muhammad said: Ibn Habib said in *al-Wadihah*: the explanation on subdividing the water with kettles is that when two persons argue on that matter, the leader (*imam*) should command two trusted men or he gathers the relatives with the consent of both persons. Both of them take a clay kettle or the like, then drill a hole at the bottom and hang both kettles over a pot chamber, and both collect some water in a jar, then in the early morning, pour the water into the both kettles and let it flows out from the hole. Whenever the water is emptied, pour again until the water flows from the hole consistently night and day till the next morning. Then count the water and divide what has been collected from the water to fewer shares of them by measuring or weighing. Next both of them give each relative certain measure that stands for their share of the water and they drill a hole on each kettle with a driller used to drill the first one. When one of them wishes to irrigate, hang his kettle and pour all the water to his land and the water poured from his kettle would irrigate his land. Then that's the way to divide; if they are greedy initially, (later) they will share it

Ibn Yunus said: Each relative is given a kettle in correspondence to the size of his share. Such is valid when their shares are equal. Whereas if their shares are not equal, then owner of the big share is cheating; for, whenever the kettle becomes heavy and big, the water becomes heavy inside and its flow becomes stronger from the hole as if what passes from a small hole is a lot more; for, one of them would have ten shares and a share for others. When he takes his share of the water, and he puts in his kettle, the water flow becomes slow and he takes a lot more than his portion. So what I believe is that the water should be divided in correspondence to the smallest share among them and the partner takes one share while the other takes ten shares.

96- Discourse On The House Whose Interior Belonged To A Man And The Exterior Belonged To Another, And They Disagreed In Changing The Door Of The Exterior House.

Master mason Muhammad said: If a house has an interior owned by a man and an exterior owned by others and there is a passageway for people of the interior house to pass through the exterior house; the owner of the exterior house wants to change the location of his door to a place closer without harming the people of the interior house, hence there are two views:

Ibn al-Qasim said in *al-Mudawwanah*: The owner of the exterior house has the right to do it and the other one has no right to prevent him except when it becomes too far from the original door, then the owner of the interior has the right to protest.

Sahnun said in *al-Majmu'ah*: they have no right and they should not change the location of the door except with the consent of the owner of the interior house.

Thereof master mason Muhammad said: If the owner of the exterior wants to narrow the door of the house, then the owner of the interior could prevent them from doing so. Ibn al-Qasim said that in *al-Mudawwanah*.

Thereof master mason said: If the interior owner subdivides his property and the new owners want to open new doors for each section, then the owner of the exterior has a right to prevent them. Master mason Muhammad also said: Except for the first door, which was used before the division, then they should not prevent them. This is a clear view of Ibn al-Qasim in *al-Mudawwanah*. Ibn Habib said: If the wall in which they wished to open doors is theirs, then the people of the exterior have no right to prevent them. And if the wall belongs the exterior owner, then he has the right to prevent them.

97- Discourse On Opening A Door Of A Jointly Owned House Through Another House Owned By One Of Them, And When Is Precedence (*tafadul*) And Donation (*heba*) Allowed[169] On That, And To Whom Belongs The Shelf Board (*al-Ajniha*) and *Fina*.

Master mason Muhammad said: From *al-Mudawwanah*, Ibn al-Qasim said from Malik regarding a house between two men who divided it, and one partner's house had a door on a side of one of two lots facing the other street. Then this man bought one of the two lots, which was attached to his house, and he opened a door toward that portion of his house. Later he began to pass through from his house to the road through this lot, so too his tenant and whoever stayed with him. He has the right if he wants to utilize it, except when he makes it as a public road (*sikkah nafizah*) for passers by entering and leaving from his house like a lane, then he had no right to do that. Ibn Yunus said: It's correct if the wall[170] is not shared. If the wall is shared, he has no right except with the consent of his co-partner.

---

[169] Precedence of one thing over another.
[170] Where the door is located.

Thereof Master mason said: If there is a house jointly owned between two men; one of the partners had his house attached to that jointly owned house, and then he wishes to open in what is owned jointly a door through which he enters his house, his co-partner has the right to prevent him.

Master mason Muhammad said: Ibn al-Mawwaz said: If he opened (a door) on his own wall to enter into a shared house, I do not see any objection and he has a right to do that.

Master-mason Muhammad said: This is an excellent opinion, for the wall in which he opened the door is his own property, which is not shared with anybody. With whatever arguments his partner argues on that matter, he has no valid argument except from the perspective of partnership that he has rights on the wall in which the door is opened. If he has no rights on the wall, then he cannot prevent him unless the opening is clearly harmful, thus in my opinion, it should be prevented. It is by analogy of what we have known from similar situations.

Thereof master mason Muhammad said: Ibn al-Qasim said in *al-Mudawwanah*: If they wished to subdivide, and one of them said: Make my share on the side of my house so it would be easy for me to open a door. This demand is not acceptable and the house should be divided by value. So wherever his portions comes about, he should take it. If it happens that his share is on the side of his building, he can open a door in it if he wishes as we have described before, but if his lot is located in another place, then he would not get another option.

Thereof Master mason Muhammad said: Ibn al-Qasim said in *al-Mudawwanah*: There is no objection on precedence (*tafadul*) in a division by consent. A man takes a portion of the house and another one takes his, on the condition that one of them should add to the other some space, or an animal as a payment, or postponement of payment for a prescribed time. It is permissible as to what is permissible in sale, and it is voided as to what is voided in sales.

Thereof master-mason Muhammad said: Ibn al-Qasim said from Malik in *al-Mudawwanah*: if two men divided a house among them and one of them wishes to donate a portion to his neighbor, then it is permissible.

Thereof master mason Muhammad said: Ibn al-Qasim said in *al-Mudawwanah*: If two men divided a house on the condition that each one should take a portion and then one of them has a projected cantilever (*jinah*, plural *al-ajnihah*) under his possession, then it is for him and it is not counted as a part of the *fina'*. However, if the *jinah* falls within the *fina'* airspace, then it is considered as part of the *fina'*, which is a part of the elements of the house, and the *fina'* of the house, in this case is for both of them.

98- Discourse On A House Between Two Men And One Of Them Built In It Something Before It Was Divided.

Master mason Muhammad said: From *al-Mustakhrajah*, I'sa bin Dinar said: Ibn al-Qasim was asked about two brothers inheriting a house and one of them built or planted something before the house was divided, what is the decree on that? He answered: division of the property is based on the following: if the newly built structure or plant becomes part of the property of the one who built it, then it is his; however, if it becomes the property of the one who did not build it, and if he desires to demolish it he can pay his brother what the demolished structure is worth. I said: what if he uses and benefits from it before the house was divided? He said: If they were present, they would have nothing (to say); for, as if they would have permitted him. But if they were not present, they would get rental from what has been built or planted equivalent to the rental of an empty land.

99- Discourse On Dispute Regarding Access From A House To Another House.

Master-mason Muhammad said: If one of the two houses has an access door through the other house, its owner does not have a right to use it for access (*al-tatarruq*) unless he has the evidence that he frequently used it for access, and the other party did not know if he owns the door or not. There are two views about that:

First opinion: There is nothing to be judged on him, for; he perhaps used it for access by the permission of the house owner or without his permission.

Second opinion: if it has been established that way, then this arrangement should continue and he should not be prevented (from using the door for access) except with a rightful reason.

Master mason Muhammad said: from *al-Majmua'ah,* Ashhab said: If a man has his entrance door attached to his neighbor's house, he has no right to use this door except if the other party knew that he used to pass through it and it does not appear that his right of passage was prohibited. However, if he did not know this arrangement, or he knew but the access door was not used for a long time, then he can prevent access, unless the owner of the door provides evidence, or the neighbor takes the oath that he did not know about the door; but if the other provides two witnesses that he used the door for access, unless a long time has elapsed for it not being used, then the neighbor can assume control and the right of passage is terminated.

Master mason Muhammad said: The same problem occurred to us in Tunis. Two men with each of them has a house attached to each other's back to back, while the front door of each house is facing a different dead-end street. And between two houses is a covered path around ten hand-spans in length and at the entrance of the path from the east direction is an old connected door with a lock that the owner of the house on the east side controled. At the entrance of the path from the west direction is also an old connected door which has a lock used by the owner of the house on the west side for locking it.

Both men brought their case to the judge and both of them claimed that the path belongs to himself, and both claimed that they have the right of passage through their respective neighbors' path. Subsequently the judge commanded that the situation be examined by experts. So we went down to the said place and we saw what we have described before, that the door of the east side house opened in the courtyard of the house, whereas the door of the west side house opened on the western side of the house. We acknowledged the condition and that both doors were very old and both men swore that the path belonged to them.

Therefore the judge ordered us to divide the path between them, each owned half of it. After that we built a brick screen in the middle of the path and it transformed the eastern part of the path into a small room in the courtyard of the eastern house and the western part was transformed into a small storage space for the other house. Such a division was confirmed after each one took an oath. This narration correlates with the opinion of Sahnun.

100- Discourse On Construction Activities Causing Damage To A Threshing Floor And Prevents Wind Circulation.

Master mason Muhammad said: If a man wished to undertake construction within his premise and adjacent to his neighbor's threshing floor that would harm its function, then there are three views on that:

Ibn al-Qasim said: He has no rights to do that. Ibn Habib said: He is not to be prevented from doing that.

Sahnun said: If the place has no other benefit except for building, then I do not see that he is to be prevented. If (without the construction) he will be harmed and he cannot get on without it, then he should not be prevented, but if he can get along without (extra building), I think he should be prevented.

Master mason Muhammad said: Text of the first opinion is from *al-'Utbiyah* through the auditioning of Yahya bin Yahya who said: I asked Ibn al-Qasim about a man whose threshing floor is adjacent to another man's land and the owner of the land wished to build a wall. The wall would harm the threshing floor and prevents the wind during winnowing time, hence it will spoil the wheat. Is the owner of the land allowed (to build the wall)? He replied: He is not allowed to build up in the place that will ruin the neighbor's threshing floor that preceded him in time and benefit. The landowner also is not allowed to damage the owner of the threshing floor by cutting his benefit. I asked him: Should the man be prevented from building on his land in a place that will cause damage to the owner of the threshing floor? He replied: Yes, he is prevented from building on his land when it is harmful to the owner of the threshing floor. Indeed already existing threshing floors are for us like *fina'* and similar things; where it is not permitted to disturb its owners or to cut their benefits.

Master mason Muhammad said: Ibn 'Abdus said: Some of our companions were asked about that and they gave the same answer, whereas they do not mention that it was narrated from Ibn al-Qassim or others. al-'Utbi said from Yahya bin Yahya from Ibn Nafi' a similar opinion; however, he added: whether he needed the building or not; for, the Prophet said: *'la darar wa la dirar'*.

Master mason Muhammad said: Text of the second opinion is from *al- Wadihah* as Ibn Habib said: I asked Mutarrif and Ibn al-Majashun about a man who wished to build in a village adjacent to a threshing floor that belongs to another, his building will prevent the wind from the threshing floor and causes disruption to its users, could he be prevented from that? Both (Mutarrif and Ibn al-Majashun) said to me: He should not be prevented to build on his property even though it will cause damage to the threshing floor, whether he found an alternative for that or not; even though his building might disrupt the threshing floor. For, the user of the threshing floor can transfer to another threshing floor and can establish another one. And if he is prevented from building within his property, his right is damaged. Ibn Habib said: I asked Asbagh bin al-Faraj about that and he gave the same answer as Mutarrif and Ibn al-Majashun.

Master mason Muhammad said: Text of the third opinion from *al-'Utbiah* is: al-'Utbi said: Sahnun was asked about someone who built something next to a threshing floor that belonged to another man and he replied: If that place has no purpose except for building, then I do not see that the man who wished to build on it be prevented from doing so, even if he has no necessity to build, but if the owner (of the building) is really in need to build for he could not get along without it, then he should not be prevented. Whereas if he would not face any damages without building, and he would be sufficient without it, I think he should be prevented if (his building) will prevent the circulation of wind to his neighbor's threshing floor. Sahnun said: Indeed Ibn 'Asim narrated from Ashhab a similar opinion.

Master mason Muhammad said: Opinion of Ibn Habib in my view is clearer; for threshing floors exist everywhere and most of the people operate their threshing floor in their land or they rent in within the *fina'* of another owner. The threshing activities are limited to a certain time, while the building and it's sites are bounded and immovable contrary to the threshing floor. Thus, it is preferable that the owner of the building should not be prevented from constructing.

Master-mason Muhammad said: Sahnun has another opinion similar to the opinion of Ibn al-Qassim.

101- Discourse On The Garden Located Adjacent To A Man's Threshing Floor And In Consequence The Straws And Dust Causes Harm To The Garden.

Master mason Muhammad said: if a garden belongs to a man located adjacent to a threshing floor of another man and then the straws and dust causes harm to the garden, we say: It is either, the garden has preceded the threshing floor, while the threshing floor was recently created, or the threshing floor preceded the garden while the garden was recently created. If the garden preceded the threshing floor: then its owner should be prevented from establishing a threshing floor by consensus of our scholars (Malikis) and they said: Establishing a threshing floor is like establishing an oven, or public bath or tannery. These all are disallowed unanimously and there is no dispute about that. And if the garden was recently established and the threshing floor preceded it, then there are two opinions:

Sahnun said in *al-'Utbiyah*: If the threshing floor preceded the garden or the building, the threshing floor should not be removed from its present place and the owner of the building or the garden has a right to build and to plant, even though the building would harm the threshing floor as previously mentioned by us on the wind that is prevented by the building.

Second opinion: Opinion of Ibn Habib in *al-Wadihah*: Mutarrif and Ibn al-Majashun said: If the garden was recently established next to the threshing floor and then the dust and straws of the threshing floor caused harm to the garden, therefore such harm is disallowed; for the threshing floor is operated all the time, at the same time it is moveable, and can be established at any time and it is unlikely to be a recently created harm. So with this fact, he (owner of the garden) has a right to prevent the owner of the threshing floor from causing the straws and dust falling into his land before setting up the garden, and that would damage what he is going to set up. Ibn Habib said: I asked Asbagh about the matter and he gave me the same answer.

Master-mason Muhammad said: The house and the garden is similar in this matter. This opinion also appeared in other primary sources.

102- Discourse On Two Threshing Floors One Is Blocking The Other By A Pileup Of Straws, And Another Threshing Floor Located In A Residential Area And Each One Claimed Its Ownership.

Master-mason Muhammad said: If a threshing floor belonged to a man located next to a threshing floor of another man where wheat straws (spike) piled up and became a mound, then the neighbor said to him: your threshing floor prevents the wind to flow into mine, causing it inoperative. Sahnun said in *al-'Utbiyah*: He (the neighbor) has no right on that since the man piles up his straws inside his own land.

Master mason Muhammad said: This is correct; if a building is allowed, then what about something which is lighter?

Master mason Muhammad said: From *al-'Utbiyah* by auditioning from Asbagh, he said: I asked Ibn Nafi' about a threshing floor located in the middle of a residential area, all the doors of the houses opened towards the threshing floor, and all the residents threshed their grains on it by themselves. But the ownership of the threshing floor was unknown; although some said that it belonged to an unknown person among them. Perhaps some of the houses there were built earlier than the others. He said: he, who owned it (the threshing floor) has a right on it, the earliest person residing there is more rightful. Perhaps the threshing floor, which is located within the residential area does not belong to them. Indeed the local authority should investigate the situation and make a determination.

103- Discourse On Limitation Of The Road Width And Disputes About That.

Master mason Muhammad said: Ibn Wahb narrated through Ismail bin I'yash through Rabia'h bin Abu 'Abdurrahman and Zaid bin Aslam that the Prophet said: If the people disagree on the road, limit it to seven cubits.[171]

Ibn Wahb said: Ibn Juraij narrated the same hadith. Ibn Wahb narrated and attributed it to the Prophet who said: 'Each road on which people pass through is seven cubits wide, and people can build according to this limit; and he who builds on a wide place (*al-baqi'*), then it belongs to him and each wide place which is not built up belongs to God and the Prophet and it is yours if you build on it'.

I'sa bin Musa said: My grandfather, 'Umar bin Yusuf narrated to me: I asked Muhammad bin Talid on the Prophet's saying about the limit of a road and he replied: Streets used by people are seven cubits wide; and if it is less than that, then it should be increased from the adjacent people's properties. Streets for cattle and cows is twenty cubits; that is what the scholars said and the Prophet has no saying about this. And whatever street like an un-

---

[171] Narrated by Bukhari through different chains and different wording. See *Fath al-Bari* 5:118, *Kitab al-Mathalim* hadith no. 2473.

noticed private lane (*al-mukhda'*), which belonged to the people, is four cubits.

Master-mason Muhammad said: from the book of Ibn 'Abdus, he said: Ibn Kinanah said: The width of a private lane (*al-aziqqah*) and a public street (*al-turuq*) should be sufficient for the largest and biggest load to pass through such as the biggest loaded camel without causing any damage.

Master-mason Muhammad said: Ibn Habib said: The interpretation is that it is (applicable) for newly constructed residential areas, so the width of a street should follow what was described by Ibn Kinanah.

104- Discourse On A Public Road, Which Was Cut Off By A River, Should A Man's Land Be Appropriated.

Master mason Muhammad said: If a public road was cut off and damaged and it is adjacent to a man's land, should a part of the man's land be appropriated for the road? We say: Either the road can be expendable because of the existence of another nearby road; or there is no other substitute road. In the case of the road is expendable due to the existence of another road, which is also easy to access, then the landowner should not be forced to allocate some part of his land (for the road). The authority also should not appropriate his land to build an alternative road. If there is no other alternative road, they differed into two opinions: Sahnun said: He should be forced (to hand over part of his land) and be compensated for that.

Ibn Habib said: He should not be forced (to hand over part of his land) and nothing to be taken from his land except by his consent.

Master mason Muhammad said: the text of the first opinion is from *al-'Utbiyah*, al-'Utbi said: Sahnun was asked about a land adjacent to a road on which people passed through in their daily life and the road was near a river which then wiped away that road, do you think that the authority has a right to build another public road by appropriating this private land, and compensate the owner and force him to accept that? He replied: If the road is indispensable, the authority has the right to appropriate the land and compensate the man using money from the public treasury. Sahnun has the same opinion as al-'Utbi as stated in the book of Ibn 'Abdus.

Master mason Muhammad said: the text of the second opinion is from *al-Wadihah,* Ibn Habib narrated that Mutarrif and Ibn al-Majashun said: nothing can be taken from the owner of the land except by his consent and permission, and he has the right to oppose them on that, if he is able to.

Ibn Habib said: I said to both of them, where are the people going to go when they have no access road, since theirs was cut off by the river and it was a public road? Both of them replied to me: Search in front of them for a solution, or they have to find a way. I do not think that one has a right to pass through private land or to build a road on it except with the owner's consent. I also think that he who passes through it, even once, should ask the permission from the owner, or to seek the permission before passing through it, and I prefer that way.

Ibn Habib said: I asked Asbagh about that and he gave the same answer as both (Mutarrif and Ibn Majishun).

Thereof master mason Muhammad said: In book of *al-Jidar* of Isa bin Musa, he said: my grandfather 'Umar b. Yusuf told me: I asked Muhammad bin Talid about a damaged road that belonged to a village, some of them wished to repair it, but some others refused, could they be forced or not? He replied: Repairing a road should not be forced on people, except those who volunteer to do so; rather, the repair is the responsibility upon the public treasury (*Baitul Mal*).

Master-mason Muhammad said: Outside our district, there was a road. It flooded when rain fell, no one was able to pass through it, and the one who rode an animal could fall down and be covered in mud, and people suffered from it. Many districts surrounded the road. I informed our master al-Faqih Abu Ishaq Ibn 'Abd al-Rafi' - Qadi al-Jama'ah - and at that time I was appointed to check roads, I said to him: O my master that particular road is inaccessible to anybody during winter and perhaps you may order people of the surrounding districts to reinforce it with stone for the width of five hand-spans wide on which people can pass through. He replied: That is not their obligation; who is in power in that district? I replied to him: He is such and such person. He said to me: Bring to me this representative. When the representative came, he advised and encouraged him to do good work. The judge said to the representative as follows: A man who removes a thorn from the street, God will thank him and forgive him, and you if you make an effort to repair that road, thus we hope God may forgive you. He (the judge) did not command him (the representative) but encouraged him to perform good work. If repairing a road is the responsibility of someone, he would have commanded me to force that person to do the repairing.

105- Discourse On A Man Whose Property Is Separated By A Public Road And He Wants To Relocate It Inside His Land.

Master mason Muhammad said: About a man who owns two parcels of land and between these two parcels is a public road. Then he wished to relocate it inside his land. Thus, we say: The new location is either far from the original one, or the change will benefit them and not cause any damage to the users. If he relocates it to a farther location, he has no right to do that. The opinion differs if he changes it to another location that does not harm the passersby, and would be better for them than the original road.

Ashhab said: If the relocation is by one cubit, then I think he can proceed with his plan. However, Ibn al-Qasim said: He has no right to do that.

Master mason Muhammad said: Text of the first opinion from *al-'Utbiyah* through auditioning of Ashhab and Ibn Nafi', both said: Malik was asked by a man: I have two parcels of lands bordering each other and people have a road between these parcels. I planted in one of the two parcels small palm trees (*al-wadiy*). The passersby would endanger my young palm trees, and thus I wished to shift the road to the other parcel that is uncultivated. Thus, the new location will be convenient for them and for me, and also nearer to them; it will cause them neither damage nor circling around.

So he (Malik) said: I do not agree with that except with people's consent. He (the landowner) said to him: I would build a road on the uncultivated land just like the previous one within a distance of one cubit. He (Malik) replied: If the distance is within one cubit and does not cause any harm to the passersby, then there is no objection, and if it is not as described, I think you should ask their permission. Ibn al-Hakam has the same opinion. Master mason Muhammad said: Ibn 'Abdus narrated the same from Ashhab from Malik.

Master mason Muhammad said: From *al-Wadihah*, Ibn Habib said: Ibn al-Qasim was asked about a man whose uncultivated land is encroached by the road. He wanted to reposition the road from its place to another place inside his land which was more convenient to him and passersby. He then replied: He has no right to change a road from its place to somewhere else, even if it's convenience is more or less similar to the first road. Although it has caused him damage; but if he bought it or inherited it or it was given as gift by a previous owner who already agreed with his neighbors (regarding the road). The road is open to the public, therefore permission of only some of them is not allowed, unless all users of the road agreed for the road to be relocated, then he can do that. If they do not give their consent, then he is not allowed to change its location, even if (the number who oppose) is small.

106- Discourse On A Man Who Has A Land Upon Which A Public Road Passes And He Wishes To Change Its Location To Another Place On His Land.

Master mason Muhammad said: If a man wished to shift a road from its place to another place inside his land it is either: the new position would be nearer from the previous one or farther. If he changes it far away from the previous location and involves a major reposition, all scholars agreed in preventing that and he should be prevented from doing so. If it is transferred to a place closer than the previous location and the reposition does not cause any damages to passersby and involves a minor relocation such as one cubit or so, then there are three opinions regarding that:

Ibn Nafii' said: If the distance is about one cubit or so, and it would be more convenient and closer, then he is not prevented, and if it is not (as described), then he is not (allowed to change it).

Ibn al-Qasim said: He is not allowed.

Mutarrif said: The matter should be referred to the authority (*imam*) and what the authority orders should be applied.

Master-mason Muhammad said: Text of the first view is from *al-'Utbiyah* through auditioning of Ibn Nafii' from Malik who said: Malik was asked by a man who said to him: I have a land being separated by a road and I want to relocate it from its present location to another location nearer and more convenient than the previous one. Thereby the damage will be taken off me by the relocation, and it does not cause damage to anybody and the scale of relocation is around one cubit. He (Malik) said: If it is as described, it is near, but if not, then he cannot relocate (the road). Master mason Muhammad said: Ibn Ashhab and Ibn 'Abdul Hakam said the same.

Master mason Muhammad said: Text of the second opinion from *al-Wadihah* as Ibn Habib said: Ibn al-Qasim was asked about a man who had an uncultivated land being separated by a road, wished to relocate the road from its place to another place within his land which is more convenient to him and users of the road. He said: No one can relocate a road from its original place to a lower or upper side of the previous one. Despite its convenience being more or less similar to that of the first road, or even though it caused him damage. This is because, when he bought it or inherited it, or it was given as a gift by a previous owner, it was already agreed with his neighbors (regarding the road) that it was to be a public road; whereby all the people have the right on it. Partial permission of some of them is not allowed; unless all the road users agreed to allow the road to be relocated, then he can do that.

Master-mason Muhammad said: Text of the third opinion from *al-Wadihah* also as Ibn Habib said: I asked Ibn al-Majashun about that and he said to me: I think the matter of the road should be brought up to the authority (*imam*) and thus he can investigate the matter. If the authority decides that the relocation would benefit the public and those staying nearby with more convenience, easier and nearer in access, I think they should allow the relocation. But if the authority decides that there is harm to the surrounding people, or all people who use it, then the authority should prevent that. If he relocates it without permission from the authority, then the authority should investigate the matter, if what he did is right, then leave it, but if not, he should restore the road to its original condition, because the authority (*imam*) is a supervisor for all the people and has the power to decide that.

Ibn Habib said: Ibn Nafii' has also a similar opinion, and he said I would prefer that and it is my opinion. Master mason Muhammad said: This is our practice, our trusted scholars informed me about that.

107- **Discourse On Litigation Among People Regarding Usage Of A Road Inside Another Person's Land.**

Master mason Muhammad said: al-'Utbi said in *al-Mustakhrajah*: Sahnun was asked about a person who demarcated a piece of land, planted it and claimed that he owned it, while adjacent people claimed that part of the land was their access road. Thus, they protested saying: you have cut off our road. He (the claimant) denied that the road belongs to them, claiming it is his property. Consequently, they brought their case to the judge. The residents presented witnesses to confirm that they had used the road for twenty years, while the claimant presented witnesses to say that it had been used as a road only recently without a right to it. So which of the two evidences should be accepted?

Sahnun said: Such cases often occurred among the residents and the people arguing over land that was cultivated leaving them without an access road. Some people tolerated their land being used as a pathway because the access road is rather far away. If this road was determined to belong to the above category then it is not necessarily under possession of the land owner. Except when the road is in a rural area (*tariq badiyah*) when it was left (to occupy the land) for a long time up to 50-60 years. But if the land is within an urban area, the landowner has no excuse when it was established.

Master mason Muhammad said: The distinction between a rural road and an urban road is that the latter originates from urban areas. The principle of a road in rural areas is that (the passersby) possessed it for something like sixty years or so.

108- **Discourse On A Man Who has A Right Of Passage To His Palm Tree In Someone Else's Land And The Landowner Prevented Him From Entering.**

Master mason Muhammad said: Ibn 'Abdus said in his book: Ashhab and Ibn al-Qasim were asked about a man whose palm tree is in another man's land and when he wants to access his tree, the landowner said to him: I will not let you pass through my land. Ibn al-Qasim and Ashhab replied: He has no rights to prevent you from that and you have a right of access to your palm tree (either) to irrigate, cutting off twigs, to pollinate, or to improve its soils, even if his entire land was fully cultivated, he still has no right to prevent you from your palm tree. However, if by passing through his farm it causes damages to him, then he has the right to prevent you. But if you insist to pass through his land then you can find someone to help you in that matter, and you can consult with him on what you really need to do (to your palm tree).

Master mason Muhammad said: Ibn al-Qasim said: I do not see that the owner of the palm tree harming the landowner by passing through to his palm tree. Rather he has rights to pass through, but he cannot bring with him a large group of people because it will destroy the farm by the treading on the plants during entering and leaving the farm.

Ibn al-Qasim said: Malik was asked about a man whose land was in the middle of someone else's land, which is fully planted. Thereupon the owner of the middle land wants to bring his cows and animals to benefit from his land. Hence Malik replied: I think he has the right on that, but he has to prevent any damage to the owner of the surrounding land, because if he brought his animals then he will destroy his neighbor's farms.

Ibn al-Qasim said: I am in the opinion that he has rights to fertilize his land, and thus he should not be prevented from that. I did not hear from Malik anything about that.

Master mason Muhammad said: This is Malik's opinion in *al-Mudawwanah*.

109- Discourse On A Man Who Owned Trees Inside Another Man's Land; The Landowner Wishes To Fence His Land.

Master mason Muhammad said: these trees are either planted together in one place, or scattered in different places, or many trees covering the entire land.

If the trees are planted together in one place, not scattered, the owner of the land should be prevented from fencing his land. He should be told: You may fence yours, but leave the part that is planted!

If the trees are only few and scattered in the land, tell the landowner: You may fence your land and owner of the the trees cannot prevent you.

If the trees are many covering the entire land, the landowner should be prevented from fencing his land. The details and explanation for that is in the rest of this discourse.

Master mason Muhammad said: Ibn Habib said in *al- Wadihah*: I have written to Asbagh bin al-Faraj asking him about a man who owned a tree or trees in the other man's land. The owner of the land, wishes to surround his land with a fence, or he wishes to build a house on his land or to foreclose the man's trees. The owner of the trees prevents him from doing so, saying to the land owner: I have the right to attend my trees without being blocked up. The landowner said: I would let you in according to your right and I will open when you wish to access to your trees to collect its fruit or to nurture it, do you think he (the landowner) has the right?

He wrote to me saying: the answer differs according to different conditions: if the trees owned by the man are planted in one place without being scattered in the land, the landowner could be prevented from fencing the trees together with all his land, saying to him: Fence up your land but leave the part that is planted with the trees.

This can be done when the owner of the trees has access to his trees whether it is near or far, or easy or difficult to access. If the tree or trees are in the middle of the land or in one side of the land or is scattered in the land whereby the landowner is not able to fence his property and it causes a lot of damage; but if the trees are not many and do not cover the entire land and the land is wide, the owner of the trees has no right to prevent the owner of the land from benefiting by fencing it.

If the planter claimed that by fencing the land, it would cause damage to him based on the Prophet's saying: (*La Darar wa la Dirar*) Harm not yourself and others and others should not harm you and themselves; for, when two harms occur on two partners concurrently; the first to bear the harm is the one who bears the lesser harm.

So in this case he is the one who caused harm to his partner, if he prevented the landowner from fencing, it will cause major harm to the landowner. So tell the land owner: fence up your land and at the same time open a gate to the tree's owner to attend his trees with a closeby access and convenient for him and the padlock should be in his hand if he requests that, and if he uses a different entrance from the one used by the landowner. And tell the landowner: you have the right to prevent anybody from entering, if you wish you could fence it.

He said: If the trees are many and scattered all over the land, then the landowner has no right to fence his land; by far, the most harm is on the owner of the trees, if he is prevented from his trees. In this case, you should follow what the Prophet said: (*La Darar wa la Dirar*) harm not yourself and others, nor others should harm you and themselves. Whenever the harm to one of them is greater, then it is harmful to him and he should find a way out from that damage. So the least harmful is to prevent from fencing. Thus seek help from the explanation of Malik's opinion on the selling of the palm trees, of those pollinated or not pollinated. If only a small number of the palm trees were pollinated then the fruits belong to the buyer.

The Prophet said: Whoever has sold a palm tree which is already pollinated, then its fruit belongs to the seller. Thus people of knowledge do not try to clarify by drawing analogous conclusions on what is totally ambiguous. So too the Prophet's saying on two harms, when the damages are concurrent, the one whose injury is greater, is avoided by the commission of the lesser harm.

110- Discourse On A Man's Land Located In The Middle Of Others Property With No Passageway; He Wished To Build In His Centrally Located Land.

Master-mason Muhammad said: Ibn Habib said in *al-Wadihah*: I asked Asbagh about a man's land in the middle of other's land, to which he goes for tilling and harvesting, passing through a farmland in which no one is working in that year. He then wished to build a building inside his land; however, other surrounding farmers prevented him from doing so. They said to him: "You pass through our farms, damaging our farms while we are cultivating", is he prevented from constructing a building as he wishes? Asbagh said to me: He is not prevented from that as he is only passing through the farms to his land and sometimes the farms are planted and in other times they are left barren. He should be prevented if his action would harm people's farms. He (Ibn Habib) said: I said: If people around him want to fence their land by building (a wall) or a garden fence; what should the owner of the land located in the middle do?

He, Asbagh said: The people are prevented from fencing their land until they reach a consensus on the right of passage for the man, which is taken from a land of one of them who is willing to do so. So too with the other owner whose land was frequented by this person to pass through to his land. I (Ibn Habib) said: If they disagreed on the passageway and the owner of the land in the middle said to them; Reserve for me a wide passage passable to my cattle, all my necessities and me; however, the people refused to obey.

Asbagh said to me: The judgment is in his favor and he has the right of passage for tilling and transferring his plant and cattle as he frequented before and according to what they had agreed. If he used to frequent without the animal, then they should not provide the passageway passable to his animal. If he is the only one wishing to build while others did not want to build on their land, and want it left for tilling and planting only as it was before. However, if his frequency of entering and leaving his property is more than previously, then he could be prevented from building; since his new claim of right is much more than his previous one.

Ibn Habib said; Ibn al-Qasim was asked about that and he said the same thing.

Master mason Muhammad said: The same opinion was also stated in *al-'Utbiyah* through Ibn 'Asim and Ibn al-Qasim.

Master-mason Muhammad said: I do not know any disagreement about this problem except that of Ibn Kinanah, who said: If his building would bring harm, then he is prevented, but if it is for his need, then he is not prevented. Ibn Kinanah narrated this from Ibn 'Abdus in his book.

Thereof master mason Muhammad said: I found in the book of *al-Jidar* of 'Isa bin Musa that 'Isa said: Ismail bin Muwassal was asked the same question and he said: If a man used to go frequently to his grape vines passing through a farm belonging to another person since long a time ago and nobody can remember what the original arrangement was, therefore he is entitled for the right of passage perpetually. Yet, if the arrangement for the access road between the land and other's land is known before it was totally shut upon him, it is incumbent on the owners of the farms to allow him a right of passage to his grape vines. The alternative way is for the owners to discuss among them and provide an access path to him. They also could reimburse him for the damage he faces (for denying him an access road), so understand what I illustrated to you previously, and open the shortest and best access path to him. Thus, this is the judgment on them, as what Ibn al-Qasim said. Those who refuse could be forced to abide. And if each one of them is able to provide an access road passing through their land, they should do that without compensating him; if not, the compensation is applicable.

111- Discourse On The Man Whose Land Is Located Inside Other's Properties, Then They Lock Their Properties And Thus Blocked His Access.

Master-mason Muhammad said: In *al-'Utbiyah*, Ashhab and Ibn Nafi' said: Malik was asked about a man who has a right of passage through (an opening in the) wall to his property located behind that wall. (An opening on) the wall has no door. Then the wall's owner wished to block his wall, by making a door on it. Malik said: I do not think that the owner of the wall has a right to do that except with the consent of that passerby; for, when he locks it by creating a door, the passerby is not able to go through whenever he wishes or if he comes at night and finds the door closed. Thus, (the owner) would say to him; during this time, the door is not open to anybody. When it is raining, he could not wait longer (for the door to be opened) and he leaves. Therefore, I consider that it should be with the consent of the passer by. He (Malik) then was asked: what do you think if he builds a fence without a lockable door? He said: I am afraid that the person who used to pass through and sees the wall will discontinue his intention. I am also afraid that with the passage of time the owner of the wall will forget the previous arrangement and askes the other: Do you know anyone who could prove that you have the right of passage through our property?

Master-mason Muhammad said: The same opinion is stated in the book of Ibn 'Abdus from Ibn Nafi' from Malik, so too in the book of Ibn 'Abdul Hakam.

112- General Discourse On The Usurpation Of Plants, And On A Man Who Built On Someone Else's Property With Or Without His Permission.

Master mason Muhammad said: The source is from what Ibn Habib narrated in *al-Wadihah*. Ibn Habib said: As'ad bin Musa narrated to me through 'Abbad bin al-'Awam through Yahya bin 'Urwah bin al-Zubair through his father: a man planted a date-palm in the land of an *Ansari* man and they brought the case to the Prophet. The Prophet judged that the *Ansari* has a right to his land and the other has to root out his date palm.[172]

He said: Ibn Habib also narrated this tradition, saying: Mutarrif reported from Malik from Hamid bin Qais from Mujahid: A man revived a wasteland. He planted in it trees and constructed a building. Afterwards another person furnished proofs that the land belonged to him. Both of them brought the case to 'Umar and he said: If you wish, we tell you the total expenditure of the person, then you will pay it (and possess your land) otherwise, he pays the price of your land (and will possess the land).[173]

Ibn Habib said: The judgment of the Prophet differed from the judgment of 'Umar bin al-Khattab; so, the judgment on the two cases is different. The planter on the land of al-Ansari is a transgressor, thus the judgment in this case is to root out the date palm unless the landowner wishes to pay him the value of uprooted tree. The planter who cultivates on someone else's property, in 'Umar's tradition, is in doubt since he believed that the land is a wasteland. Therefore, 'Umar imposed upon the owner to pay the expenses of the other's cultivation and building, and the tree and building should remain without being taken down.

Ibn Habib said: likewise, everyone who built or planted on someone else's property without knowing that the land belongs to someone else is entitled to his effort.

Master-mason Muhammad said: Ibn Habib also narrated (another tradition), saying: Mutarrif and 'Abdul 'Aziz al-'Uwaisiy narrated to me through al-Umari through Hamid bin Qais through Mujahid, saying: A man came to Abu Bakr al-Siddiq, asking him for an allotment of a piece of land. Abu Bakr then allotted the land for him and the man later planted and developed the land. Subsequently some people claimed that the Prophet granted them the land before this man and claimed ownership on that. They brought their case to 'Umar bin al-Khattab during his reign. 'Umar judged that the man should be given his expenditure on the land and move out. They said that: We do not have anything to give him; 'Umar then asked the man to pay the price of the land. The man also said: I do not have anything. For

---

[172] Narrated by Abu Daud 3:178, hadith no.3074 and in al-Baihaqi in *Sunan al-Kubra* 6:142. See also Ibn Ubaid, *Kitab al-Amwal* p. 244, hadith no 703.

[173] Narrated by Abu 'Ubaid in *Kitab al-Amwal*, pp. 366, 367, Hadith no 707.

that reason, 'Umar judged that they become co-partners in the land; one is based on the value of the land and the other is based on the value of his investment to revive the land.

Ibn Habib said: I asked Mutarrif and Ibn Majishun: Did Malik apply this tradition and used it in his judgments? Both said: Neither Malik nor other scholars; neither al-Mughirah nor Ibn Dinar applied this tradition that is to ask the owner to discharge his ownership whenever someone else unintentionally developed their land. However, if the landowner refuses to pay the developer his expenditure, they would be considered as partners; the landowner based on the value of his undeveloped land while the developer is based on his construction, and the developer must not be compelled to pay the land's price and expell the owner.

The author mentioned Ibn Habib's interpretation of their partnership by saying: The undeveloped land is assessed, without the value of any building in it, after they become co-partners; hence, the value can be known. Then the developed land is evaluated. Therefore, whatever increase in the value of the land belongs to the developer as his share. Therefore, they are partners if they wished, or they could divide their shares or, if they like, they could stay as partners.

Master-mason Muhammad said; Ibn Habib said: Ibn al-Qasim based his judgment on that tradition.

Ibn Habib said; the opinion of Malik is also the opinion of *al-Madaniyyun* (those who follow the traditions of Medina), which is the most preferable, and on that, I base my opinion.

Master-mason Muhammad said: from *al-Mudawwanah*, Sahnun cited Ibn al-Qasim, who quoted what Malik said regarding dead land: if a man revived a land, that he assumed is a wasteland without an owner, then another man claims ownership, Malik commented on 'Umar's judgment, saying: I accept that and I think if both refused to compensate each other then both will be partners, one is based on the value of his investment while the other is based on the value of the land. Thus, both become partners in the land and building. Master-mason Muhammad said: Ibn 'Abdul Hakam has the same opinion except that he did not mention 'Umar's judgment.

Master-mason Muhammad said: Sahnun narrated that Ibn al-Qasim said: The opinion differed in this case but ('Umar's judgment) is better and preferable to me since I think that one who buys a land, and constructs a building, then someone else claimes ownership of the land, has to pay him his expenditure and repossess it. Alternatively, tell the purchaser: compensate him the value of his plot. If he refuses, both would be partners; the landowner with the value of his plot and the purchaser based on the value of what he had revived. Both become partners according to their capital; whether they divide or bought either one's share.

Likewise, whoever wishes to claim the right of pre-emption on what he deserves, it is said to him: pay him the value of what he developed and possess it by way of pre-emption. If he refuses, say to the purchaser: Pay him half of the value of the plot that he deserves. And if he did, then that belonged to him and he (the purchaser) should claim compensation from the vendor for another half of the price. However, if both (the buyer and the owner) refuse; consider half of the value of what he built recently in the plot of the claimer, and the value of the plot itself. So, both are partners in that half; the share of the owner of the building is based on half value of his building, and the claimant (owner) is based on the value of his right on the plot. Accordingly, both are partners in half of what was calculated based on their capital.

113- Discourse On Someone Who Built On Someone Else's Property With Or Without His Permission, Could He Claim The Total Value Of His Building Or The Cost Only.

Master-mason Muhammad said: The opinion differed about someone who built inside someone else property with or without his permission; could he claim the total value of his building or the cost only?

Ibn Habib said in *al-Wadihah:* I heard Mutarrif and Ibn Majishun saying: We heard Malik say more than once: Whoever built inside someone else's property with his permission and knowledge, has a right to the current value of his standing building. Whoever built in someone else's property without his permission and knowledge, would be given the cost of his work only, and the building being demolished.

Malik said: Similarly, whoever rented or was granted a land to a certain period or unknown period, then he asked the landlord permission to construct a building and they allowed it; or he built with their knowledge, but not with their permission, and they asked him to move out, he is entitled to the cost of his building and work; and the building is allowed to stand.

So to whoever built on a shared property with his partner's permission or knowledge, is entitled to the value of his building standing and work. Equally, whoever built inside his wife's property with her permission or knowledge is entitled to the value of his standing building. In addition, whoever builds inside his wife land or on a shared land or in any land without the owner's permission and knowledge is entitled to his expenditure on the building in its demolished state and work.

Ibn Habib said: I said to Mutarrif and Ibn al-Majishun that it was mentioned to us that Malik said: Whether he built with the owner's permission or not, he is only entitled to the cost of his work. Both, Mutarrif and Ibn al-Majishun said to me: This is a misinterpretation from the transmitter to you and be careful with that. We never heard that Malik said contrary to what we had told you. Moreover, none of us dispute his opinion, and neither of his companion say (contrary to that) be it Ibn Abu Hazm, al-Mughirah, and Ibn Dinar and others. Indeed, this opinion remains applied in judgment among judges of the Madinah from earliest times to the present.

Master-mason Muhammad said: Asbagh said in *al-Wadihah* through Ibn al-Qasim: That he is entitled to the cost of his work (and the building being demolished). Ibn Habib also said: Ibn al-Qasim used to say; He is entitled to the cost of his work, when the building is in its demolished state. He narrated this from Malik; yet, we did not accept it; while the opinion of Mutarrif and Ibn Majishun is preferable to me and on that I based my opinion.

Master-mason Muhammad said; Ibn Nafi' and Ibn Kinanah together with all *al-Madaniyyun* have the same opinion.

114- Discourse On Someone Who Built On His Wife's Property.

Master-mason Muhammad said: The opinion differs about a man who built inside his wife's property into two: From *al-'Utbiyah*, Yahya bin Yahya said: I asked Ibn al-Qasim about a man who is planting on his wife's property or building in it or in her house. Then one of them died; is the value of that cultivation or building belongs to the woman or who bequeaths her? He said: Yes the value of that belongs to her or who bequeaths her if she dies.

Indeed, the husband has only the right of servitude on his wife's property. It is like a commodity loan (*'ariyā*) when he cultivated and built on her land, unless if the woman or those who bequeaths her have evidence that he spent his wife's money in constructing a building or did repairs for her. Therefore, the woman is more deserving on her property and on whatever her husband developed inside her property using her wealth.

He said: The husband is entitled to the cost of his building in its demolished state, if the woman does not come with evidence on what I have mentioned.

Second opinion: Ibn Habib said from Mutarrif and Ibn Majishun: The value of the building standing, and not in its demolished state.

115- Discourse On A Man Who Allowed Another Man to Build Inside His Property For A Certain Period, And When The Time Expires The Building Is Demolished.

Master-mason Muhammad said: The opinion differed on someone who allowed another person to build in his property (*a'rsah*) for a certain time; when the time expires, could he claim the value of his building standing, or the value of the building in its demolished state?

Ibn Habib said: He is entitled to the value of his building in its standing state.

Ibn al-Qasim said: He is entitled to the value of the building in its demolished state.

The text of the first opinion from *al-Wadihah:* Ibn Habib said that I asked Mutarrif and Ibn Majishun about a man who allowed another man to build in his property on the condition that he would stay for a period. When the period expired, he demolished the building and the property was returned to him (landlord) as it was on the day he occupied it. Both Mutarrif and Ibn Majishun replied to me: The condition is void and he is entitled to the value of his building to remain on the ground where it is, when the period expires. For the condition is damaging (to the lessee) and is irregular.

Ibn Habib said: I said to both: If he sets a condition on him that when the period is completed, he is entitled to the value of his building to remain on the ground. If he did not put that condition, do you consider such a condition as flawed? Both said to me: Yes! Such a condition causes the contract to be void. For, it is

217

like he rented his property without the building while the value is delayed at that time. So that is the risk and it's like the contract of *salaf* (advance payment) that brings the benefit. Thus, when he built on that, he is entitled to the price of the building approximately on the day when he finished and completed it (building) or from the expense that he spent on it. Later on, the property owner has rights on the land rental effective from the day of his staying.

Ibn Habib said: I asked Asbagh about that and he gave the same opinion: if he set the condition on him the value of a standing building; but it is permissible if he sets the condition on the value of the demolished building.

Ibn al-Qasim said: He is entitled to the value of the building in its demolished state and flattened to the ground, be it stipulated or not. Ibn Habib and others reported that.

Ibn Habib said: our opinion is as the opinion of Mutarrif and Ibn Majishun and it is also the opinion of *al-Madaniyyun*. I do not know any dispute between them in it. There is a narration (*athar*) from the Prophet who said: whoever built in a property of people without their permission has only the right of taking the material of the demolished structure.[174] It is narrated by 'Abdullah b. al-Hakam through Bakr bin Mudar through Hamzah from the Prophet. Ibn Wahb also narrated it through Bakr bin Mudar through Hamzah from the Prophet.

116- Discourse On What A Builder Could And Could Not Take From The Remains Of What He Built In Another Man's Property, With or Without His Permission.

Master-mason Muhammad said: From the book of 'Abdullah bin Abd al-Hakam, he said: Whoever built on other's property without their permission, and the owner of the property claimed ownership on that, and then if the owner wishes he can give him the value of his building after it is demolished. He has no right to take the rubble, which is not beneficial for him, after demolishing or destroying something that the house owner had repaired. He is also not obliged to put back the soil that he removed from the original place. However, if the tenant (the man who built without permission) removed a beam, he should put it

---

[174] According to Ibn Hajar this hadith is week, see *al-Tahzib*, 3:39.

back to its original place. And if he destroyed a wall, he should rebuild it; if the house owner prefers that he put back a beam similar to the previous one or bricks similar to his bricks, he should do it; if he (house owner) preferred to take the value, then he should pay. A usurper is not entitled to pull out a marble (*jir*) or any decoration (*tazwiq*) including anything that would not benefit him.

Master-mason Muhammad said: Things that are not beneficial to him when the building is torn down: Bricks which are not valuable after being destroyed or the price is equal to the wages paid to the worker to demolish; what I meant is the brick wall built either with baked brick or mud brick, semicircle roof (*damus*), decoration (*tazwiq*), a huge pool (*jabiyah*)[175], if it was built using baked brick or *astak* [176] on the ground, painted walls or underground storage (*matmurah*). If the building is constructed with stones, he has no right to demolish it. For, by demolishing it, it would damage the ground and it could cause a landslide. All this is of no benefit in demolishing it, but if the landowner wants to demolish and repossess (the site), he could take it and pay its value.

Thereof master mason Muhammad said: Whatever renovation the tenant did on the house either by plastering or whatever for his convenience and the landlord did not deny it and allowed it. But both disagreed on the value when the period is completed, therefore the tenant is entitled to the cost of his work, when the house owner want to repossess it. He has the choice in that, and anything which has no value, he will get nothing when the house is demolished, he also cannot leave it to the landowner to demolish (for him) if he wishes to tear it down.

Ibn Habib said: Ibn al-Qasim used not to differentiate between what the house owner permitted the tenant to plaster or rebuild and what he did not permit him to do. For him the tenant is entitled to the cost in its demolished state. This opinion differs with the opinion of *al-Madaniyyun*.

---

[175] a huge pool to collect water for camel
[176] a layer of roof made from mud to protect the roof from cracking.

117- Discourse On A Man Who Leased A Land To Another Man To Develop It For A Certain Period, Then The Land Was Reclaimed Before The Period Was Completed.
Master-mason Muhammad said: Sahnun said in *al-Mudawwanah*: I said to Ibn al-Qasim: What do you think if I rent a land from a man for several years for the purpose of building, cultivating, and living on it. I then built, cultivated and tilled; then, the man claimed the right of ownership on the land before the period was completed. He replied: The claimant has a choice on the rest of the uncompleted periods; if he likes he could allow the contract to be completed or he could nullify it. If he allowes the period to be completed, he has a right to possess the building and plants based on the value in its demolished state. If he likes he can ask the owner to demolish it. However, if he (the landlord) refused the option and wants the agreement to be nullified, he is not entitled to demolish the building or to possess it based on the value of the building in its demolished state. Nevertheless, he has an option: If he likes, he could pay him based on the value of the building to remain on the ground, where it is; if he refuses, tell the builder or cultivator: pay him the value of his land. If both refuse, they become partners; this is a principle in building and cultivating.
Master-mason Muhammad said: This opinion is contradictory to the opinion of *al-Madaniyyun* as previously mentioned.

118- Discourse On Whoever Purchased Date-Palm Trees Or Rubbles (Derelict Building) To Be Pulled Down, And What If The Land Was Sold Before Or After That, And Was That A Subject Of Pre-emption.
Master-mason Muhammad said: Regarding someone who purchased date-palm trees or derelict building to be pulled down, Ibn al-Qasim said as in *al-Mudawwanah*: if someone purchased date-palm trees to be pulled down, then purchased the land, and the trees remained therein, then another man claimed ownership on half of the said property. The man thus has a right to take half of the trees and land by right of preemption and he should pay half of the total price of those (trees and land) of its original value. The purchaser has no right to argue that he bought the date-palm trees to be pulled up; for, the claimant became his partner of all dates-palm trees. If the claimant did not want to

exercise his right of pre-emption, the purchaser could choose either to hold to his purchase or to return it.

Master mason Muhammad said: Muhammad bin al-Mawwaz said in his book from Ashhab: He has the right of pre-emption to the land, and possess it without the date-palm trees; for the man bought the trees for the purpose of pulling them up.

Master mason Muhammad said: Sahnun said in the book of Ibn 'Abdus: The claimant is told: You could choose either to let your portion be sold or you could take the price from your partner with no argument for the purchaser. For, the transaction is completed on him (the deal is safely in his hand); if he does not allow his share to be sold, he can take it and the purchaser should ask the seller for refund for half of the price. Regarding the trees: if its species are of superior quality like *Saihani* or *Burniy* [177], small or big or the like, the transaction, then is void on half of the purchaser; for, if he bought the date-palm trees for the purpose of pulling out, it was an unknown transaction, not known what would happen in the division because the land was divided with the date-palm trees. Therefore his portion would be abundant with the date-palm trees, but with a smaller land portion or he will get a small number of date-palm trees with the larger land area with grapevine and *Daba*[178]. If the land and the date-palm trees can be divided equally, then the transaction is legitimate and the purchaser may have options. According to the opinion of Ashhab, either to hand over what is remaining in his hand or to keep it. If the purchaser withholds his share, then *al-shafii'* (holder of the right of pre-emption) can exercise the right of preemption in the land and the trees by half of the price. As Malik said on the pre-emption for the purpose of pulling out if the land did not belong to either one of them. Ibn al-Qasim said: The pre-emptor should begin with the option, either to exercise his right or to let go.

Thereof master-mason Muhammad said: from *al-Mudawwanah* Ibn al-Qasim said: If a man purchased a property including a portion of a house in which there is a derelict building that its rubble belongs to the house owner and after that he purchased the derelict building (rubble) first and then he purchased the

---

[177] Names of two types of dates.
[178] A kind of fruit.

property; then the pre-emptor, who deserves half of that property, asked for the right of pre-emption. Ibn al-Qasim replied: He, the pre-emptor has a right to take the property and the derelict building (rubble) altogether, by the right of pre-emption, and pays the price for the property and the value of the derelict building (rubble) standing without being demolished.

Master-mason Muhammad said: In the book of Muhammad bin al-Mawwaz: If a man purchased trees or derelict building (rubble) for the purpose of demolishing and then he purchased the land, with all those remaining on the land; and after that a man claimed a right on half of all (of lands and trees), he has the right of pre-emption by paying half the price of all things.

Asbagh said: up to this we refer to Ibn Qasim and his opinion is preferred. Meanwhile, Ashhab believed that the man has the right of pre-emption on the land only, but not on the trees and building.

Ibn al-Mawwaz said: The opinion of Ibn al-Qasim is correct and is applied by our companions; for, the purchaser's situation is as if he bought that wholly, and if it were not like that, the sale is void.

Master-mason Muhammad said: Ibn al-Qasim said in *al-Mudawwanah*: Whoever purchased part of a jointly owned property of a man or of his portion of date palm trees for the purpose of pulling out that portion, while his partner is not present, then the transaction is void; for, neither he nor the seller are able to pull it out except after division. If the seller wished to divide the trees with his partner for the purpose of pulling out, he cannot do that except with the land.

Ibn Mawwaz said: Another feature is that he purchased tree trunks unknown what he would be getting from the trees because the transaction is not completed without the land. Perhaps he might get fewer trees because his portion contains less, or his land portion is not fertile. And he (Ibn al-Mawwaz) said: If the date palm trees are equal in its division because of similarity in the quality of trees and the land, thus the division becomes one in quantity, I will accept it.

Ashhab said: I consider it like sheep, cloth, and beast, when one of them sells his portion. Ashhab continue saying: Then there is no right of pre-emption on the trees; for, it (trees) are sold for the purpose of pulling out; whereas the removal could not be valid except after the division, it looks like as if the transaction is negotiated after the division. The trees are (firstly) subject of division and (after that) the transaction can be done, so if he takes the tree by the right of preemption, he should pull it out like the purchaser would do (if he bought it).

Ashhab said: Likewise, if he purchased a portion of land from the tree's seller after purchasing his portion of the trees, the transaction is void.

Master-mason Muhammad said: Ibn al-Mawwaz said: The transaction of the land and the tree separately is void. Ibn al-Mawwaz said: If he does not lay down any condition except his portion of the land only, the transaction is void; for, the land is not yet divided with his partners and whoever purchases a jointly owned property, is not allowed. For, (in one instance) his purchase (real value) will be less after he divided with him and then (in another instance) his purchase would increase. Except when he purchases all his portion of the trees and the land in one transaction; then it is allowable. As buying a portion after another, both are void because it could contain deceit.

Ashhab said: Except the land and the trees are similar in quality, quantity, and places. If he bought one share or portion after another, he is entitled to claim the pre-emption on the land only, the buyer is obliged to divide the trees and pull it out.

Ibn al-Mawwaz said: I do not like this opinion. I think that when he purchased his portion of the trees before (buying) the land, he has the right of pre-emption of the trees and land; if he bought the land before the tree, he has the right of preemption on the land only, but not the trees because before that, the right of pre-emption is applicable on trees only since they were partners in the land. If he sells the trees first, his partner is entitled to the right of pre-emption on the trees; since both were partners in the land. If he sells the land first after their partnership on the land was broken and the trees remained but not the land, thus he has no right of pre-emption on that. It is like someone who sells his share of a jointly owned garden and fruit and a well and the slave, thus he has no right of preemption in the well and the slave having been sold afterward. And if he sells the well and the slave before, both are entitled to the right of preemption.

Ibn al-Mawwaz said: When he sells his share of the trees in one deal and then he sells his portion of the land from the tree purchaser or others, thus the purchaser has a right to take the trees only and surrender the land or take the land and surrender the trees or he takes all. If one of them takes (either land or trees), then it is inevitable to divide the rest. If he takes the trees, his partner may divide (*qasama*) the trees and the land entirely; whatever became his possession by half of his possession, he could take it with his trees and whatever became possession of his partner, he could pull out his trees and hand over his land to his partner. However, if he took the land, they only could divide the trees; for the deal is one and if not that its transaction would not have been allowed and whatever belonged to his partner, his partner was forced to pull it out.

Master-mason Muhammad said: Many opinions of this kind is found in the book of Ibn al-Mawwaz.

Master-mason Muhammad said: Ibn al-Qasim said in *al-Mudawwanah*: If a man purchased a standing derelict building to be pulled down and later a man claimed the right of ownership on half of the house, then the purchaser could give back the rest of the derelict building. There is no right of pre-emption to the claimant; for, it was sold for the purpose of pulling it down and he did not buy the land. If he is entitled to all the land without the derelict building or the date palm trees were sold to be pulled up and then a man claimed the land, but not the date-palm trees; therefore, such a transaction on the rubble and the trees is complete. The claimant has the right to take that (rubbles and trees) from the purchaser by paying him the cost in its pulled out state, not its value. It is not subject of preemption, but (to lessen) the damage. The purchaser cannot prevent that; for, to prevent it is harmful. If he, the claimant, refuses to take those on the cost of its pulled out state, then tell the purchaser: Pull them out.

Master-mason Muhammad said: Sahnun rejects this view, by saying: If the seller takes the land illegally, the claimant will get the land by judgment and if he wishes, he should pay the usurper (*ghasib*) the cost of his building and the rubble belongs to the purchaser. If he, the claimant, wishes, he *can* hand over the rubble to the purchaser. If the seller of the rubbles is the purchaser of the land, he (the claimant) can give him the value of the rubble while the building is still standing on the site and later the transaction is invalidated. Thus the purchaser of the rubbles should not say: I take this value which the seller took it with, such as someone sold goods for a hundred and he bought it from another for seventy. Then the first purchaser wished to take it [merchandise] with seventy and this he cannot do. If the claimant of the land said: I don't give him the value of the building, it is said to seller of the rubbles: Give him the value of his land and thus his buying of the rubbles was legitimate. If he refused, both become partners and buying of the purchaser was invalidated when it becomes his possession from half of the rubbles of the claimant of the land [but] his buying was legitimate, as it became possession of the rubbles. When the seller of the rubbles got half of what he bought, so more than that was like goods which he bought and thus he deserved some of the goods; for, what the claimant of the land took, was for reasons as if he deserved more than the purchaser.

Thereof master-mason Muhammad said: As of *al-Mudawwanah*, Ibn al-Qasim said as what Malik said: About someone who rented a land for years, cultivating trees and later the period was completed, the landlord has the right to give him the value of the trees after being pulled out, or he asks him to pull out the trees.

He said: If someone built in a land which he believed to be his, but was reclaimed by someone else, the claimant ought to be paid the value of the standing building because of *shubhah*. If he refuses, he should hand over the building that he erected. If he again refuses, both become partners, one is based on the value of his land and the other by the value of his trees, not on the basis of being a tenant, but because he toiled to a certain period.

119- General Discourse On Plantation; And Discourse On Someone Who Cuts Or Destroyed Someone Else's Trees.

Master-mason Muhammad said: Ibn Wahb narrated through Yunus that he asked Rabia'h about the damage to the land and trees. Rabia'h said: look at the price of the cultivated land, and the price after the trees were destroyed. The difference between these two prices will tell the damage caused. Let us say the price of the cultivated lot was twenty thousand, but after the damage occurred, its price decreased to four or five thousand. Thus, the difference will tell the value of the damage caused to the farmland. The leader (*imam*) might also consider extra punishment relevant to the action.

Master-mason Muhammad said: Ibn Habib said in *al-Wadihah*: I asked Asbagh bin al-Faraj about a garden or a cluster of olive trees or a garden with any kind of trees, which was destroyed by a hostile act, so how to evaluate what was damaged and destroyed? He replied to me: If the destruction of the tree is minor, it is evaluated on what has been damaged and destroyed and the value is paid according to that. If the destruction is comprehensive, it should be evaluated based on the most expansive value. It is by evaluating the value after the destruction; and the value of the garden, or farm or cluster of the olive trees before the destruction. So after deducting that, the real value should be known plus some value as a punishment for the misdemeanor. That is what Ibn Wahb narrated to us from Yunus bin Yazid from Rabia'h bin Abu 'Abdul Rahman and this is the better opinion in this case.

Thereof Master-mason Muhammad said: also from *al-Wadihah* Ibn Habib said: I said to Asbagh: Regarding the opinion which says that the value should be double on the destroyer of the tree, is such an opinion applicable in this case? He said to me: Malik has been asked about that and he rejects it, saying: There is no other value except the value of what has been destroyed. Ibn Wahb narrated the same opinion from Malik.

Ibn Habib said: Asbagh narrated what Malik said: Whoever destroyed the fruits before it matured, he has to pay the value of the fruits that he destroyed. Ibn Wahb said from Malik: He has to pay the value at the time of destruction, i.e. the value of the fruits when sold at that time.

120- Discourse On Someone Who Usurped Plants from A Man's Garden And He Planted It In His Garden.

Master-mason Muhammad said: Discourse on taking the plants is two kinds: Sometimes, it is for pruning (*dalalah*) and sometimes it is for usurpation (*ghasb*) and theft. If he took the plant by way for pruning, the plant's owner has no right to take the plant, but he should take its value on the day when the man took it out of his garden. If he took the plant by way of usurpation and theft, should the plant owner take his plant or its value? For this, four opinions:

Rabi'ah said: The plant owner can choose either to take the price of the plant higher than the sale price on the day when it was illegally taken or to take a similar plant, if he is able to get higher than what is sold.

Ibn Habib said: The plant owner has the right to pull out his plant even though the plant was planted a long time ago in the usurper's land.

Third opinion: Ibn al-Qasim said: If the tree was taken out legally according to the experts because of too many trees, he said: I do not think that he has a right to pull it out, and I think the owner can take its price, if there is a price for that, but if not, I think he has the right to pull it out.

Fourth opinion: Muhammad narrated from his father, Sahnun: If the date-palm tree or any tree can survive in the land of the owner after being uprooted from the usurper's land, then they can uproot it and plant it back at the owner's farm. If the tree will not survive after being uprooted, the value with a stern punishment should be imposed upon the usurper.

Master-mason Muhammad said: Text of the first opinion, Ibn Wahb said from Yunus from Yazid from Rabi'ah, he said: regarding a man who took a seedling of date palm tree or tree of another man, and he then replanted it in his land, or he bought it from someone who stole it. Rabi'ah said: If he took the plant in aggression without the consent of the owner, he should be punished severely and the owner of the seedling could have a choice whether to take the highest price on the day that his seedling was taken from his land or he is given a similar seedling if he is able to get the highest price for that seedling. If he bought and grew a stolen seedling, the owner can take from him the value of the seedling when someone claimed ownership on that seedling on his land.

It is not necessary to return a man's date palm seedling, which was cultivated by a person in his land since it will cause destruction to his land. It is like someone who went to the market and bought a plank or two planks of woods and used them to support his roof and built on it. Later, another person claims ownership on the planks. If he returned the planks, it would damage his house, which would cause him four hundred *dinars* while the price of the planks is ten *dinars*. If he paid the price of the planks so there is no cruelty on him. So too with the usurped seedling, the owner has a choice whether to take the value of the seedling or to take something similar to it with a higher price.

Master-mason Muhammad said: Text of the second opinion from *al-Wadihah* Ibn Habib said: I asked Asbagh about a man who took from another man's garden a trunk (of a tree) illegally and unjustly and planted it in his land. He (Asbagh) said: The plant owner is more rightful over his plant even if the plant grew in the land of the usurper for a long time; it is like a boy who was abducted and the owner later found him grown up and became a young man. He (the owner) is still the rightful owner, and similarly the plant because the root is still alive, whether the plant survives and grows after being replanted from the usurper's land or the plant does not survive. In this case, he still has a right over the plant; if he wishes, he could leave the plant to the usurper, and ask the value of the plant on the day that it was uprooted.

Master-mason Muhammad said: Text of the third opinion from *al-'Utbiyah* via auditioning of Asbagh from Ibn al-Qasim. Asbagh said: Ibn al-Qasim said: If the date palm seedling on the day it was uprooted is a necessary action according to the experts because of too many saplings, I do not think that it should be re uprooted again, and I think he (the owner) is entitled to the price of the seedling, if the seedling has a price on it. He said: If it is not like that, I think he has a right to uproot it, unless he wishes to accept the price.

Master-mason Muhammad said: Text of the fourth opinion is from the book of Ibn Sahnun: Sahnun was asked about someone who took a date-palm seedling of a man who did not claim the right of ownership until the seedling grew and became a date palm tree inside the land of the usurper or thief. He said: See if the tree or the date palm can survive after being pulled out of the usurper land and replanted at the owner's property, then he must repossess it. The growth of the plants in the land of the usurper or thief did not deny his (the owner's) right. If the plant would not survive in the land of its owner, then the usurper should pay its value.

Master-mason Muhammad said: If the usurper says: I do not need your date-palm tree, nor would I pay you its value but take it as it is and pull it out. Sahnun said: He could not do that. It is like someone who kidnapped a child and later his guardian claimed him after he grew up and became a young man. The growth of the baby does not invalidate his right. The claimant does not have to pay anything to the usurper on what he spent on the child.

Master-mason Muhammad said: Two opinions regarding the punishment of a usurper: Rabi'ah said: He should be severly punished. Ibn Wahb said: He should be punished according to what the leader (*imam*) thought suitable for the act.

Thereof master-mason Muhammad said: From the book of Ibn Sahnun, Muhammad said: I said to my father: If a man commanded his slave to plant for him a tree and the slave usurped his neighbor's plant and replanted it in his land. My father replied: This case is similar to what I have described to you before.

121- Discourse On A Man Who Took A Tree Of Another Man And Then Sold It To Someone Who Does Not Know That It Was Illegally Possessed; Should The Plant be Repossessed From The Buyer?

Master mason Muhammad said: Ibn Habib said in *al-Wadihah*: I said: If a man usurped a tree from another man's land, then he sold it to someone who does not know that it was illegally possessed and he planted it within his land; later on the owner of the plant claimed ownership of the firmly rooted plant. Ibn Habib said to me: The claimant has three options:

If he wishes, he could take the value of the plant from the usurper based on the day when he (the usurper) took out the plant whose value is fixed at that time in accordance to its condition.

If he wishes, he could take the price that is similar to the price if he had sold it. He should take it from the usurper.

If he wishes, he could repossess and pull out the plant on the condition that the time has not passed too long since the plant was planted in the land of the purchaser. If the time passed is too long he can then ask the buyer to pay him the value based on the day he planted it, not its present value; since he (the buyer) had to irrigate, cultivate and attend to it. Because of all his work, the plant reached its state of maturity. If he (the owner) takes the price of his plants from the purchaser, then the purchaser should ask the usurper for reimbursement for what he paid the owner.

Master-mason Muhammad said: The opinion of Asbagh differs in this problem; for his opinion about someone who usurped a plant of another person and then cultivates it. The owner of the plant, thus has a right to pull it out and take it, whether the time has passed too long or not. Except in this problem, he said: He has the right to take his plant if the time did not pass too long and he must consider his (the cultivator's) work for irrigating and taking care of the plant as his right; for, the cultivator is not the usurper. However, the real owner should excuse him (the cultivator). The matter is a burden on the plant owner when time passes too long in the land of the cultivator and he should be excused and do not cause him any harm, but ask him to pay the value (of the usurped tree).

122- Discourse On A Man While He Was Absent His Land Was Usurped By A Person, And Another One Usurped A Seedling And Planted It In His Land.

Master mason Muhammad said: Ibn Habib said in *al-Wadihah*: I asked Asbagh: If a man whose land was usurped by another man while he was absent, and a second man usurped a seedling then cultivate it in his land. Afterward the landowner stood against usurper and claimed his ownerships on the land, while the seedling owner claimed his, which is rooted and became a big tree. He replied to me: The land owner could take his land and the seedling owner could take the plant after being pulled out whether it will survive or not, and the only benefit he would get is its wood. I said to him: you have not agreed with the one who judged that since the land belonged to him, he should pay the value of the tree (to the owner); for, he is not the one who usurped the tree. He is like a purchaser who knew nothing (on what he bought). He replied to me: it is not like that, if he is the buyer, then he is also the grower. However, in this case the usurper planted it as his own, so the owner of the plant has a right to take it back if he liked, as he is rightful to it even if the usurper grew it in his land. There are no differences (in these two cases) except if he (the owner) wishes to let the plant grow in the land of the usurper. So the plant owner could claim the value (of his plant) from the usurper based on the day he took it from the usurped land. Or else the landowner, where the usurped tree is located, agrees to pay the value (of the tree); or another option that is lawful for both of them.

123- Discourse On Someone Who Pulled Out (a stem) Of A Tree That Belonged To another Man and Then Nurtured It In His Land.

Master mason Muhammad said: about a man who pulls out a stem of a tree that belonged to another person and then grew it in his land. It is either: that he did that by way of usurpation or by way of pruning. If he does that by way of usurpation, he is an aggressor. His action is either harmful to the tree or not. If it is harmful, he should be chastised, punished severely and pay the damage caused to the tree by his action. It is disputed whether he should pay the value or to pull it out and give it back to the owner. Regarding this, there are three opinions:

Ibn al-Qasim said in *al-'Utbiyah*: If the plant is of no value according to the custom of their country, I think that it is to the cultivator. I do not think that the tree owner should get anything.

Asbagh said: He (the owner) should be paid the value of the twig pulled out.

Ibn Habib said in *al-Wadihah*: If he claimed his right on what the other person grew, if it has value – then he has the right to take it. If time passed too long and after the tree grew, I think there is no way for him to take it. However, he is entitled to the value of the tree based on the day when it was pulled out and did not harm his trees, based on its value as broken twigs.

Master mason Muhammad said: How about if he cut the stem for pruning, not as an aggressor or usurper? Asbagh said: He should legitimize it, if he wished to do so, and if not he (who cut the stem) ought to pay the value of it as broken twigs, the value based on the day when he cut it.

Master mason Muhammad said: The value is inclusive on whatever damage is caused to the tree, illegally taken or for pruning. The punishment is imposed upon the usurper, not upon the one who prunes the tree.

Master-mason Muhammad said: The difference between the tree and a cut off twigs (*amlakh*) are as they said: *Amlakh* is different from the plant. For us, the plant is a living root, which is taken and planted live. The plant also remains firm and grows. It is like a small boy who was abducted by a man and later grows to become a young man, yet his guardian/parent is the rightful owner forever.

As for *amlakh / imtilakh* (cuting off twigs or branches), it is dead like a seed that was usurped by a man who then cultivates it in his land and it grows. Thus, the tree is for the usurper and he ought to return back a similar seed from whom he has taken illegally. Likewise, the usurper is responsible. Master-mason Muhammad said: The dominant opinion is based on the value of the twig the day it was cut off.

124- Discourse On Someone Who Usurped Saffron's Corm and Then Cultivates It In His Land.

Master-mason Muhammad said: Two different opinions on someone who stole saffron's corm and then cultivates it in his land:

Al-'Utbi said in *al-Mustakhrajah*: Asbagh asked Ibn al-Qasim about someone who steals saffron's corm of a man and then cultivates it in his land. The plant flourished and blossomed then the owner found out and he did not make a report on that or report it. Ibn al-Qasim said: If he knew that it was his plant that was flourishing and maturing and it was confirmed by the thief in front of people or the Sultan, the owner of the plant could choose either to take the value of his plant or to take the onions itself. If he could not recognize whether it was the corm, which was stolen, or not, the owner of the plant could take the price of his plant based on the day that the corm was stolen.

Second opinion: Asbagh said in *al-'Utbiyah*: This case in my opinion is like the case of the flourishing and maturing plant that was claimed in someone else property. The man, who claimes ownership, is rightful to buy the plant or to pay its value and he has no option regarding its cultivation.

125- Discourse On A Tree Owned by A Man And It's Roots Protruded into His Neighbor's Land.

Master mason Muhammad said: regarding a tree owned by a man in his land, its roots protruded into neighboring land and sprouted shoots. Thus, the owner of the tree has a choice on that; if the tree is still useful for him, he can uproot it and plant it somewhere else inside his property: and if it is not useful for him and without the shoots he will not face any damage, then the tree shoots belongs to his neighbor. Except if, the neighbor cut down the tree shoots, the tree owner has the right on the price of the wood or firewood. However, he has to pay his neighbor the cost of cutting down the tree shoots. This is the opinion of 'Isa b. Dinar from Ibn al-Qasim in *al-'Utbiah* and Ibn 'Abdus said from Ibn al-Qasim. 'Isa b. Dinar said: If the existence of the new shoot would endanger the root of the original tree, then he has no right to (maintain the new shoot) except by consent of the owner of the tree.

Ibn 'Abdus and others said: The tree shoot should be left to him (the neighbor), especially if its existence is not harmful to the owner of the old tree. If the roots of the old tree supplies water to the new one sprouting shoot inside the land of his neighbor then he has the right to remove the tree shoot. Except, if the owner of the land where the shoot is located, wishes to cut off the connection between the old and the new tree so there will be no damage to the old tree. In that case he has to pay the value of the new sprout and he can keep it.

Ibn Habib said in *al-Wadihah* from Asbagh: If he thinks that the new sprouting shoot would harm the first tree, causing lack of water to it, then the tree owner is right to cut it off if he wishes. If he opted to leave it and believes that it is not harmful to the tree, then he (the neighbor) can choose whether to pull it out from his land or to pay the owner of the old tree price of the sprout being pulled out. He can choose either one.

Thereof master mason Muhammad said about a tree growing on a mound between two walls; the mound either belongs to one of them, or the ownership is uncertain, but both of them claim it as theirs while the tree is heavily intertwined or (its root) is deeply penetrated. Ibn al-Qasim said in the book of Ibn 'Abdus that, if the mound belonged to one of them then whatever grows on it belongs to him. Hence, the root of that tree should be examined (if it is possible to dig it without damaging the tree), then the owner of the tree has the right to the value of the tree; or he is ordered to remove it from his land if the tree has value.

He said: If the owner of the mound cannot be identified and both men claimed full ownership, while the tree is divisible, the mound and the trees should be divided equally between them. He said: If the trees become intertwined and its fruits fall down by the wind, and it could not be identified from which of the two trees are the fruits, then I think the fruits should be sold by one of them and its price divided between them.

126- Discourse On The Tree Owned By A Man Causing Damage To His Neighbor's Wall, Could The Tree Be Cut Off?

Master mason Muhammad said: If a tree owned by a man, harmed a neighbor's wall, then it is either the tree was planted before the construction of the wall or the tree was planted later than the wall. If the tree is new while the wall was built earlier, then whatever harms the wall should be cut, be it minor or major and I did not see any dispute about that.

Master mason Muhammad said: So too with its roots. However, if the tree preceded the wall, and the wall was built later, then they differed in two views:

'Isa bin Dinar said in his book, *al-Jidar*: if the tree preceded the wall, then examine its present condition, how extensive are its branches spreading. If it is established that the wall was built after the tree, then the tree should not be cut down. However, for the branches that sprouted after the wall was constructed and caused damage to the wall, they should be pruned. Ibn Habib narrated the same opinion from Mutarrif. Ibn Habib said in *al-Wadihah* from Ibn al-Majishun: If the tree preceded the wall, then it should be left alone. As for the expanding branches, they should be left untouched, even if they damaged the wall. Because this is the nature of the tree with its ever-expanding branches, also because the tree possessed it's surrounding area (*harim*) and its airspace. Ibn Habib said: I asked Asbagh about that and he replied to me similar to Mutarrif's view, which I favor most and applied in my judgment.

127- Discourse On The Tree Belonged To A Man, Its Huge Branches Are Harmful To His Neighbor's Property.

Master mason Muhammad said: It is either that its huge branches are growing upward or its branches are growing sideways encroaching onto his neighbor's land.

If its branches are growing upward towards the sky, shadowing his neighbor's land or house, then the tree should not be cut down; for, it is as if a building built by a man inside his property, and his house obstructs his neighbor's house from the sun and the wind. His neighbor has no right to protest, so too with the tree as long as it does not bend over toward his neighbor's airspace. The author said: I do not know any different opinion about this. They differed when the branches are slanted towards neighbor's airspace.

Master mason Muhammad said: Ibn al-Qasim said: If both of them, nurtured the tree, then there is no harm on each other's, i.e. none would harm each other. If both of them inherited it or bought it or it (tree) benefited both of them and later divided the tree, then the tree expanded inside the neighbor's property and shadowed his house and prevented him from benefits (like sunshine or air circulation), the tree should not be cut down. This is because, when they divided it, or they bought it, they knew already that the nature of the tree is to grow and gets bigger. If the tree grows and gets bigger inside the property of one of them as described, I do not think that the tree should be pruned or pulled out from its present place, even if it's getting bigger, because they already knew this since dividing or buying it.

Second opinion: Asbagh said in *al-'Utbiyyah* that Ibn Nafi' was asked about that and he replied: this matter to me is the same, either they acquired the tree by way of growing it or purchasing or others; if the tree gets bigger or shadows (the neighboring house), then the tree should be trimmed down. For the tree should not be divided as described before. Rather, what can be divided is the land with the tree and later the land's value, addition, and measurement should be adjusted.

Ibn Nafi' also said: In our opinion when the date palm gets larger, its height could be known by comparing (the length of) its shadow with its trunk, when the current shadow is longer. May this be a guide to the problem.

Ibn Mazin said: I asked Asbagh about that and he gave the same opinion like Ibn Nafi': for the tree, that causes damage because of its growth has to be prevented from damaging others.

Master mason Muhammad said: In the book of 'Isa bin Musa, he said: 'Umar bin Yusuf told me, He said: I asked Muhammad bin Talid about an old tree whose history is unknown. He replied: (an old tree) is not subject to anything, whatever happens because of it does not account for, neither what became dry because of it. As for the recently (planted) tree whenever it damages, or shadows someone's property, the cause should be eliminated. 'Isa b. Musa said: Ismail b. Mawsil has the same opinion. Ibn Talid said regarding the tree in the garden shading a man's property and the landowner then bought that tree from its owner. Then he told the owner of the garden, saying: cut it down for me whenever the tree grows since I bought it already. The tree was recently planted; do you think he (the landowner) has right on that? Meanwhile the owner of the tree said to him: Indeed, you have bought it and you know that this tree is growing. Does (his action by buying the tree) will benefit him or not? What if the garden was divided between people, and the tree gets bigger and shadows (others' properties) after the division? He replied: As to the tree which has been divided among the heirs, nobody can prevent the owner from nurturing his tree to grow and generates new branches and shoots, for by the increase of the new branches they could divide it, so too with an old tree with an unknown history or origin.

Master mason Muhammad said: Asbagh narrated the same opinion from Ibn al-Qasim, on a man who noticed that his neighbor's land is being sold whereas there is a big tree overshadowing his property belonged to the said neighbor. The man did not complain until the transaction was completed. He thus had no right to ask (the new owner) to cut it off, for (the new owner) would argue that: I will adhere to whatever complain you have but there is none, so it is not your right and I have an argument on that. He said: This is the view of 'Isa bin Musa from Ibn Talid.

Master mason Muhammad said: This is contrary to Sahnun's view; for, he said: Whatever comes out from the tree protruding into a neighbor's land, the neighbor has a right to cut the protruding branches up to the land's border, because the airspace that the branches protruded into belongs to this neighbor.

Thereof master-mason Muhammad said: Ibn 'Abdus said in his book: Sahnun was asked about two men who grew two trees in their land which borders the other, and one of the trees harmed the other. He answered that both should remain as it was; for, each one is working on their own land as they like, and each one should avoid from creating anything which causes damage to the other. If one of the trees was planted before the other, then damage to it from the other later tree should be prevented.

Master mason Muhammad said: If the distance is too close and it damages the newly planted tree, how far should the distance between them be? Abu al-Hasan al-Lakhmi said in *al-Tabsirah*: I asked the experts regarding the *harim* of fruit trees, they replied: The protected area (*harim*) of a fruit tree is twenty cubits from each direction.

Master-mason said: Ibn Habib said in *al-Wadihah* as Asbagh had said: As for the tree located in a man's land by way of inheritance or purchase or (planted) in an open space or in whatever other condition, while its height and branches are growing and damaging the land, the owner has no right of dispute on that. Ibn al-Qasim was asked in another book, and he gave the same opinion.

Master mason Muhammad said: I did not come across any different opinion in this matter and I do not know whether any exist or not.

128- Discourse On The Tree Or The Date Palm Belongs To A Man Inside Someone Else's Property And The Tree Falls Down, Could He Replace It With Another One? Or A Date Palm Which Belongs To A Man In Another Man's Property And Damages Him (The Landowner), Could It Be Sold to Him?

Master mason Muhammad said: Ibn Wahab narrated from Jarir bin Hazim that Wasil, *maula* of Abu 'Uyainah bin al-Mahlab, reported to him that he heard Abu Ja°far Muhammad bin 'Ali bin Husain saying that Samrah bin Jundab owned an *al-'Adhidah* (an offshoot from palm tree) in a walled garden of a man from *al-Ansar*. Then he (Samrah) entered the walled garden without permission and the owner later complained to the Prophet. And the Prophet called upon him, saying: Sell it to your brother, however he refused. He (the Prophet) said: Give it (as a gift) to him; but he also refused. The Prophet said: Go away you are damaging (others), go (owner of walled garden) to his date palm and cut it down and throw it away.[179]

Master mason Muhammad said: Ibn Wahab also narrated that Jarir said: Muhammad bin Ishaq told me from 'Asim bin 'Amrah that Qatadah al-Ansari said: Abu Lubabah bin al-Munzir had a date palm in an *al-Ansar* man's walled garden. And the owner of the tree would enter the garden and annoy its owner. Thus the man said to him (Abu Lubabah): Indeed, you irritate me, so sell me your date palm or you may remove it to your property; but he refused. Then the man went to the Prophet and the Prophet replied: O! Abu Lubabah sell it to your brother or take a similar tree from his land. He (Abu Lubabah) said: I will not do that. The Prophet said: You will have the same in paradise, he replied: I will not sell the date palm. The Prophet said: Go! Remove the date palm from his garden and plant it in your garden, and build a wall between you and him.

Master mason Muhammad said: Regarding on the tree or date palm, which belonged to a man and it died, could he replant

---

[179] Narrated by al-Baihaqi in *Sunan al-Kubra*, Vol. 6, p. 157

another tree in its place. Thus, we replied: either the newly planted tree would be like the previous one in the sense of size, branch diffusion, and harmfulness. The scholar unanimously agreed that he has the right to replant without looking at differences the in type of tree, such as the former is a fig replaced with an olive tree, or the former is an olive replaced with a walnut or similar to that, thus he has the right to do that. However, if what is re-planted is bigger and more harmful than the former, then he has no right to do that.

The opinion differed if he wants to replace it with two trees.

Ibn al-Qasim said: He has no right for that, except one. Ashhab said: He has the right to plant two trees if there is no harm to the owner of the land.

Master mason Muhammad said: from the book of Ibn 'Abdus: Ibn al-Qasim was asked about a man who had a date palm which died. He then wished to grow in its place an olive or a walnut or a date palm, or two date palms or two trees. He said: He is allowed to plant, according to local custom, what is similar to his date palm. However, he has no right to add anything else, and he has no rights to grow what is, according to local custom, anything bigger that might harm the land. I did not hear that from Malik but that is my opinion; for Malik has allowed him to replant in place of his date palm.

Master mason Muhammad said: Text of the second opinion. Ibn 'Abdus said Ashhab had said in the case of replanting two date palms, if it is not harmful then he has right to do that. If it would damage his partner's date palm, then he is forbidden. As for growing an olive or walnut or other type of tree, if the damaging effect is similar to the date palm or almost the same on other nearby trees, then he has the right to do that, and if not then he cannot do that.

Thereof master mason Muhammad said: From *al-'Utbiyah*, Ibn al-Qasim said: Malik was asked about a man who had a tree in a land and the tree fell down and shoots from it grew in that location, do they belong to the owner of the original tree? He said: Yes. Ibn 'Abdus has the same opinion, which he narrated from Ibn al-Qasim from Malik.

Master mason Muhammad said: From *al-'Utbiyah*, (al-'Utbi) said: I asked Ibn al-Qasim: Do you think the owner of the tree has a right to plant another tree in the place (of the previous tree)? He replied: Yes, I believe he has the right on that. Ibn

'Abdus said from Ibn al-Qasim and Malik the same. Ibn Kinanah and Ashhab have the same opinion.

Ashhab said: That is like the palm tree and land both belong to you. Similarly, one who has one palm tree or many palm trees is same in this case. Ibn Kinanah said: Unless the date tree is an endowment (*hubs*) property, or he only has the right to its fruits, but he did not own the tree, then he has no right on that.

129- Discourse On A Fruit Tree That Belonged To A Man Whose Fruit Falls Inside His Neighbor's Garden and Damages His Property.

Master mason Muhammad said: From the book of 'Isa b. Musa: Ismail bin Mawsil was asked about a man having a grape vine and another man having a fruit farm in a village, planted with walnut tree whose branches are leaning toward the grapevine. Thus, whenever the tree owner harvested his walnut, the walnuts dropped onto the grapevine and on the *dawali* (a kind of grapes) of the man and damages his property. Does he have the right to stop the harm or not? He replied: The grapevine owner has no argument against the fruit farm owner while the latter is harvesting, entering into it, and going out without ruining or damaging anything. If his action causes obvious destruction and damages the grapevine, then he could have been prevented and told: you can enter and leave and harvest your fruit (walnut) as people would do, without harming my grape vine.

Master mason Muhammad said: This judgment applied if the fruit farm preceded the grapevine or he bought the grapevine and the fruit trees were leaning toward the grapevine. Thus the problem described by Ibn al-Qasim, is valid as previously mentioned.

If the two owners setup their farms in their property at the same time, and the tree owned by one of them grows bigger and protrudes into the neighbor's land, it should be trimmed once it encroaches on the airspace of the other, as Sahnun and others have said.

130- Discourse On The Tree That Belonged To A Man Inside His House Overlooking His Neighbor.

Master mason Muhammad said: From *al-'Utbiyah* through audition of 'Abdul Malik bin al-Hasan narrated from Ibn Wahab, Abdul Malik said: Ibn Wahab was asked about a man who grew a tree inside his house which then became tall until it overlooked his neighbor's house. When he climbed the tree to collect the fruit, he can look inside his neighbor's house. His neighbor feared that he (the tree owner) could enter his house or he could overlook/view his family, this harmful effect becomes an issue that should be prevented. The tree was there for so many years and it keeps growing each year. When he brought up the matter to the authority, of what is harmful to him, the question that arrises: should he (owner of the tree) be forced to cut what was damaging (his neighbor) and what was used to overlook him and his family? He replied: If there is no other necessity except based on what he complained and feared of overlooking by the person who was collecting the fruit, then he can not do that and he has no case to prevent someone from collecting the fruit for the sake of the fear of overlooking.

Master mason Muhammad said: From the book of *al-Jidar* written by 'Isa bin Dinar: He was asked about a tree in a man's house, when he climbed up to collect the fruit, he could overlook what was inside the house of his neighbor, is he prevented from that? He replied: He is not prevented from that and I do not see it as similar to overlooking from a room.

Master mason Muhammad said: They differed on whether the tree owner must get permission (from the nighbor) to climb the tree; in two opinions:

Ibn Wahab said in *al-'Utbiyah*: He should get permission to climb the tree to pluck the fruit. Ibn Habib said the same in *al-Wadihah* from Mutarrif, Ibn al-Majishun, and Asbagh, it is the predominant opinion. 'Isa bin Dinar said: He does not need to get permission.

Thereof master mason Muhammad said: If a tree is damaging the wall by its branches, and the roots beneath the ground also damages a well or cistern, then Ibn Wahab said in al-'Utbiyah: What is causing the harm should be cut off.

Master mason Muhammad said: This occurred to us in Tunis, of a man who grew in his house a fig tree, and there was a cistern behind the wall that belonged to his neighbor. The roots of the tree crept toward the cistern, piercing its wall and causing the water to dry up. Therefore, both of them (the tree owner and his neighbor) brought their case to al-Sheikh al-Fakih al-Qadi Abu Ishaq bin 'Abdul Rafi'. We were asked to look into the matter and we told him about the damage to the cistern from the roots of the tree. He said to us: If by cutting the roots the harm can be eliminated, then cut off the roots but save the tree. If the harm to the cistern cannot be eliminated by cutting the roots, then eliminate the harm to the cistern as God inspires you to do. We then said to him that by cutting down the tree we could prevent the damage. For the roots of a fig tree move along under the ground towards wherever there is water and neither building or anything else can stop it, in contrast to other trees. In fact, no matter how the root is cut, the rest of it would creep towards the water. Thus, the tree ought to be cut down.

131- Discourse On The Tree Adjacent To A Public Street, Which Is Harmful To Passersby.

Master mason Muhammad said: From *al-'Utbiyah* through audition of Asbagh from Ibn al-Qasim, who said: He was asked about a tree close to the road and its growth and nurture by its owner or he bought it, then it harmed the street, do you think what was harmful to the street from the tree, should be cut off? He said: Yes! I think so; the public street should be cleared off from any damaging elements from whatever direction.

Master-mason Muhammad said: This differed from what he said regarding a tree growing and leaning towards a neighboring garden.

132- Discourse On A Parched River; Could Someone Nearby Reclaim The Parched Land?

Master mason Muhammad said: Opinion differed on the parched river adjacent to a village, when parts of it becomes dry each year until it turns into a vacant land; could someone adjacent to it reclaim the land? Two opinions:

Ibn al-Majishun said in *al-Wadihah*: My opinion is that the landowner located next to the parched river can reclaim it since the adjacent land belongs to him. If the land is uncultivated (*al-bur*) and owned by people, then it becomes part of fallow land. Someone asked: If the flow of the river deviates from its stream, swallowed the adjacent land, and carried the soil away, so the deposited land belongs to whom? He replied: To the two men who were staying along the river. God has transferred its course to his land, and then he could irrigate the land with the river.

Second opinion: master mason Muhammad said: Ibn Habib also said in *al- Wadihah*: I asked Mutarrif about that, and he replied:

Whether part of the river or all of it dries up or the river changes its course, and its former stream becomes virgin land in which it is worked and tilled, that land does not belong to anybody except the authority (*imam*), and they will decide to whom it should be allocated. The land is considered as a surplus land (*al-ᶜafa*) and dead land (*al-mawat*) because the river was not created by man, it is not owned by anybody, rather it is like a public street, accessible by all, where water might come to the place one day or the place remains uncultivated and thus it belongs to all the people to benefit from. Moreover, it is the duty of the leader (*imam*) to look into the matter. Mutarrif aso said: It is not the right of someone staying next to a river to operate a mill or something like that, because they alone would benefit from the water. When the river dries up, its watercourse becomes ground, and its condition changes from the present, so it is up to the leader to look into the matter.

Ibn Habib said: If the surrounding area around a river is an uninhabited or uncultivated place, then it is owned by people of that village or adjoining villages. Yet, why is it not considered to belong to them, but considered as a fallow land? He said to me: It cannot be treated like a fallow land; for if the place was considered as fallow land, then it would be treated like their pasture and under their possession. However, if the river continues to exist as a river, the water would benefit them and others, like setting up on it something or to irrigate their land or as a waterway, thus, all people have equal access to it. Therefore, if the place dries up, it becomes an '*afa* land (surplus land) and it is up to the authority to allocate it.

Abdul Malik bin Habib said: I asked Asbagh about that and his reply is similar to Mutarrif's opinion.

Abdul Malik said: It is an analogy; the principal is that people should follow the leader's (*imam*) determination, if they have one, on matters like this or similar to it. If not, then al-Majishun opinion is more preferable to me.

133- Discourse On The River Running Between People, They Compete For Its Water, How Should The Water be Allocated.

Master mason Muhammad said: from *al-Wadihah*, Abdul Malik bin Habib said as Mutarrif and Ibn al-Majishun, on rivers which the surrounding people were competing with each other to draw water from. If it is not a man made river, but a natural one and is not owned by anybody who is staying near it, or at upstream or downstream from it, rather it is a bounty which God sent down to his servants for their benefit: then the first to benefit is the one nearer to it. He would utilize it to operate his mill or to irrigate his farm. Then he would pass it to someone downstream who would benefit from it with blessing as he wishes. Therefore, someone downstream, who gets less than others, has no right to claim neither to protest on the advantage of people upstream, which was made by God to be close to the river. Our reference on that matter is the judgment of the Prophet regarding the flood-channels of *Mahzur* and *Muzaynib*[180], both are two oases in Medina, while the upstream has a right to dam the water up to the ankle level, and then he should release it to the downstream user and so on, until the water reaches the last person. The water might be abundant for all or could be insufficient for some. Mutarrif and Ibn al-Majishun said: That is the rule among us regarding rivers that are naturally flowing as a bounty from God to his servants, but not on a man-made rivers. The ones who are closer to the river are more deserving to benefit either for milling or irrigation purposes; then followed by the ones below and so on. If the last one receives insufficient water, the Prophet already said that: The upstream (user) does not cause any harm. Thereby this proof justifies our explanation.

Abdul Malik said: I said to both: Is it the same if the upstream user used the water to operate their mill, but not for irrigation, or for irrigation, but not for running their mill and the downstream user also has the same pattern of usage or differed from that? They both answered: When the need for the water is equal between the upstream user and the downstream user, the upstream user still has the right to use it first as we have described to you. For example, both of them are in need of water for operating the mill or irrigating their fields, or the need of the upstream user is to irrigate the field and the need of the downstream user is to operate the mill and thus the upper has the right to use the water first.

If the need of the upstream user is to operate the mill and the downstream to irrigate the trees after the upstream takes his

---

[180] Narrated by Malik in *Muwatta'* 2:744 *Kitab al-Aqdiah*, hadith no: 28.

portion to operate the mill; however the upstream user still has priority in using the water first. If the trees do not receive the water from upstream user or the upstream user dams it for himself to operate the mill so the downstream user is left dry for a few days, in this case the trees have the priority (to receive the water). Since the downstream users have a right on the water that were used by the upstream user for their mill and they blocked the water from flowing downstream, then they should be prevented from doing that. This is applicable for the trees that depend on water to survive before the water dries up. It is not applicable if the seedling is just begun or for the yearly cultivation of vegetable like onion and watermelon and the like of which there is no fixed principle.

Thereof master mason Muhammad said: from *al-Wadihah*, Mutarrif and Ibn al-Majishun said: As for collecting water from piping (*al-khuruj*) and irrigation channel (*al-sawaqi*) which was built by the villagers to be used in their mills or to irrigate their fields according to their right of the amount that they are entitled to. Their location on the channel has no influence since their share was determined, whether their need for it is equal or not.

Master-mason Muhammad said: Ibn Wahb, Ibn al-Qasim and Asbagh and Ibn Nafi' have similar opinions.

134- Discourse On A Flowing Irrigation Channel, Which A Man Wished To Split It and Direct The Upstream Water To His Mill And Return The Water To Its Origin, Could He do That? And On The Spring That Belongs To A Man, From Its Water His Neighbor Planted And Then The Spring Owner Wished To Divert His Water.

Master mason Muhammad said: On an irrigation channel flowing through a property of a man to people downstream for their irrigation, the man either takes drinking water from it or not, but he wishes to build a secondary channel at the upstream location since it already flows through his land. This secondary channel will be connected to another channel for running a mill. The water will then be released back to the main channel to be used by people downstream. Does he have the right to do that?

Therefore, we say: Either his action will harm them or not.

If his action would harm and damage them, he is prevented from doing so and there is no difference of opinions on that. If his action does not harm or damage them, the scholars differed into two opinions:

Ibn al-Majishun said: If it is a natural channel and not dug by them, and if the downstream users do not think that it would damage them by cutting off their water supply at any time, then he can create another channel. However, if that is not according to this feature or they dug the channel to run the water, then he has no right to do that.

Second opinion: Mutarrif and Asbagh said: He has no right to do that whether it is harmful to them or not; whether it is a natural channel or not.

Master-mason Muhammad said: If the irrigation channel was not dug by the people, and it was something bestowed by God and it will not be cause any damage by splitting it and the water would be returned back to its original course; then he can do that, since he has the priority on the water over the downstream users due to his location. And if the people created the channel, and they owned it and not him, they have the right to prevent him; for the irrigation channel is theirs and (the water) cannot be transferred without their permission. This is an analogy to what Ibn al-Qasim said in another section.

Thereof, the author said: Ibn al-Qasim said on a water spring that belonged to a man in his garden which is at the top of a hill while there is another man's house located below. He (the owner of the house downstream) then dug a channel to supply the water to his house and garden using the water from the upstream spring. He drinks and irrigates his farm from the water spring for a long time. Thereupon the water spring owner wishes to remove it from the downstream owner who was utilizing it and to stop it from him without any reason. He replied: He (the owner of the spring) has the right on that. The downstream owner who planted and utilized the spring water to irrigate his farm without permission has no right to prevent the spring's owner from changing his watercourse. If he (the owner downstream) was allowed (by the spring owner) to utilize the water and establish plants, he (spring's owner) cannot reverse his permission.

Master-mason Muhammad said: Asbagh and Ibn Nafi' gave the same opinion in the book of Ibn Habib after the spring's owner takes the oath - that he knew (the downstream user is utilizing his water) - that this happened without his permission. If he did not know (about the downstream owner utilizing his water), he should not take an oath. Then he has a right to remove the watercourse except if the tree is bearing fruits; fearing that by removing the water, it could destroy the fruit. Moreover, if it is vegetation, let it be harvested first (before removing the watercourse).

135- Discourse On Fishing Areas In Lakes, Rivers, Pools, And Small Lakes. Is It Possible For The People Around Those Natural Resources To Prevent Others From Fishing?

Master-mason Muhammad said: Fishing areas in the sea, rivers, pools, and small lakes; is it possible for the people surrounding those fishing places to prevent others (from fishing) or not?

Three opinions differed:

Ibn Habib said in *al-Wadihah* from Mutarrif and Ibn al-Majishun: Whatever belonged to them or under their possession they have a right to prevent others from it and whatever from the rivers and gulfs that are not owned by anyone, whomever staying adjacent to such places has no right to prevent others from fishing. Ibn Habib said: I said to both: If they erected fishing traps using wood or reeds or whatever technique known by the fishermen; do they have any right to prevent people in those areas from using those areas for fishing? Both of them replied to me: They have no right to refrain others (from fishing) at all. After they achieved their need, it is said to them: Allow others to fish in it.

Second opinion: Asbagh said from Ibn al-Qasim in *al-Wadihah*: All of that is the same for Ibn al-Qasim; whether it is possessed by them or not. Thus, it is not appropriate for them to prevent others from fishing in those areas. It is similar to grazing land.

Master mason Muhammad said: In a narration of Sahnun from Ibn al-Qasim regarding someone who had a pool or a small lake with fish, inside his land. He has no right to prevent others from fishing in it, and such a place cannot be sold to someone who is fishing there for a year; because (the fish) can increase or decrease.

Third opinion: Ashhab said: If they added fish and they multiplied, then they have the right to prevent others from fishing until they are able to satisfy their need from fishing. If it is not like that, then they have no right to prevent others.

Thereof Master mason Muhammad said: Asbagh said on fishing devises: One who wished to make a fishing trap over a fishing trap of others who preceded him, has the right to do so. The one who has preceded others, has no right to prevent someone after him (to catch fish). And if he said: You caused the fish to run away or turn them away from my fishing trap; as long as he does not place his fishing trap at the opening of the earlier fishing trap in such a way that it would block some fish from the trap or blocks all of them. As for what was placed above or under the earlier fishing trap, if that is considered as a way of fishing and the fishing area is extensive that enables the hunt to be flexible, then he (the earlier one) has no right to prevent him (the one who came later).

Asbagh said: As for fishing traps the owners have the right to fish and satisfy their needs first. Whatever is left after that, they cannot prevent others from fishing as I explained to you before.

136- Discourse On A Damaged Mill Owned By A Group Of People, And One Of Them Calls For Repair While Some Refused.

Master-mason Muhammad said: 'Isa bin Dinar was asked about the mill owned by a group of people, which was damaged, one of them called to repair it while some of them refused. He said: Tell the ones who refused: whether you do or you hire someone to work with him, they are obliged to repair. This is also the opinion of Malik. Someone said to him: If some of them repaired and spent some money on it and when they finished their work and started to operate the mill, the one who refused to repair said: This is half of what you have spent and I should have my share fom it. 'Isa said that the one who refused is entitled to his share because he shared on the repair (after paying what was due to him).

Master-mason Muhammad said: I do not know any opinion differing from that. However, the opinion differed to whom the profit belongs before the partner pays half of the expenditure; Muhammad bin Ibrahim bin Dinar (al-Madani) said: It belongs to the one who repaired first according to what he spent on it and what his share was before that. One who did not contribute to the repairs work will get the profit according to his share before the work was done.

Master mason Muhammad said: Ibn al-Qasim has a different opinion about that, saying: The profit belongs entirely to the one who repaired and none for one who refused to work with him until he pays his share of the expenditure of what was done. It is similar to the case of the well whose water is seeping or part of it is damaged and one of the two co-partners wished to repair it while the other refused. Therefore, it is said to the one who refused to work: Work with him or hire someone to work with him. If he still refuses to contribute, all the water is for the one who repaired the well until he pays his share for the cost of repairing. This rule is also applicable to the mill as was mentioned in the section on the water well.

Master-mason Muhammad said: 'Isa bin Dinar said that he saw Ibn Bashir[181] judging according to this view.

Ibn al-Qasim said on the mill: Offset the expenses incurred from the generated yield. If he did not pay half of the expenditure, his share of the profit will be considered as his capital for repairing purpose so he will get nothing from the yield.

Master-mason Muhammad said: 'Isa bin Dinar said: And what I think is that the entire yield belongs to the one who has done the repairs. The one who did not participate is still entitled for the rent of his share on spaces from the mills and what remained from the work. If he wants to share with them, he should contribute to their expenditure; based on the value when he entered in the partnership, not the value of their expenditure.

'Isa said: It was informed to me from Ibn Wahb that his opinion on the yield is like Ibn Dinar al-Madani's opinion: that the yield is for the worker according to what he spent on it and what was for him. The one, who did not participate, is still entitled to his share from the site of the mill and the rest of the mill's operation.

Master-mason Muhammad said: The interpretation of that is to assess the value of the damaged mill and the value after its repairs. If its value before the operation is ten and after the operation is fifteen, then one third of the yield is for the worker (who restored it) and two thirds of the yield is between him and his co-partner. Then the one who refused to work has to pay the wage to the worker (restorer) during the day he carried out the work. If the one who refused to work later wishes to join with the one who restord the mill, he should pay the equivalent of the

---

[181] He is Abu 'Abdullah Muhammad b. Said b. Bashir b. Sharahil (d. 198/814). He travelled east and heard directly from Malik, then returned to al-Andalus and became the Qadi of Cordova. See *Tartib al-Madarik* 3:327-339, and *Tarikh Qudat al-Andalus* 47-53.

value of the mill based on his share. The payment is based on the value on the day he pays him.

Master-mason Muhammad said: Yahya bin Yahya gave the same opinion regarding all of that in dividing the yield and paying the value. He narrated from Ibn al-Qasim a different opinion.

Mutarrif said: the entire yield is for the one who repaired the mill whereas the rental fees of the space is upon his friend including the remaining of what was from the space that can be utilized. When he rejoins him, he ought to pay the approximate value based on the day he rejoins or based on the expenditure.

Master mason Muhammad said: Ibn al-Majishun said: He can offset the expenses incurred with the generated yield. When he reimburses him on the expenditure so that each one ownes half.

Master mason Muhammad said: This is one of the two opinions of Ibn al-Qasim narrated by Ibn Habib. Ibn Habib also narrated another opinion of Ibn al-Qasim that is similar to the opinion of Mutarrif. Asbagh bin al-Faraj also has a similar opinion.

Ibn al-Majishun said: In my opinion, it is like a damaged house and shop shared between two parties and later one of them rebuilt it. That is a contract of *salaf*[182] to his partner; if his companion likes, he can pay him half of the price and they can divide the yield and rent. If he likes, he can hold his payment and compensate it with his yield until all the expense incurred is fully paid. After that, the yield can be shared equally between them.

Ibn al-Majishun said: If the mill, shop, or the dwelling is a *waqf* property, the one who refused, cannot be forced to sell if he did not want to join the renovation. It is said to the other: Work alone, and when your partner gives you half of what you have spent, then he is your partner.

Ibn al-Majishun said: If he made his mind to rebuild, he should find a trusted expert (*amin*) who knows the total expenditure and its shares.

Master-mason Muhammad said: If a judge's decree is based on either one of the two opinions and judged according to one of them, I mean the opinion on which Ibn Dinar al-Madani and Ibn Wahb have agreed upon and the other one on which Ibn al-Qasim, Mutarrif and Asbagh have agreed upon, both opinions are

---

[182] To buy by payment in advance (contract of future sale).

based on *Ijtihad* from *'Ulama* and both based their opinion on *qiyas* and the argument.

137- Discourse On An Established Mill Belonged To A Man, And Another Person Wanted To Build A New One Over Or Under It.

Master-mason Muhammad said: Regarding a man who has an established mill and another man wants to build a new one over or under (it could imply: in front of or behind) his mill. The opinion differed in three:

Ibn al-Qasim said in *al-'Utbiyah*: If the experts think that the new one would cause damage to the established one in the sense of decreasing his wheat for processing or would increase his expenditure, or anything that would cause a clear damage to the owner, then the man should be prevented from creating a new mill. Asbagh said: If the harm is not so damaging, he is not prevented.

Ibn Habib said in *al-Wadihah* from Ibn al-Majishun: He is prevented due to the tradition that says: there is no harm from the later to the first.

Master-mason Muhammad said: If the experts say that it (the new one) does not harm (the earlier), then let him (build). If the new mill caused difficulties to them, it is said to them: Operate your mill, if it will cause harm (to the first mill), we would cancel your operation. If they said: There is no harm to the first from the newly operated mill, then the judgment is in his favor to continue his operation. When he completed his work and the harm appeared to be affecting the earlier mill, the permit is cancelled and he is prevented from continuing his operation. If he operated without any authority while the (established) mill owner is watching, and does not complain until the work is finished, and then the harm is seen affecting his established mill, then the first man said: don't you think that it is damaging. He replied: examine it carefully; if it was the same and no damage would be expected on the first one, then there is no argument for him (the owner of the first mill) and the newly built mill can stay. If it is uncertain, but he is afraid that it would not be the same, then he (the first owner) should swear on his silence and he thinks that it is damaging him, then the newly built mill that is causing harm, should be eliminated.

Master mason Muhammad said: These are all the opinions of Asbagh, Ibn Wahb and Ibn Nafi'.

Ibn Abi Zaid said: This also applies to rivers that are not owned.

Abu Muhammad (Ibn Abi-Zaid) said: In *al-Majmu'ah* some of our companions said: When the experts say that it does not cause any damage to the first mill, and then permission is given to him to build, and when completed it is found that the new mill causes damage to the earlier mill. He said: When the authority used *ijtihad* and gave him permission to build, the judgment cannot be nullified. If the first owner has abandoned his mill, and someone rebuilt and operated his mill, he (the first owner) then appeared and complained about the damaged caused; I do not think that the authority has the right to demolish it; for, he has abandoned it until someone spends a lot of money (to restart another operation).

Others said: He cannot be left to suffer continuously either with the permission of the ruler or not, and I think the harm, when clearly visible, should be eliminated.

138- Discourse On A Damaged Mill That Belonged to A Man, And Another Built A Mill Close By (Under Or Above It That Caused Harm); Could He Be Prevented Or Not?

Master-mason Muhammad said: From *al-Wadihah*, Ibn Habib said from Asbagh: If a mill belonged to a man that broke down, then another man wanted to build above or below it (it could imply: in front of or behind) another one which is harmful to the first one if its owner wanted to start operating it. He said: If the mill was damaged and out of operation for a long time, then he has no right to prevent him. If the mill was recently damaged, and it was not left out of order, then he has a right to prevent someone from renovating it when he has declared that he wants to rebuild his mill and put it in operation. However, he has no right to prevent him if he has no plans to rebuild his old mill in the near future. For this is considered as preventing people (from their benefit). 'Umar said: 'Do not refrain people'. For example, if one revived a dead land and then left it and another one later revived it, the dead land is for the later reviver.

Thereof: Master mason Muhammad said: From *al-'Utbiyah* and book of Ibn 'Abdus, `Asbagh said: If on the opposite sides of riverbanks are located two mills owned by different persons, and when one is in operation, the other cannot be operated (due to lack of water). Do you think they should divide the water? He said: If both of them are greedy, then each of them should be entitled for half of the river. If the mill is able to operate with (the water) from half of the river, so it is their right. It's wrong to encroach on the other side except by permission of the owner of that side, be that harmful to them or not; for, half of the water is (divided) between them. If the mill is ineffective using half of the water, both should be prevented to operate their mills until they agree with each other (on how to divide the water).

Master mason Muhammad said: in *al-Wadihah*, from Asbagh about two men setting up two mills inside their property and one of them earlier than the other. When the two operated their mills, one of them caused damage to the other. If one of them began the operation before the other, and his mill went out of action or becomes less effective than the other one (who built it later) operates his mill after that and is able to finish (the job), and if it turned out that the latter caused damage to the earlier one, then he should be prevented (from continuing his operation), however, if he (the first to start operation) causes damage to the latter, then he can continue to operate.

Master mason Muhammad said: this is similar to the man who dug a well inside his property and then his neighbor dug another one inside his property causing the water of the first well to dry, therefore the neighbor of the second well is prevented from doing so.

Asbagh said: If two men began operating their mill together at the same time with no one clearly ahead of the other, and both did not use much expense, and if they are located further apart, then none of them can prevent the other. However, if the two locations are close to each other and there is a clear harm, then both should be prevented; for both were competing to harm each other, unless they are separated and kept away from each other.

Master-mason Muhammad said: Ibn Habib said in *al-Wadihah*: I asked Asbagh about people who dam their mills to accumulate water and prevent people from (transporting) wood using the river. He (Asbagh) replied: They have no right to do that; for, the rivers are public ways and no one can prevent others as previously mentioned. In addition, he said: Nor do they have a right to establish something harmful to the people on their route. The leader (*imam*) ought to command (someone) to demolish whatever is preventing the wood (from being transported) by any blockage of the waterway, and the cost of that is upon the owners of the dams and not on those who provide the wood, whether the dams are recent or old.

Master mason Muhammad said: Sahnun also said regarding the dams that are used for fishing and then people complained that the said dams are harmful to them, their property and for watering their cattle, the barrier also causes inconvenience to the servants and womenfolk from taking the water due to the frequency of fishing. He thus replied: such harm ought to be prevented wherever it is.

Thereof master mason Muhammad said: from *al-Wadihah*, Ibn Habib said: Mutarrif and Ibn al-Majishun said regarding someone who reserved a site to build a mill inside his property but without water, because a neighbor's land separated his mill from the river. He then asked him (the neighbor) to allow him to run a channel through his land. The neighbor allowed him to do so and he built the mill. The water flowed to the mill through the neighbor's land and then he (the neighbor) reverses his permission. He said: He has no right to reverse the permission, which was considered as a donation. He too has no right to reverse it at any time, so too with his inheritors after his death as long as he does not limit the permit for a period. If it was considered as a loan, he has a right to reverse that after the period is completed. If the channel was dug up on the neighbor's land purposely for supplying water to the mill, then he (the landowner) reversed his decision, is it right for him to do that? Both Mutarrif and Ibn al-Majishun replied: Yes, that is his right whenever he wished as long as that was not a gift or has a time limit. There is no difference whether his permission to the man is to run the channel through his land or only for getting the water. The judgment in both cases to me is the same.

Ibn Habib said: I said: Regarding the spring water used for planting, both of them said that the permission is forever and he has no right to reverse it. Both (Mutarrif and Ibn al-Majishun) replied: since it will cause destruction if the water was cut off from the plants. Whereas to establish a mill station without water would not bring destruction to the mill, but its benefit would be lost.

Master mason Muhammad said: Asbagh has a different opinion about that, he said: He has the right to reverse in these entire situations as long as it is not considered as a gift. This is also the opinion of Ibn al-Qasim.

Master-mason Muhammad said: Abu Bakr bin Muhammad bin Yunus said in his *diwan:* The most desirable to me is that he does not have any right to reverse that, except when the period is completed or it was a loan and he mentioned to him the lending period. Or when it is a gift and its value is explained. On the other hand, if the permission was unclear, then it is advisable that he does not reverse that because he allowed him to use his resources. It is as if he said to the man: Build for me this wall and in return you will get one hundred *dinars* and after he builds it he is entitled for the hundred *dinars*.

139- Discourse On The Procedural Implementation Of The Mill.

Master mason Muhammad said: From *al-Nawadir*, he said: 'Isa bin Dinar was asked about a man whose mill or mill site was ruined, then wished to employ a man to repair it, what is necessary for that? He replied: It is necessary for him to say to the employee: Build for me a mill like this and this and it can grind this and this, by stone like this and this, by wood of this and this and he describes to him the building in detail. When the mill is completed, half of the mill is mine and the other half is yours or two thirds of it is mine while one third of it is yours, this is permitted. Or he can say to him: Build for me a mill according to this and this with the expenditure like this and this and you can use it for this number of years. This is also allowed. 'Isa said: A reliable river and unreliable river (for water supply) is the same in this contract.

Master mason Muhammad said: Ibn 'Asim has the same opinion in *al-'Utbiyah* except he added: It is not permitted except with a reliable river.

Master mason Muhammad said: Ibn Habib said: 'Isa bin Dinar was asked about a man who said to another man (a worker): operate my mill with features like this and this. When the operation is completed, the yield of the mill is divided among us or the Friday's day and night yield belongs to you. Therefore, the employee worked on that contract and he takes the proceeds for some time. Then they realized that the contract is invalid to both parties; how to legalize it? He ('Isa bin Dinar) replied: The worker has a right for the expenditure that he brought into the mill like its rock, stone and wood at the cost based on the day he started working in the mill. He also should get the payment for his service at that time, wages, and others. All the yields belonged to the owner of the mill. He, the worker, should return all the proceeds he took from the mill. If he takes food he must give back its like; if money (*dinar* or plural *dananir*), he must give back its sum; if he took some food that cannot be measured, he must bear its cost but not the goods itself. He added: this happened because the owner employed the worker to work in the mill, but he (the worker) bought his own tools without the owner's permission. Therefore, the worker is entitled to the value that he brought into the mill including payment for his employment. In consequence, all yields belonged to the mill owner. The worker is obliged to return what he took illegally and he should be paid his wages as if someone told him: Work on this mill of mine and when it is completed, you would get half of the proceeds from another mill of mine. Alternatively, the Friday's proceeds will be yours or you would get fruit from my garden before it matures for sale. If the contract proceeds as agreed and completed, he (the worker) is entitled to the cost that he brought into the mill and his employment wage; for, he had purchased the rock, the stone, and what he brought into the mill from the wood and other tools. He was hired with a void contract and therefore he ought to be given what is owed to him and he should return what he took illegitimately.

Master mason Muhammad said: The opinion differed on the remains (*naqd*), should its value be based on its standing value or the value in its demolished state? Yahya bin Yahya said from Ibn al-Qasim: All the proceeds belong to the worker and the worker is accountable for the rent of the mill site. He is also entitled to the value of his work in its demolished state. Yahya bin Yahya said: My opinion is that he should be paid the value of his work (in setting up the mill) standing.

Thereof master-mason Muhammad said: 'Isa bin Dinar said regarding the previous problem of a man who built a mill and extended its dam onto the neighbor's land with the pledge that he will grind their food for them every month. He ('Isa b. Dinar) answered: The condition is valid if they agreed on how many months it should be. However, it is disallowed if there is no fixed time. He ('Isa b. Dinar) was asked: What do you think if he does not fix the time for preparing the food. He replied: That is not legitimate. Again, he was asked: If it happened? He replied: The landowner should pay the value of what's left for him from half of the water and he could remove the dam from his land. He also should pay the cost of grinding to the owner of the mill based on the condition that both had agreed. If it were not like that, he (the land owner) would have prevented the miller from doing so and he (land owner) would request to divide the water; for, half of the water is for him and the other half is for the worker.

He was asked: What do you think if the mill owner sold his mill before they nullified the condition and he stipulates upon the purchaser that he has to abide to the condition set by the landowner. Or the purchaser has known that and later he bought it without being told about the condition as he already knew that. He replied: For that reason, the transaction is void and thus the arrangement is between the mill founder and the landowner as to what I have explained to you except if the mill is abandoned and thus he is accountable to pay the value of the mill. He was also asked: If the buyer does not know that, and there is no condition stipulated? He answered: For that reason, the transaction will be legitimate and the arrangement is between the buyer and the landowner in all that as what I have explained to you.

Master-mason Muhammad said: 'Abdul Malik said: 'Isa was also asked about a man who built a mill and protruded part of his dam through a people's land, reserving certain days of the month for them to grind their food on the condition that they allow him to extend part of his dam into their land. He ('Isa) said: If their partnership in the mill came after the mill was built based on the calculation of those days of the month and they laid down several conditions to the miller and then they become a partner in the mill. Then they are responsible to repair the mill if it gets damaged, including working on the mill just like it belonged to them on those agreed days, then it is legitimate. If the proceeds belonged to them only in the agreed days, but they did not own the mill itself, then it is not good. When the period is completed, and the dam was removed from their land, they are entitled to the value of their land, and they should return whatever proceeds they took.

140- Discourse On The Pre-emption (*Shufʿah*) On the Mill, Hammam, Threshing Floor, and Water; And On Someone Who Purchased A Land That Includes Plants Or Date-Palms, Are They Considered Part Of The Purchase?

Master-mason Muhammad said: Malik said: No pre-emption on mills. Ibn al-Qasim said: The mills are not part of the building; it is like dumped stones; if the land and the house were sold together with the mill which was placed therein, there is pre-emption (*shufʿah)* therein except the mill, whether the mill is operated by water or the beast.

Master-mason Muhammad said: In *al-Mawaziyya*, Muhammad said from Ashhab and 'Abdul Malik: If they set up the mill in their land, then there is *shufʿah*; if they set up the mills not in their own property, then there is no *shufʿah* when one of them sold his portion of the mill or his portion of the house.

Ashhab said: The mill operated by water or beasts is the same if it is located in water owned by two people. If one of them sold his portion, his co-partner would be entitled to *shufʿah*, and if he wished, he could nullify the transaction except when the seller invited him to divide, then the transaction could not be nullified until he makes the division. If the mill falls inside the portion owned by the seller, the transaction is legitimate. If the mill falls inside the portion that belonged to his co-partner, the transaction is void. He (Ashhab) said: Malik had said: No *shufʿah* on the mill. He did not consider it like a building. The mill in our view is like a door in a building, which could be taken out, if he wished without harm and if he wished, he can refits it easily. Then there is *shufʿah* in it if it is sold with the house. And if *Shufʿah* is also applicable on the wall that is made with palm-leafs then should it not apply to the mill? Ibn al-Mawwaz replied: It is my opinion.

Thereof: Master mason Muhammad said: Ibn al-Qasim said in *al-Mudawwanah* that Malik said: *Shufʿah* is applicable to the *Hammam* (bath house).

Ibn al-Mawwaz said: The *Hammam* is more appropriate for pre-emption (*shufʿah)* than a residence or plots of land due to the harm in dividing the *Hammam,* which is what Malik and his companions said.

Master-mason Muhammad said: Ibn al-Majishun said in *al-Wadihah*: Malik denied *shufʿah* in *Hammam* because it cannot be divided except by changing it function to other things, and thus I think there is *shuf'ah* in *Hammam*.

Master-mason Muhammad said: 'Abdul Wahab[183], the judge, reported from Malik two opinions about *Hammam* and the property that is not divisible. He then said: No *shuf'ah* in that, and he also said: there is *shuf'ah*.

Master-mason Muhammad said: So the reason of the prohibition is based on the Prophet saying that (the pre-emption is on something that is indivisible, but if boundaries can be set up, then it is not subject to pre-emption), i.e. according to its divisibility. The basis for proof is that boundaries can be set up so the division can be implemented according to God's saying (of what is few or many from it as an obligated share). That is based on the existence of division; for pre-emption depends on division in determining its permission or prohibition.

Thereof master mason Muhammad said: Sahnun said in *al-'Utbiyah*: The threshing floor is not subject to pre-emption; because it is like an *afniyah*,[184] not entitled to pre-emption.

'Abdul Malik bin al-Hasan narrated from Ibn Wahab that he said: If they share the cost of the threshing floor, then it is subject to pre-emption like any other site.

Ashhab said: Pre-emption is applicable, whether it is (used as) a threshing floor or not; few or many when possessed by two persons.

Master-mason Muhammad said: Ibn al-Qasim said from *al-Mudawwanah*: Malik said: There is no pre-emption on a well having neither uncultivated land nor date palms. Ibn al-Qasim said: Malik's opinion does not differ in the well. Malik said: If this well (is supplying water) to a land or date palms, which is indivisible and later one of them sells his portion of the well or water spring, then it is subject to preemption, contrary to when he sold the well to a purchaser after the division of the land.

---

[183] He is al-Qadi 'Abd al-Wahab b. Nasr al-Baghdadi (d 422/1031) the author of 'al-Talqin'. *Tarikh Qudat al-Andalus* 40-42.

[184] *Fina* (plural *afniyah*) is the term used for the interior courtyard of a building and to the exterior space immediately adjacent to the exterior wall or walls of a building. The latter type is allocated for the daily temporary use of the inhabitant(s) of the house to which it abuts, without allowing occupation of the space.

Thereof master mason Muhammad said: Ibn al-Qasim said: Nothing is wrong with his purchase, for drinking for a day or a month or two months and watering his plants in his land without buying the original water resource. He said: If the water becomes scarce or less up to one third of drinking needs, he who bought could take from him (the owner of the sources) like necessities of the fruit trees.

Ibn al-Qasim said: I think that it is like what happened to the fruit before watering, one can obtain from him (seller) if his water becomes scarce as long as there is no clear damage. If it is less than one third, there is no harm to him; nothing should be demanded (from the seller). This is the opinion of Sahnun.

Thereof master-mason said: Ibn al-Qasim said: If a man bought a land in which there is plantation, then it is for the purchaser unless the seller makes a condition. However, if one purchased a land without being told about the trees, then the trees are included in the transaction, unless the seller says: I will sell the land to you without trees. Malik said about someone who donated trees without mentioning the land or he donated the land without mentioning the trees, then the land is included with the trees in his donation.

141- Discourse On The Rights Of Pre-emption On The Wall, Does The Upper Floor Owner Has Pre-emption Rights? (Or Does The Upper Floor Owner Of A House Has Pre-emption Rights?).

The author said: Ibn al-Qasim said in *al-Mudawwanah*: If there is a wall between two men and one of them sells his portion of the wall, then his partner will get the right of pre-emption in the wall.

Master-mason Muhammad said: Ibn Yunus added in his *diwan*, saying: If there is a wall between a group of people and one of them sells his portion, then his partner will get the right of pre-emption.

Master-mason Muhammad said: his saying that "If there is a wall between two men and one of them sells his portion" it is not possible to sell his portion of the wall to someone else (not his partner) without selling the house altogether. However, what Ibn al-Qasim meant is that: If he sells his house with a wall jointly owned between him and his neighbor, his neighbor will get the right of pre-emption on half of that wall that is jointly owned, the wall should be valued at a proportionate to the price of the house and then he pays the price, and own the wall by the right of pre-emption.

Master-mason Muhammad said: If there are beams owned by the seller attached to the wall, it will belong to someone who takes half by right of preemption and the other has the right to the inserted wooden beams as it was before.

Thereof master mason Muhammad said: Ibn al-Qasim said in *al-Mudawwanah*: He, who inserted wooden beams in the wall, has no right of pre-emption when he does not own the wall. He also said: If one owned an upper floor of a house while the other owned the lower floor, the owner of the house has no right of pre-emption when the upper floor owner sells his upper floor. Likewise, when the house owner sells his house, the upper floor owner has no right of pre-emption to the house. Ibn al-Qasim also said in *al-Mudawwanah*: If someone has street access to a house and the house is sold, then he has no pre-emption to the house. He also said: No pre-emption on the wall and the attachments adjunct to an access, and no partnership on the access itself.

Master-mason said: If a man built inside someone else's open space (*a'rsah*) with his permission and then one of them sold his portion of the rubble (interpreted as either of what is left of building materials, or as a result of demolishing the building). The owner of the open space has the right to take the rubble at a reduced price or at the selling price. If the other party refuses, he then has the right to take it by right of pre-emption due to the concept of *darar* and *dirar*, on which the principle of pre-emption is based.

142- Discourse On Damage Caused By Cattle On The Farm; Is The Owner Of The Cattle Responsible; And About The Camel And The Predatory Dog.

Master-mason Muhammad said: From *al-Wadihah*, Ibn Habib narrated from Mutarrif and Ibn al-Majishun from Ibn Shihab from Said bin al-Musayyab from the Prophet who decreed: That the owners of walled farms should take care of their farms during day time, and owners of cattle should take care of their cattle during the night[185]. In another tradition narrated by Malik from Ibn Shihab: Anything that is destroyed by cattle at nighttime becomes the responsibility of the owner. Malik said: We follow that rule.

Master mason said: Sahnun was asked about all this and he replied: The interpretation of the tradition is that owners of walled farms should secure their farms at daytime. So the owner of the cattle that are attended would not be responsible for any damage caused by their animals as long as it was not due to their negligence. That is the explanation of the tradition, as we understand it; however if a man who opens his farm's door and releases his cattle or animals without a guardian or shepherd, he will be liable for any damage caused by his animals and he must bear the penalty.

Master mason Muhammad said: from *al-Nawadir* Ibn al-Qasim said: Whatever damage caused by the cattle at night becomes the responsibility of its owners; whether the farm was fenced or not. Moreover anything destroyed at daytime, is not subject to the responsibility of its owners, be it fenced or not.

Master-mason Muhammad said: Yahya narrated from Asbagh who said: The cattle owners should not take out their cattle to the farmlands without a shepherd to guard the cattle. It is their responsibility to keep the cattle away from the farm. When the cattle reach their grazing place, whenever they stride toward the gardens and farms, the owners of the gardens and farms should steer them out.

Master mason Muhammad said: 'Isa said as narrated by Yahya: Except in the case of a camel or a cow or an animal which is accustomed to eat plants and harm the farm. If he (the farm owner) is unable to prevent it, he could propose to the owner to slaughter their cow or camel, or to send them far away to a place which has no farms therein. So anything destroyed after the objection, becomes the responsibility of the owner whether during the day or night.

Master-mason Muhammad said: So too with a predatory dog, if the owner keeps it as part of his animals, whatever damage it causes before the owner is warned, there is no liability on him.

---

[185] Narrated by Malik in *al-Muwatta* 2:747-748, Abu Daud in *Kitab al-Buyu* 3:298 hadith no: 3569 and 3570.

However anything caused by the dog after its owner was warned is his responsibility. 'Isa said: If he brings the dog to a place which is not proper for the dog being there, then the owner is responsible, whether he was warned or not; particularly if the dog is of a predatory type. Master-mason Muhammad said: It is similar to the opinion of Ibn al-Qasim in all these cases.

Thereof master mason Muhammad said: Ibn al-Qasim said about whatever is damaged by the cattle at night, even if the value of the damage is many times the value of the cattle, the owner is responsible to compensate it. They have no right to give the cattle up as a substitute for whatever is damaged; for, the offense came from the cattle owners and not the cattle.

Thereof master mason Muhammad said: Ibn Kinanah was asked about a man who found some cattle on his farm, and he later drove the cattle to his dwelling, and some or all of the cattle died inside his compound. He then answered: The man is not responsible for that, unless he cruelly struck the cattle or did something that caused the cattle to die.

Master mason said: Malik said: If the cattle destroyed the plants or the walled farm at night and the man, who is considered as a just and honest person, took the cattle that are within his farm at night, his word is accepted. He should take oath on the damage caused by the cattle and if the cattle died while under his protection, he is not liable for that.

Thereof master mason Muhammad said: Ibn Habib said in *al-Wadihah*: I asked Mutarrif regarding how to assess vegetation (vegetables), which was spoiled by the cattle? He replied to me: I heard Malik say: assess it based on the hope that it will mature, and the fear that it might not mature. Therefore, he should pay the value of destruction to the farm owner, and he should not assume that the plants will grow. Abdul Malik said: I said to Mutarrif: If after this decree the plants grew again to its original condition does the fine imposed on the cattle owner still belongs to the farm owner? He said: Yes, because the decree came into force and elapsed. I said to him: If the decree was not assessed and the plant returns to its original form. He said: So the penalty, which I described to you, is abolished and there is nothing on the offender except chastisement (*adab*) from the ruler in proportion to his stupidity and his unlawful act. However, if he benefited from the destroyed property, then he is responsible to pay its value. Ibn Habib said: I asked Asbagh about that, and he then said to me from Ibn al-Qasim from Malik like the opinion of Mutarrif. Master mason Muhammad said: Yet, Asbagh does not apply that; for, he said: If the plant returns to its original form before the decree was passed, in my opinion, it should be assessed based on hope and fear, whether it would grow or not, before or after the decree.

Master-mason Muhammad said: Ibn Habib does not accept what Asbagh said; however, he agrees with the opinion of Mutarrif, saying: That is the truth by God's will.

Thereof master mason Muhammad said: 'Isa said to Ibn al-Qasim: What do you think about the camel, predatory dog and the bull whose owners were warned, and their beast killed a man while there was no witness except for one person only? He said: His relatives should take an oath and claim the blood money from the owner of the camel, bull, or dog.

Yahya said: Asbagh said: nothing could be determined in this case unless two witnesses witnessed it. Yahya said: That is all Asbagh said when we asked him about the problem and when we informed him about the narration of 'Isa on that, he completely disagreed with that, arguing with lots of arguments and demonstrating lots of examples. He said: The blood money of a free Muslim man cannot be determined by one oath of a witness because there is no *qasamah*[186] on something connected with beasts (*'ajma'*).

143- Discourse On The House Of Pigeons And Birds Kept By A Man In A Rural Area, Is He Allowed to Do So. And About A Neighbor's Pigeons mixed With His Pigeons, Can He Consume The Chicks?

Master mason Muhammad said: From *al-Majmu'ah*, Ibn Kinanah was asked about a man who kept a pigeon house, damaging his neighbor's farms and their fruits. Ibn Kinanah responded: He should not be prevented to do so, but I do not like him causing damage to others.

Master mason Muhammad said: In *al-Majmu'ah*, taken from *al-Nawadir* from Ibn al-Qasim, he said: If pigeons and sparrows causing damage to the surrounding neighbor's farms in the village or whatever below the pigeon house, for the sparrows

---

[186] Procedure of taking oath imposed on a group of people because of a killing.

always cause extensive damage to the farm like the damage caused by locusts or similar to that, do you think that he should be ordered to shut the entrance to their nesting place? He said: I do not think that he should, and I think that he should benefit from his wall and tower. It is the responsibility of the farmers to protect their farms at daytime by taking care and protecting them from harm. Mutarrif's opinion differed from that.

Master mason Muhammad said: if we say that he is not prevented from keeping pigeons and sparrows, is he then prevented from keeping geese and chicken? The geese or chicken could cause harm to plants and the farm. If it is harmful, the owner should be prevented from keeping it.

This happened to us in Tunis. A man kept chickens within his house and let them free in the street picking and collecting whatever on the ground; and at the same time the chickens burrow holes at the foundation of the neighbor's wall, destroying the lower part of the wall. Consequently, the matter was brought up to the judge and the judge then passed an order to confine the chickens inside an enclosure and prevent them from moving freely. Subsequently, we based our practice on that because of the harm they created.

Ibn al-Qasim was asked about whether chicken are not harmful to a grazing land, farm and trees, and if the chicken and geese, kept by a man, have damaged the farm, do you think the owner should be prevented from keeping it, and ordered them to be caged in? He replied: I do not think so; they and sparrows for me are the same. Thus, the farmers are responsible to protect their farm at daytime from everything. He was asked: Hence, bees in your opinion are the same as pigeons? He said: Yes.

Thereof master mason Muhammad said: Ibn al-Qasim said in *al-Nawadir* about a tower used as a pigeon house having a small window that allows the pigeons to enter and exit freely. The pigeons then intermixed with his neighbor's pigeons, which has its own tower put up by the neighbor. Thus, the man could not identify which one is his, what is your opinion if he consumes the young pigeons sheltering inside the tower. He answered: If both could identify theirs, then each person has to return the pigeons to its owner, if both are unable to identify their pigeons and he knows its breeding place, he should give up the young pigeons to the owner after its hatching. He said: If his pigeons coupled with the neighbor's pigeons and he recognizes that but unable to separate and return it to the owner, but he knew their breeding place, then he should give up the hatching to his neighbor. I said: If his neighbor's pigeon is a male? He said: Yes, for it is considered from the aspect of hatchling, not from the aspect of laying eggs.

Master mason Muhammad said: Mutarrif said in *al-Wadihah:* If his pigeon and his neighbor's pigeon coupled, and he recognized his pigeon and knew their breeding place but unable to separate them. Once they breed, he should give up the chick to his neighbor, whether his pigeon is male or female. For, it is considered from the aspect of hatchling, not from the aspect of laying the egg.

Thereof master mason Muhammad said: From *al-Mustakhrajah* through auditioning of Sahnun from Ibn al-Qasim: Malik said: Regarding a man who has a female pigeon while another has a male; they agreed that once their pigeons breed, the two will share the chicks. He said: the chicks are to be divided between them, because both of them are helping each other's in hatchling. He was asked: If a man came to another man with eggs, saying to him: let your hen hatch these eggs, so we divide the chicks. Later on the eggs hatched. He said: The chicks are for the hen's owner and the egg owner will get similar eggs. Indeed to me, it is like someone comes with some wheat to another man, saying to him: Sow this in your land and we divide the produce. Therefore, the plants are for the landowner and the wheat owner is entitled to similar wheat.

144- Discourse On Keeping Bees In A Village And They Are Harmful To Trees That Belong To People, And What If A Person's Bees Get Mixed With His Neighbor's Bees.

Master mason Muhammad said: Ibn Habib said in *al-Wadihah*: Mutarrif was asked about the bees kept by a man in the village and the bees are harmful to the trees that belong to the surrounding inhabitants especially when they blossom. He said: I think that he is prevented from keeping what is harmful to the people's farms and trees; for, they are a flying creature which is very hard to control, contrary to cattle, geese, and flying fowl. Pigeons and the bees are similar and he is not allowed to keep these animals. I said: Why are you are saying that the cattle are allowed on farms, even if it causes damage to people's trees, the owner of the cattle is not prevented from keeping them and not ordered to keep them out. It is the responsibility of the farms and tree owners to protect their trees and farms during the day. He replied: The bees and pigeons are unlike cattle because they are flying creatures and it is very hard to control them whereas it is possible to control the cattle.

Malik opined that violent beasts that cause damage to farms, and could not be protected from, should be expelled and bought from the owner. Thus, bees and pigeons are more dangerous. Similarly, wild fowls, geese, and the like, are difficult to control. An animal that easy to control is similar to cattle. Master-mason Muhammad said: 'Isa bin Dinar has the same opinion.

Ibn Habib said that it was narrated that the Prophet was asked about a man who kept the pigeons in the village, the Prophet then said: If he is planting similar to what they are planting (he can keep it), if not, then he could not.

Master-mason Muhammad said: Ibn Dinar narrated from Ibn al-Qasim contrary to that: A man is not prevented to benefit from his walled property, and it is the responsibility of the farmers to look after and protect their farms during the day. This has already been mentioned in the previous section.

Master mason Muhammad said: Ibn al-Qasim said: If bees that belong to a man enter another man's beehive and they get mixed up and he could not recognize his bees from the others. He said: He may say to the beehive's owner about his bees that encroached into his beehive: If you can recognize yours then take it, otherwise you may get nothing. Asbagh and Mutarrif have the same opinion.

* * *

Ibn al-Rami's closing statement on completing his treatise

And Allah is the Helper, Who suffices me and He is the best Guardian, and there is neither power nor strength except in Allah, The Mighty and The Great; and Praise be to Our Master Muhammad, The Noble Prophet and to his family and companions with the best praise and the purest greetings, Amin.

The book is complete by praise to Allah, by His assistance and His guidance, and the last of our supplication that all praise is to Allah, Lord of the Universe, Amin.

List of all 144 Discoursed Cases

Introduction by Ibn al-Rami, the Treatise's Author............1

1- Discourse On The Wall Between Two Neighbors.........3
1a- Discourse On The First Wall................................3
1b- Discourse On The Second Wall..........................20
1c- Discourse On the Third Wall..............................23

2- Discourse On The Method Of Dividing A Wall And Method Of Balloting And Whether A Man Has The Right Of Pre-emption (*Shuf'ah*) In The Wall................26

3- Discourse On A Man Who Allows His Neighbor To Insert Wooden Beams In A Wall, Or Who Opens A Door Or Passageway And Who Sells The Support For The Beams. Is He Allowed Repossessing It Or Not?..28

4- Discourse On A Man Who Lends His Courtyard (To Another) Who In Turn Develops It and Then the Owner Decides To Remove Him (Or To Sell A Main Beam)..32

5- The Book on the Negation of Harm, And The Discourse On The Harm And Other (Bad) Things That a Man Can Inflict Upon His Neighbor...................35

6- Discourse On the Harm Of Smoke And The Judgment On It...38

7- Discourse On The Harm Of Bad Smell and Judgment On It...40

8- Discourse On The Harm From The Tailor (*Kammadin*) And The Vibration Of The Mills..............41

9- Discourse On A Man Who Builds A Stable To Secure Animals..44

10- Discourse On The Harm Caused By Overlooking From Small Windows And Doors And The Judgment Therein……………………………………………..47

11- Discourse On The Vacant Lot without Any Building……..50

12- Discourse On Someone Who Creates A Small Window (*kuwa*), Which Enables Him To Look At The Courtyard Of His Neighbor…………………………….........51

13- Discourse On Two Small Windows *(kuwa)* Facing Each Other…………………………………………………..52

14- Discourse On Small Windows For Light And Doors Of Roof Terrace……………………………………………..53

15- Discourse On A Man Who Wants To Close The Window *(kuwa)* That Harms Him While The Owner Does Not Benefit from It……………………………………………54

16- Discourse On A Man Who Wants To Renovate (His House) And By Doing So It Blocks His Neighbor's Window *(kuwa)* And Cuts Him From Fresh Air And Light…...55

17-Discourse On Shutting The Window By Judgment………..58

18- Discourse On Someone Who Opened A Window *(kuwa)* On A Rented House……………………………………………59

19- Discourse On the Window of Towers in the Gardens and Vineyards……………………………………...59

20- Discourse On Someone Who Builds On Higher Ground Overlooking Neighboring Houses……………………………..61

21- Discourse On A Man Who Builds A Minaret That Overlooks Neighboring Houses Or From The Roof Terrace Of A Mosque……………………………………………………...63

22- Discourse On A Man Who Wants To Create A Door On The Main Road………………………………………………63

23- Discourse on A Man Who Wants To Open A Shop
Or Shops Opposite His Neighbor's Door……............................67

24- Discourse On A Man Who Wants To Open A
Door On A Dead-End Street And His Neighbor Protests……..70

25- Discourse On A Man Who's Building
Encroaches Onto A Public Street………………………………...75

26- Discourse About A Man Who Makes A
Protrusion Onto The Road Without Damaging Others………..79

27- Discourse On Renting And Dividing The *Fina'*…………..82

28- Discourse On Building A Gate On A Dead-End Street…...83

29- Discourse On the Residents Of A Dead-End Street
Who Want To Repair Their Gate While Some Of them
Refuse (And About Those Who Want To Protect
Their Houses With Walls Or Others)……………………….84

30- Discourse On The Defamation (*tajrih*) On Someone
Whose Building Protrudes Onto A Public Street
(And Is It Possible To Reclaim A Part Of The *Fina'*
To Expand The Street)……………………………………………87

31-Discourse On Someone Who Possesses The
Right Of Precedence (*Hiyazah*) Over His Neighbor On
Building Or Damaging Act, Which Is Limited For Several
Years, Does He Have The Right To Claim Ownership On That
Or Not?...89

32- Book Of Defects In Houses………………………………….94

33- Discourse On A Minor and Major Defect
And The Evaluation Of Its Price……………………………….96

34- Discourse On The Disagreement Of The Experts
On Defects And Harm, And The Testimony
(*Shahadah*) On It……………………………………………..106

35- Discourse On The Rented House, When It Is Completely Or Partly Destroyed, Should The Owner Be Forced To Rebuild It Or Not?...................108

36- Discourse On A Tenant Who After Completing His Leasing Contract, Claims That Part Of The House Is Built By Him But It Is Denied By The Landlord..............113

37- Discourse About Two Floors That Are Owned By Different Persons, To Whom Does The Roof Belongs?..........114

38- Discourse On The Obligation Of The Owner Of The Lower Floor To Rebuild And Renovate, And Can The Owner Of The Upper Floor Build An Extra Structure In His Air Space..119

39- Discourse On Who Is Responsible for Building The Supports Of The Upper Floor, And Who Is Responsible If The Supports Fall and Destroys Other Structures...122

40- Discourse On The Cleaning Of The Restroom Between The Upper And Lower Floors, And Who Is Responsible For Building It?...............124

41- Discourse On The Cleaning Of The House's Water Channel Between Two Partners...................125

42- Discourse On The Grievance Between A Landlord And A Tenant On The Cleaning Of The Water Channel........125

43- Discourse On Cleaning The Filth And Wastewater Of Residential Channels That Are In Lanes And The Main Road..128

44- Discourse On The Maintenance Of Waterways In Farms..131

45- Discourse On The Construction Of A Channel On The Main Road Between Residences And How The Financial Responsibility Should Be Determined............132

46- Discourse On A House Which Has No Water
Channel And The Owner Wishes To Build One……………..133

47- Discourse On Someone Who Wants To Discharge
His Rainwater Onto The Street………………………………....134

48- Discourse On An Old Channel That Causes
Harm To Neighbors………………………………………………..134

49- Discourse On A Man Whose Rooftop Water Flows
Down To His Neighbor's House,
And He Wants To Cut It Off……………………………………135

50- Discourse On Water Spouts Pointed Towards
Neighbor's Houses…………………………………………....136

51- Discourse On A Man Who Wants To Create
A Room In His House And Wants To Direct The
Rainwater Towards The Neighbor's House…………………137

52- Discourse On A Land Which Its Water Flows
To Another Land…………………………………………..138

53- Discourse On Two Neighbors Regarding Rainwater
That's Flowing From One Roof Top
Onto the Other…………………………………………………..138

54- Discourse On Rainwater Being Contested Between
Owners Of The Upper And Lower Floors…………………….139

55- Discourse On The Ownership Of Water Collected
In A Cistern Between Tenant And Landlord…………………141

56- Discourse On the Well Located in A Man's Land
But The Access To It Is Located Inside
Someone Else's Property……………………………………...142

57- Discourse On An Existing Unused Channel From
A House On A Private Lane, Whose Owner
Wants To Reclaim It……………………………………………..143

58- Discourse On A Man Who Owned A Water Channel Running Through The Neighboring House, Whose Owner Wants To Renovate It……………………....144

59- Discourse On Distribution of Rainwater From Streets between the Gardens…………………………………….145

60- Discourse On Drainage Running On The Surface And Disposing Waste Water Onto The Street……………..146

61- Discourse On Overhanging Ledge Of Houses And Usage Of Its Airspace……………………………………....148

62- Discourse On Protruding Cantilevers and Ledges Onto The Street…………………………………………………….150

63- Discourse On What Is Allowed And Disallowed In The Street……………………………………...151

64- Discourse On Building Columns And Benches In The Street…………………………………………………..152

65- Discourse On What Is Disallowed And Allowed In The Street……………………………………....153

66- Discourse On The Wall And Room Feared To Collapse, If It Is A Shared Property Or Under the Trustee Of A Legal Guardian…………………..154

67- Discourse On A Man Who's Building Is Slanting Toward The Neighboring Airspace…………………………...156

68- Discourse On A Ruin In A Residential Area With Huge Garbage And Harmful To The Neighboring Houses……………………………………...157

69- Discourse On Dirt From A Man's Property Brought By Rainwater To Neighboring Doors Or Someone Else's Door That Blocked The Water Channel……………….159

70- Discourse On The Ground Floor Belongs To A Man And Upper Floor Belongs To Another And The Road Was Heightened Making The Door On The Ground Floor Shorter...159

71- Discourse On A Shared Well And House Between Two Persons, Both Properties Collapsed But One Of The Partners Refused To Participate In Rebuilding And They Quarreled About That..................................160

72- Discourse On A Shared Vacant Lot Between Two Men One Of Them Wants To Build...............................161

73- Discourse On A Jointly Owned Grapevine Wall That Is Falling...161

74- Discourse On Somebody Who Alters The Boundary.......162

75- Discourse On Disagreement On Land Boundary...........164

76- Discourse On The Protective Area (*harim*) of The Well...164

77- Discourse On A Man Who Prevents Others To Benefit From The Surplus Of His Well Water....................166

78- Discourse On A Man Who Sells His Pasture.................168

79- Discourse On A Well Shared Between Two Neighbors Is Feared To Collapse....................................169

80- Discourse On A Well Shared Between Two Persons With Decreased Water, Shall One Of Them Be Forced To Repair It Or Not?..170

81- Discourse On The Method Of Digging A Well And Its Preparation...171

82- Discourse On A Man Digging A Well In His House, Whether He Should Be Prevented Or Not?..............................173

273

83- Discourse On The Water Spring That Belongs To A
Man And Its Water Leakes Into A Neighboring Plot………...175

84- Discourse On A Man Who Wants To Channel His Water
Through Neighboring Land To His Other Property………….176

85- Discourse On What Is Essential On *Ijarah* And *Ju'l*
In Digging A Well……………………………………………178

86- Discourse On A Man Hiring Two Men To Dig A Well
For Him, One of Them Fell Sick After Starting
Their Work……………………………………………………182

87- Discourse On Hiring (*Ijarah*) And Wage (*Ju'l*) In A
Construction Work……………………………………………183

88- Discourse On Dividing The House By *Muzaraah*
And On Dividing Building And Courtyard And
What Is Necessary To Be Included…………………………...184

89- Discourse Between Partners In Utilizing the Courtyard…186

90- Discourse On Dividing A Double Storey House And
What Is Necessary For That…………………………………..187

91- Discourse On Division Of The House And The
Silence About The Entrance, Water Channel, And
Screen, And What Is Necessary For That……………………189

92- Discourse On Unacceptable Conditions In Division
Due To Its Harm……………………………………………...190

93- Discourse On The Litigation Between Two Partners
On A Chamber (Of The House) After Division………………191

94- Discourse On All Divisions And What Is
Necessary For That…………………………………………...191

95- Discourse On Indivisible Things,
And How To Divide Water…………………………………...192

96- Discourse On The House Whose Interior Belonged To A Man And The Exterior Belonged To Another, And They Disagreed In Changing The Door Of The Exterior House...193

97- Discourse On Opening A Door of A Jointly Owned House Through Another House Owned By One of Them, And When is Precedence (*tafadul*) And Donation (*heba*) Allowed on That, And To whom Belongs The Shelf Board (*al-Ajniha*) and *Fina'*...................................194

98- Discourse On A House Between Two Men And One Of Them Built In It Something Before It Was Divided.............196

99- Discourse On Dispute Regarding Access From A House To Another House..196

100- Discourse On Construction Activities Causing Damage To A Threshing Floor And Prevents Wind Circulation.........197

101- Discourse On The Garden Located Adjacent To A Man's Threshing Floor And In Consequence The Straws And Dust Causes Harm To The Garden.................199

102- Discourse On Two Threshing Floors One Is Blocking The Other By A Pileup Of Straws, And Another Threshing Floor Located In A Residential Area And Each One Claimed Its Ownership...200

103- Discourse On Limitation Of The Road Width And Disputes About That...201

104- Discourse On A Public Road, Which Was Cut Off By A River, Should A Man's Land Be Appropriated...........202

105- Discourse On A Man Whose Property Is Separated By A Public Road And He Wants To Relocate It Inside His Land..204

275

106- Discourse On a Man Who Has a Land Upon Which A Public Road Passes And He Wishes To Change Its Location To Another Place On His Land......................205

107- Discourse On Litigation Among People Regarding Usage Of A Road Inside Another Person's Land................206

108- Discourse On A Man Who Has A Right Of Passage To His Palm Tree In Someone Else's Land And The Landowner Prevented Him From Entering......................207

109- Discourse On A Man Who Owned Trees Inside Another Man's Land; The Landowner Wishes To Fence His Land...208

110- Discourse On A Man's Land Located In The Middle Of Others Property With No Passageway; He Wished To Build In His Centrally Located Land............................210

111- Discourse On The Man Whose Land Is Located Inside Other's Properties, Then They Lock Their Properties And Thus Blocked His Access........................212

112- General Discourse On The Usurpation Of Plants, And On A Man Who Built On Someone Else's Property With Or Without His Permission...............................212

113- Discourse On Someone Who Built On Someone Else's Property With Or Without His Permission, Could He Claim The Total Value Of His Building Or The Cost Only..215

114- Discourse On Someone Who Built On His Wife's Property...216

115- Discourse On A Man Who Allowed Another Man To Build Inside His Property For A Certain Period, And When The Time Expires The Building Is Demolished..........217

116- Discourse On What A Builder Could And Could Not Take From The Remains Of What He Built In Another Man's Property, With or Without His Permission...............218

117- Discourse on A Man Who Leased A Land To Another Man To Develop It For Certain Period, Then The Land Was Reclaimed Before The Period Was Completed………...220

118- Discourse On Whoever Purchased Date-Palm Trees Or Rubbles (Derelict Building) To Be Pulled Down, And How If The Land Was Sold Before Or After That, And Was That A Subject Of Pre-emption……………...220

119- General Discourse on Plantation; And Discourse On Someone who Cuts or Destroyed Someone's Else Trees…......225

120- Discourse On Someone Who Usurped Plants From A Man's Garden And He Planted It In His Garden…………………………………………………226

121- Discourse On A Man Who Took A Tree Of Another Man And Then Sold It To Someone Who Does Not Know That It Was Illegally Possessed; Should The Plant Be Repossessed From The Buyer?........................229

122- Discourse On A Man While He Was Absent His Land Was Usurped By A Person, And Another One Usurped A Seedling And Planted It In His Land……………………...230

123- Discourse On Someone Who Pulled Out (a stem) Of A Tree That Belonged To Another Man And Then Nurtured It In His Land……………………………………………….230

124- Discourse On Someone Who Usurped Saffron's Corm And Then Cultivates It In His Land…………………………...232

125- Discourse On A Tree Owned By A Man And It's Roots Protruded Into His Neighbor's Land………………232

126- Discourse On The Tree Owned By A Man Causing Damage To His Neighbor's Wall, Could The Tree Be Cut Off?..233

127- Discourse On The Tree Belonged To A Man, Its Huge Branches Are Harmful To His Neighbor's Property............234

128- Discourse On The Tree Or The Date Palm Belongs to A Man Inside Someone Else's Property And The Tree Falls Down, Could He Replace It With Another One? Or A Date Palm Which Belongs to A Man In Another Man's Property And Damages Him (The Landowner), Could It Be Sold to Him?...237

129- Discourse On A Fruit Tree That Belonged To a Man Whose Fruit Falls Inside His Neighbor's Garden and Damages His Property...…..239

130- Discourse On The Tree Belonged To A Man Inside His House Overlooking His Neighbor...........................239

131- Discourse On The Tree Adjacent To A Public Street, Which Is Harmful To Passersby……………………………..241

132- Discourse On A Parched River; Could Someone Nearby Reclaim The Parched Land?......................................241

133- Discourse On The River Running Between People, They Compete For Its Water, How Should The Water Be Allocated…………………………………………….242

134- Discourse On A Flowing Irrigation Channel, Which A Man Wished To Split It And Direct The Upstream Water To His Mill And Return The Water To Its Origin, Could He Do That? And On The Spring That Belongs To A Man, From Its Water His Neighbor Planted And Then The Spring Owner Wished To Divert His Water……………………………..244

135- Discourse On Fishing Areas In Lakes, Rivers, Pools, And Small Lakes. Is It Possible For The People Around Those Natural Resources To Prevent Others From Fishing?..246

136- Discourse On A Damaged Mill Owned By A Group Of People, And One Of Them Calls For Repair While Some Refused...247

137- Discourse On An Established Mill Belonged To A Man, And Another Person Wanted To Build A New One Over or Under It..250

138- Discourse On A Damaged Mill That Belonged To A Man, And Another Built A Mill Close By (Under Or Above It That Caused Harm); Could He Be Prevented Or Not?.............251

139- Discourse On The Procedural Implementation Of The Mill………………………………………………....254

140- Discourse On The Pre-emption (*Shuf'ah*) On the Mill, Hammam, Threshing Floor, and Water; And On Someone Who Purchased A Land That Incudes Plants or Date-Palms, Are They Considered Part Of The Purchase? ………………..257

141- Discourse On The Rights Of Pre-emption On The Wall, Does The Upper Floor Owner Has Pre-emption Rights? (Or Does The Upper Floor Owner Of A House Has Pre-emption Rights?)…………………………………………….259

142- Discourse On Damage Caused By Cattle On The Farm; Is The Owner Of The Cattle Responsible; And About The Camel And The Predatory Dog………………………….260

143- Discourse On The House Of Pigeons And Birds Kept By A Man In A Rural Area, Is He Allowed To Do So? And About A Neighbor's Pigeons Mixed With His Pigeons, Can He Consume The Chicks?....................................263

144- Discourse On Keeping Bees In A Village And They Are Harmful To Trees That Belong To People, And What If A Person's Bees Get Mixed With His Neighbor's Bees……………………………………………..265

Ibn al-Rami's Closing Statement To His Treatise……………266

Glossary of selected terms

Harm: *La Darar wa la Dirar* – A saying of the Prophet Muhammad that emphasized the negation of harm, translated as: 'Do not harm others or yourself, and others should not harm you or themselves'.

Qadi: judge; *Qadi al-Jama'ah*: the highest ranking judge in a district or region.

Mufti: a specialist on law who can give an authoritative opinion on points of doctrine; his considered legal opinion is a *Fatwa*.

Madhhab: an Islamic School of Law. The Maliki school of law was the predominant school in North Africa and al-Andalus (Islamic Spain).

Urf: the established custom and practice in a district or region; or the habit, custom, of a people in their sayings and acts.

Hiyazah: the right to posses, such as possession of potential damage that might occur in the future. The person who builds first has the right to exercise 'control over potential damage' from a neighboring structure that is built in the near or distant future. See case # 31.

Fina (plural *Afniyah*): the space immediately adjacent to the exterior wall or walls of a building. It is allocated for the daily temporary use of the inhabitant(s) of the house, or building, to which it abuts, without allowing the occupation of the space. It extends vertically to create an airspace that allows projections from the wall, and by extension room(s) bridging the public-right-of-way (sabat). See cases 61 to 65.

Qimt / Aqd: the wall bond, at its corners, with the adjacent wall(s). The bonds at the corners can determine if both walls were built at the same time, and thus establishes ownership of the walls.

Kuwa: small window or aperture in a wall.

Bios of the Editor and Translator

Besim S. Hakim is a former professor of architecture and urban planning; a consultant and independent scholar. He has been researching and writing about traditional rules from the Mediterranean region since 1975. His goal is to articulate how those rules shaped the traditional built environment, so as to provide lessons and models for contemporary and future architects, urban designers, city administrators and officials, and lawyers. He is the author of *Arabic-Islamic Cities: Building and Planning Principles*, 1986, KPI, London, and *Mediterranean Urbanism: Historic Urban/Building Rules and Processes*, 2014, Springer, Dordrecht.

Mohd Dani Muhamad is an associate professor at the Academy of Contemporary Islamic Studies, Universiti Teknologi Mara in Selangor, Malaysia. He has an MA in History of Art and Architecture of the Islamic Middle East from the School of Oriental and African Studies, University of London, UK, and a PhD in Islamic Civilization from the International Institute of Islamic Thought and Civilisation (ISTAC), International Islamic University, Malaysia.

www.ingramcontent.com/pod-product-compliance
Lightning Source LLC
Chambersburg PA
CBHW060112170426
43198CB00010B/861